D0564258

THE
TYRANNY
OF
SILENCE

HOW ONE CARTOON IGNITED A
GLOBAL DEBATE ON THE FUTURE
OF FREE SPEECH

THE
TYRANNY
OF
SILENCE

FLEMMING ROSE

CATO
INSTITUTE
WASHINGTON, D.C.

© 2010 Jyllands-Postens Forlag, JP/Politikens Forlagshus A/S
Translation © 2011 Martin Aitken
International Rights Management: Susanna Lea Associates

Library of Congress Cataloging-in-Publication Data

Rose, Flemming, 1958-
    The tyranny of silence / Flemming Rose.
        pages cm
    Includes bibliographical references and index.
    ISBN 978-1-939709-42-4 (hardback : alk. paper)
        1. Freedom of speech. 2. Muhammad, Prophet, -632—Caricatures
    and cartoons. 3. Caricatures and cartoons—Political aspects—
Denmark. 4. Morgenavisen jyllands-posten. I. Title.

JC591.R67 2014
323.44'3—dc23
                                                                2014032590

ISBN: 978-1-939709-42-4 (hardback) ISBN: 978-1-939709-99-8 (paperback)
eBook ISBN: 978-1-944424-04-6

Cover design: Jon Meyers.
Printed in the United States of America.

CATO INSTITUTE
1000 Massachusetts Avenue, N.W.
Washington, D.C. 20001
www.cato.org

Contents

FOREWORD ... vii

1. FROM WHERE I STAND ... 1

2. MASS MURDER AND SATIRE ... 17

3. FROM MOSCOW TO MUHAMMAD ... 29

4. THE INFAMOUS ABILITY OF HUMANS TO ADAPT ... 67

5. THE PATHWAY TO GOD ... 93

6. AFTERSHOCK I ... 103

7. AFTERSHOCK II ... 139

8. FROM RUSSIA WITH LOVE ... 169

9. QUESTIONING THE HARASSERS ... 195

10. A VICTIMLESS CRIME ... 225

AFTERWORD ... 279

NOTES ... 301

INDEX ... 315

Foreword

As a longtime proponent of free speech, however controversial, and as a senior fellow at the Cato Institute, I am delighted the Cato Institute Press is publishing *The Tyranny of Silence* by Flemming Rose. As features editor of the Danish newspaper *Jyllands-Posten*, Rose commissioned and published satirical cartoons about Muslims, some of them of Muhammad, that led to violent demonstrations in some Muslim countries as well as vehement protests elsewhere in the world, along with death threats and at least 200 actual corpses.

In this vivid book, Flemming Rose tells why he was responsible for publishing these cartoons as well as the long-term threatening impact they have had on him. *The Tyranny of Silence* documents the continuous multidimensional war elsewhere on free speech. I hope that among other effects, *The Tyranny of Silence* will lead to open discussions and debates in America and elsewhere on the growing amount of self-censorship among individuals and societies confronted by highly combative cultures that allow no criticism of their sacred beliefs.

Such a culture created the fierce and fatal demonstrations against the cartoons in the Danish newspaper.

Or, as Rose put it in a Fall 2007 *Middle East Quarterly* discussion by him and Naser Khader ("Reflections on the Danish Cartoon Controversy"):

> When the twelve cartoonists and I received death threats, newspapers were closed in Russia and Malaysia, and newspaper editors were jailed in Jordan and Yemen, at that point it became an issue exclusively about free speech.

Amid the violent responses elsewhere to the publication of the Danish cartoons, in the United States reactions were so intimidating that while the *New York Times*, *Washington Post*, *Los Angeles Times*, and *Chicago Tribune* described these bristling cartoons in words, these newspapers—in the land of the First Amendment guarantee of a free press—refused to print the cartoons themselves.

But a very few U.S. newspapers did: the *Philadelphia Inquirer*, the *New York Sun*, and the *Village Voice*. I was then a columnist at the *Voice*, and my story on the cartoons included the most controversial of the cartoons—Muhammad with a bomb in his turban.

It never occurred to me not to publish the cartoon, nor was I surprised when I too received death threats. For some weeks afterwards, walking the streets of Greenwich Village, where the *Voice* was published and where I live, I occasionally glanced quickly into passing baby carriages to see if machine guns were nestled there.

Also, as a reporter, I traced in the *Voice* and other publications— as I wrote in my February 2, 2009, *Washington Times* column—how the Organization of the Islamic Conference, which has permanent status at the United Nations, got the UN General Assembly to pass a nonbinding resolution urging nations to provide "'adequate protections' in their laws or constitutions against 'acts of hatred, discrimination, intimidation and coercion resulting from defamation of religions and incitement to religious hatred in general.'" Only Islam and Muslims were specifically mentioned in the resolution. The vote was 83 to 53, with the United States among those in opposition.

In "Why I Published Those Cartoons" (February 19, 2006), Flemming Rose wrote:

> We have a tradition of satire when dealing with the royal
> family and other public figures, and that was reflected in
> the cartoons. The cartoonists treated Islam the same way

they treat Christianity, Buddhism, Hinduism and other religions. And by treating Muslims in Denmark as equals they made a point: we are integrating you into the Danish tradition of satire because you are part of our society, not strangers. The cartoons are including, rather than excluding Muslims.

Tell that to the majority of the UN General Assembly that voted against the defamation of religions. And tell it to the 57 nations that are members of the Organization of the Islamic Conference who supported that resolution to punish defamation of religion worldwide.

Further evidence of how valuable this book will be for generations to come is Flemming Rose's stalwart account about how infectiously widespread the visceral hostility to free speech can be:

> Everywhere I go, I seem to provoke controversy. At American universities, I've been met by placards and students protesting against my speaking. When I was scheduled to lecture at a university in Jerusalem, a demonstration called for my removal. When I talked about freedom of speech at a UNESCO conference in Doha last spring, local media branded me the "the Danish Satan," the authorities were inundated with angry emails, and the Ministry of Internal Affairs set up a hotline for citizens who complained about my having even been allowed into the country.

Flemming Rose, welcome to the Cato Institute, where free speech is as natural as the weather. It's a climate you will find hospitable.

You, sir, are a model to the world of unyielding individual liberty.

—Nat Hentoff

1. From Where I Stand

It's a Sunday morning in 2009, and I'm standing under the shower in a hotel room in Lyon. Rain drums against the window; at the end of a narrow street, I can just see one of the two rivers that flow through the city. In an hour, I'm due at city hall to participate in a panel discussion organized by the French newspaper *Libération* on challenges to free speech in Europe. I've been doing a lot of that kind of thing in the past several years. Yesterday, I was in Paris. Earlier in the week, I was involved in a heated exchange at a conference in Berlin about Muslims and Islam in the European media.

As I began speaking, a member of the audience stood up, approached the panel, and in a voice trembling with fury demanded to know who had given me the right to tell Muslims like her about democracy. She then turned toward the organizers, angrily asked how they could even consider inviting someone like me, and then stormed out of the room.

Everywhere I go, I seem to provoke controversy. At American universities, I've been met by placards and students protesting against my speaking. When I was scheduled to lecture at a university in Jerusalem, a demonstration called for my removal. When I talked about freedom of speech at a UNESCO conference in Doha last spring, local media branded me the "the Danish Satan,"[1] the authorities were inundated with angry emails, and the Ministry of Internal Affairs set up a hotline for citizens who complained about my having even been allowed into the country.

In the spring of 2006, I was invited by the Oxford Union to take part in a discussion on freedom of speech, democracy, and respect for religious sentiment. That body is accustomed to controversy. Nevertheless, my visit turned into what local media alleged was the biggest security operation the city had seen since Michael Jackson's visit in 2001.

When I was invited to the World Association of Newspapers' forum in Moscow a few years ago, Russian authorities politely yet firmly implied that they would like me to stay away. I didn't fully comprehend their hints, so I went to Moscow oblivious. Since then, I have been unable to secure a visa, although I am married to a Russian and lived in Moscow under Soviet rule as a foreign correspondent for 12 years. During that time, though I was clearly anti-communist and openly socialized with dissidents, visas were never a problem.[2]

I could go on citing similar incidents, but what would be the point? On this autumn morning, the picture seems clear. I have become a figure many love to hate. Some would like to see me dead. I have wracked my brain trying to figure out why. I am not by nature a provocative person. I do not seek conflict for its own sake, and it gives me no pleasure when people take offense at things I have said or done. Nevertheless, I have been branded by many as a careless troublemaker who pays no heed to the consequences of his actions.

How did that happen? To the world, I am known as an editor of the Danish newspaper *Jyllands-Posten*. In September 2005, I commissioned and published a number of cartoons about Islam, prompted by my perception of self-censorship by the European media. One of those cartoons, drawn by the artist Kurt Westergaard, depicted the Muslim prophet Muhammad with a bomb wrapped in his turban. Among the other cartoons we published was another that mocked the newspaper and even myself for commissioning them, but it was Westergaard's image that would change my life.

The Cartoon Crisis, as it became known, spiraled into a violent international uproar, as Muslims around the world erupted in protest. Danish embassies were attacked, and more than 200 deaths were attributed to the protests.[3] I came to symbolize one of the defining issues of our era: the tension between respect for cultural diversity and the protection of democratic freedoms. This book is an attempt to reconcile that public symbolism with my personal story.

How did the publication of a few cartoons prompt an upheaval so extreme that, five years on, I was still grappling with it? As with most monumental events, there seems to be no simple explanation. Some believe that my newspaper, *Jyllands-Posten*, carries the main responsibility for the uproar, while others point to Danish imams who traveled around the Middle East inflaming Muslim opinion. Some believe Danish Prime Minister Anders Fogh Rasmussen is the main villain because he did not criticize the cartoons and refused to discuss them with ambassadors from Muslim countries. Still others feel the Organization of the Islamic Conference played a decisive part in orchestrating a conflict to promote that body's rather specific take on human rights, involving an effort to criminalize criticism of Islam under the somewhat ambiguous label "Islamophobia." Many say countries like Egypt, Saudi Arabia, and Pakistan took advantage of the cartoons to divert attention from domestic problems. Yet others view the clash as part of a broader struggle between Islam and the West, exploited by radical Islamists to spur followers toward a holy war. Finally, there are those who blame the secular unbelief of most Danes for their failure to understand the religious sensitivities of Muslims.

Even though the drawings were conceived in a Danish and European context, the debate is global. It touches on issues fundamental to any kind of society: freedom of speech and of religion, tolerance and intolerance, immigration and integration, Islam and Europe, majorities and minorities, and globalization, to name but a few.

What do you do when suddenly the entire world is on your back? When one misunderstanding leads to another? When what you have said and done has the world seething with anger and indignation? What do you say to people who ask how you can sleep at night when hundreds of people have died because of what you have done?

What do you say when you are accused of being a racist or a fascist, and of wanting to start the next world war?

In the past five years, I have spent most of my energy trying to address and to understand the criticism that has been leveled at my newspaper and at me. Physically and mentally, it has been an arduous journey: educational, but on occasion overwhelming. I have engaged with people on all sides of the political spectrum, with friends and enemies, believers and nonbelievers of every stripe. Oddly enough, the dividing lines between us don't coincide with the kinds of political, religious, cultural, or geographic categories one might expect. I don't claim that most Muslims have been on my side, but some have supported publication of the cartoons, while some Christians and atheists have strongly condemned them.

I have compiled an enormous archive of comments and analyses on the Cartoon Crisis from all over the world. At first, I wanted to document that I was right and that others were wrong. But along the way, I found that I needed to look inward, to reflect on my own history and background. Why was this debate so important for me? Why was I from the outset, almost instinctively, able to identify the core issue?

Why did the abstract principle of freedom of speech speak to me more than it apparently did to other people?

I do have strong opinions when it comes to certain things. But I am not a person who takes an instant stand on just anything. I am a natural skeptic. I ponder at length and lose myself in layers of meaning and the many sides of an issue. I don't see that trait as a flaw: it is the condition of modern man and indeed the core strength of secular democracies, which are founded on the idea that there is no monopoly on truth. Doubt is the germ of curiosity and critical questioning, and its prerequisite is a strong sense of self, a courage that leaves room for debate.[4]

Of course, doubt is by no means unequivocally a good thing. Questioning everything may lead to the point where there seem to be no truths and everything appears equally right or wrong. In a world of such relativity, there is no fundamental difference between the prisoner in a concentration camp and the regime that incarcerates him, between perpetrator and victim, between those who defend and those who suppress freedom.

That existential dimension of politics first became apparent to me when I traveled to the Soviet Union as a student in 1980. I had no strong preconceptions about the country; politics was peripheral to my youth. What occupied me most were the more esoteric challenges of philosophy, and I was eager to learn more about Russian culture. A long time passed before I began to draw conclusions.

I met my wife that first year and later spent a decade as a correspondent based in Moscow. Over the years, the gravity of life gradually dawned on me. Growing up in Denmark in the 1960s and 1970s during a time of youthful rebellion, I was naturally imbued with the era's atmosphere of freedom and community. Now, it struck me that freedom could not be taken for granted. People paid a high price for expressing their views. Words meant a great deal—they involved consequences. People were so fearful that official censorship was almost an afterthought. There reigned a tyranny of silence.

All stories begin and end with individuals, their choices and decisions. When I interviewed the author Salman Rushdie in 2009, he articulated a problem with which I had struggled in the wake of the Cartoon Crisis.[5] I had difficulty coming to terms with the fact that others were telling my story and interpreting my motives without, I felt, knowing who I was. When we spoke, Rushdie observed that from childhood, we use storytelling as a way of defining and understanding ourselves. It is a phenomenon that derives from a language instinct that is universal and innate in human nature. Any attempt to restrict that impulse isn't just censorship or a political violation of freedom of speech; it is an act of violence against human nature, an existential assault that turns people into something they are not. What differentiates open and closed societies is the right to tell and retell our own and other people's stories.

In the open society, history moves forward through the exchange of new narratives. Think of slavery in the United States, National Socialism in Germany, and communism in the Eastern Bloc, each overcome by challenges to the conventional way of telling the story. In closed societies, the narrative is dictated by the state, and the individual is reduced to a silent, passive object. Dissident voices are punished and censored.

In a democracy, no one can claim the exclusive right to tell certain stories. That means, to me, that Muslims have the right to tell jokes and critical stories about Jews, while nonbelievers may skewer Islam in any way they wish. Whites can laugh at blacks, and blacks at whites. To assert that only minorities may tell jokes about themselves, or criticize other minorities, is both grossly discriminating and foolish. By such logic, only Nazis may criticize Nazis, since in present-day Europe they are a persecuted and marginalized minority. Today, a majority of the world opposes female circumcision, forced marriages, and ritual violence against women. Should we be unable to criticize cultures that still adhere to those practices because they are minorities? According to some of Europe's militant multiculturalists, the answer is yes. But people in democracies should not be forced to live inside echo chambers in which the like-minded tend only to reinforce their own opinions. It is vital to transgress borders between societal groups through dialogue, and it is important to be exposed to the opinions and beliefs of others. People who talk to one another, exchange views, and tell conflicting stories will affect one another's way of thinking.

Rushdie told me that the conflict over the right to tell a certain story was at the center of his own freedom-of-speech controversy. He said:

> The only answer you can give from my side of the table is that everyone has a right to tell their story in any way they wish. This goes back to the question of what sort of society we want. If you wish to live in an open society, it follows that people will talk about things in different ways, and some of them will cause offense and anger. The answer to that is matter-of-fact: OK, you don't like it, but there are lots of things I don't like either. That's the price for living in an open society. From the moment you begin to talk about limiting and controlling certain expressions, you step into a world where freedom no longer reigns, and from that moment on, you are only discussing what level of un-freedom you want to accept. You have already accepted the principle of not being free.

Rushdie's words came just at the right time for me. They opened my eyes and helped me define my own project. We all are entitled to tell whatever story we wish about the Muhammad cartoons. Thus, this book doesn't attempt to cover every aspect of what happened. I am fully aware that other versions exist that are no less true than my own; in some cases, they may be even more complete. I am simply recounting the events as I experienced them and other stories that I deem to be relevant to that experience. My personal quest is to create coherence and meaning out of events that have taken up a lot of room in my own life and in the lives of many others since September 2005.

So this book is also about my own values, about things that are significant to me—books I have read, countries I have visited. It tries to position individual experience within the wider perspective, to explore the relation between my own story and the Cartoon Crisis as a series of events played out on a global scene. In the space between the big picture and the small lies the answer to my own conflict—the image I have of myself as a person who is not fond of conflict—against the wider, global view of me as a dangerous and irresponsible troublemaker. So I also look back to the historical forces that have shaped my attitudes, to European history and its sweeping debates on issues such as faith and doubt, knowledge and ignorance, which have shaped the very notion of tolerance.

My experiences have confirmed my basic belief that people have a lot more in common than whatever divides them. Apparent differences of culture, religion, and history are significant factors, but they are by no means constant; they change, however slowly. Think of countries such as Spain, Greece, Portugal, South Korea, Chile, and South Africa: until only a few decades ago, brutal authoritarian and oppressive regimes; now open, constitutional societies. Such examples show that we should be hesitant about writing off any culture as innately incompatible with liberty and democracy.[6]

Current discussion concerning Islam and Muslims reminds me of the debate about communism and the Soviet Russians during the Cold War. At the time, it was often said that whereas we in the West emphasized freedom and the rights of the citizen, in Eastern Europe, more weight was attached to social rights—the right to work, to housing, and to free health care and education. That distinction was put forth as intrinsically cultural; thus, criticism of the Soviet Bloc for civil rights violations was an expression of Western imperialism. I watched a parallel sentiment emerge in the wake of the Cartoon Crisis: a willingness to compromise what we in the West consider fundamental rights because of supposedly intractable "cultural differences."

My impression was that my friends and acquaintances in Soviet Russia wanted the kind of constitutional freedom and equality encompassed in the notion of universal human rights. But many scholars in the West accepted the premise that Russians were fundamentally different from people in the West; therefore, on the issue of the way it treated its citizens, the Soviet regime could not be judged by Western standards. That notion explains why they were completely unable to foresee the collapse of the regime after popular revolt: to justify their dubious premise, those scholars were compelled to marginalize the Soviet human rights movement and other dissident groups. They claimed that such groups were just manipulated by the West as part of a global political maneuver.

Exactly the same is claimed now about human rights activists and critics of Islam in the Muslim world. It's true that real incompatibilities and disparities of culture between the Islamic world and Europe played out during the conflict.

The truth, however, is that the jury is out as long as the population is prevented from speaking freely and without fear of reprisal. Freethinking forces exist in the Islamic world, insisting on free religious exercise and freedom of speech. That was confirmed during the uprisings throughout the Arab world in 2011.

While the Cartoon Crisis raged, a number of newspaper and magazine editors were arrested, and their offices were closed down because they had printed the cartoons—because, although they may have found them distasteful, they believed their readers should have the chance to make up their own minds about the now-notorious drawings. One of those people, Jihad Momani, editor-in-chief of the Jordanian weekly *Shihan*, wrote the following with reference to a terrorist attack on three hotels in Amman in November 2005: "Muslims of the world, be sensible. . . . What is more damaging to Islam? These cartoons, images of a hostage-taker cutting the throat of his victim in front of a camera, or a suicide bomber blowing himself up at a wedding in Amman?"

I note, too, that large parts of the Iranian population rejected an Islamic take on "constitutional rights" put forward in elections in 2009, and many Iranians in the West were actively supportive of *Jyllands-Posten* during the Cartoon Crisis. They knew from experience what was at stake if censorship of religious satire and criticism should be accepted.

The Cartoon Crisis provides insight into the kind of world that lies ahead in the 21st century. It was a crisis about how to coexist in a world in which old boundaries have crumbled. Today, societies everywhere are becoming more multiethnic, multicultural, and multireligious. And for the first time in history, a majority of the world's population now inhabits urban areas. Increasingly, we live side by side with people who are different from ourselves. The risk of stepping on someone's toes, of saying or doing something that exceeds someone's bounds, is steadily increasing. Moreover, advances in communications technologies have meant that events even in the remotest regions of the world are no longer perceived as being distant. All notion of context disappears. Everything that appears on the Internet appears everywhere. For humor and satire in particular, the loss of context opens the door to myriad possible misunderstandings and sources of offense.

Thus, in 2006, the Iranian authorities demanded an apology for a satirical drawing in the German newspaper *Der Tagesspiegel* showing four Iranian soccer players strapped up with bombs and being watched by German soldiers. The accompanying text read, "The German army should definitely be deployed during the World Cup."[7] The joke was aimed at German politicians who wanted armed forces to patrol the tournament that was taking place in Germany. But the Iranian religious leadership saw things differently. Molotov cocktails were thrown at the German embassy in Tehran, while the artist responsible for the work was forced into hiding because of death threats. Another German paper once printed a cartoon poking fun at the private parts of the heir to the Japanese throne—unthinkable in Japan, where the royal family is almost religiously revered.

Comedians are often keenly aware of the fine line between dangerous and harmless provocation. During a live television show in 2006, Norwegian comedian Otto Jespersen set fire to the Old Testament in the town of Ålesund, a strong bastion of Christian sentiment. Later, when asked to repeat the stunt with a copy of the Koran, Jespersen declined, joking that he would prefer to live longer than another week. It seemed that Christianity was being treated preferentially. Or was it Islam? In any case, the Norwegian prime minister leveled no criticism of the public burning of Christianity's holy book—which is fine by me, but why then did he find it so necessary to condemn a small Norwegian newspaper when it reprinted the Muhammad cartoons?

I believe I know the answer to that. But back in September 2005, I certainly did not, which is one of the reasons why *Jyllands-Posten* and I decided to draw attention to the issue of self-censorship in the public debate on Islam in the first place.

If we believe in equality, it seems there are two available responses to threats against freedom of speech. One option is, basically, "If you accept my taboos, I'll accept yours." If one group wants protection against insult, then all groups should be so protected. If denying the Holocaust or the crimes of communism is against the law, then publishing cartoons depicting the Muslim prophet should also be forbidden. But that option can quickly spiral out of control: before we know it, hardly anything may be said.

The second option is to say that in a democracy, there is no "right not to be offended." Since we are all different, the challenge is then to formulate minimum constraints on freedom of speech that will allow us to coexist in peace. A society comprising many different cultures should have greater freedom of expression than a society that is significantly more homogenous. That premise seems obvious to me, yet the opposite conviction is widely held, and that is where the tyranny of silence lurks. At present, the tendency in Europe is to deal with increasing diversity by constraining freedom of speech, whereas the United States maintains a long tradition of leading off in the other direction. Following the collapse of the Eastern Bloc, many European countries have outlawed Holocaust denial, for example, and it appears that the United States will increasingly stand alone with its tradition of upholding near-absolute freedom of expression on that issue.

My personal view is that the Americans are right. Freedom and tolerance are, to me, two sides of the same coin, and both are under pressure. As noted earlier, the world is undergoing rapid change. Taking offense has never been easier, or indeed more popular: many have developed sensitivity so exquisite that it has become excessive.

It almost tempts one to ask Europe's welfare states to spend some money, not on "sensitivity training"—learning what not to say—but on insensitivity training: learning how to tolerate. For if freedom and tolerance are to have a chance of surviving in the new world, we all need to develop thicker skin.

Certain regimes, including Russia, China, some former Soviet republics, and numerous Islamic governments, agitate in the United Nations and other international forums for laws banning offensive speech. Perversely, although such laws are often put forward in the name of minorities, in practice, they are used to silence critics and persecute minorities. Unfortunately, such petitions have traction in the international community. Their proponents are prepared to sacrifice diversity of expression in the name of respecting diversity of culture, a contradiction they clearly fail to perceive.

They feel they will further social harmony by maintaining a delicate balance between tolerance and freedom of speech—as though the two were opposites.

But tolerance and freedom of speech reinforce each other. Free speech makes sense only in a society that exercises great tolerance of those with whom it disagrees. Historically, tolerance and freedom of speech are each other's prerequisites rather than opposites. In a liberal democracy, the two must be tightly intertwined.

This book comprises nine additional chapters. Three of them consist largely of interviews with individuals who in one way or another have been close to the Cartoon Crisis, and who here shed light on some of its most significant aspects. The first is a Spanish woman whose husband was killed in the Madrid terrorist attack in March 2004, and who later appeared at the trial of the perpetrators wearing a T-shirt showing Kurt Westergaard's cartoon of Muhammad with a bomb in his turban. Next, I speak with Westergaard himself about his upbringing, his background, and his work, in the light of Denmark's history of free speech and censorship. I include an interview that took place in a detention center south of Copenhagen with Karim Sørensen, a young Tunisian who in February 2008 was apprehended by Danish police on suspicion of planning to assassinate Kurt Westergaard. As Muslims, Karim Sørensen and two of his associates felt offended by Westergaard's depiction of the Prophet.

I interweave my own version of the Cartoon Crisis and events before and after publication of the drawings in September 2005 with the story of some of the constraints that have been imposed on freedom of speech. I take a look at efforts today to reestablish so-called violation codes: blasphemy legislation, laws against the incitement of hatred and discrimination, and laws criminalizing the denial or trivialization of genocide or specific historic events.

I look at my encounters with Russian dissidents in the Soviet Union. In my view, the history of Russian dissidence is highly relevant to the Cartoon Crisis—even though the Soviet Union no longer exists, and the Cold War long ago ended—because I feel it mirrors the emergence of new dissident communities within Islam. Included are interviews I have conducted with Ayaan Hirsi Ali in New York, with Afshin Ellian in Leiden, and with Maryam Namazie in Cologne and London.

What those critics say is by no means new: in many ways, there is nothing to add to the discourse on liberty and human rights. Nevertheless, their stories are of immense importance for Europe and the West in general, demonstrating that the desire for freedom is by no means exclusive to the West, and that individuals in other cultures run enormous risks to stand up for "Western" values of freedom and tolerance.

In the book's final chapter, I examine the global struggle for universal human rights. I tell the story of the heretic Michael Servetus, who was burned at the stake in Geneva in 1553, triggering the first great debate in Europe on the issue of religious tolerance. It is a debate that I had thought was won, after the collapse of the Berlin Wall and the communist empire. I failed to see that Ayatollah Khomeini's call to all the world's Muslims to kill Salman Rushdie because of something he wrote in a novel was another major historical turning point. Today, it seems clear that the Rushdie affair was the first collision in a global conflict that seems likely to shape international relations in the 21st century. Nowhere are freedom and tolerance as deeply ingrained as in the West. That I endeavor to illustrate in the final chapter of the book with stories from Afghanistan, Pakistan, Egypt, Russia, and India, which outline how individuals and groups of individuals suffer violations of their right to free speech and free thought.

Well-meaning people in the West claim that democracies can and should sacrifice a little free speech in the name of social harmony: those stories may lead them to reconsider. Measures ostensibly designed to protect religious symbols, doctrines, and rituals in order to prevent discrimination can lead to horrible persecution of the right to speak freely. That is one of the main reasons I continue to defend our right to publish the Muhammad cartoons. If I relinquish that right, I also indirectly accept the right of authoritarian regimes and totalitarian movements to limit free speech on grounds of violation of religion and religious sentiments. I find that unacceptable.

2. Mass Murder and Satire

I woke up this morning to an empty sky.

—*Bruce Springsteen*

It's October 2007, and I'm sitting with Maria Gomez[1] in the café of the Gran Hotel Canarias across from Madrid's Prado Museum. She's wearing jeans, a loose-fitting white blouse, and sunglasses to shade her eyes from the sharp glare of the afternoon sun. I order coffee with cold milk while Maria lights a cigarette. She seems restless. Tears well in her eyes as she recalls what happened three and a half years ago. During the course of our conversation, her mood swings from sorrow to anger, from dark humor to helplessness.

Since the death of her husband in an explosion that ripped through a train on the outskirts of Madrid in 2004, Gomez has been unable to work. A year ago, she and their baby daughter traveled to the island of Menorca to make a fresh start, while her first husband took care of their two sons. The vacation was a disaster; Maria fell into a depression. Her mother, to whom she feels especially close, developed cancer and is terminally ill. Maria's only source of income is the tiny widow's pension she receives from the state. All that and much more she reveals to me that warm autumn day, taking me back to March 11, 2004, a day she and 46 million other Spaniards will never forget.

It was a Thursday. As usual, Maria Gomez was up early. She prepared breakfast for her children. The modest little home in a sleepy suburb north of the city was quiet. No television or radio—at that time of day, Maria Gomez wasn't interested in what was going on in the world outside. She loved the calm that filled her home in those early morning hours.

Shortly after 7:00 a.m., Maria texted her 34-year-old husband Carlos, who had been working all night as a welder doing some construction work in a supermarket in Alcalá de Henares.

"Good morning, my love, looking forward to you getting home," she wrote.

The supermarket remained open while the construction was under way, so Carlos had to work at night. It was his second night working there; the next day, he would move on to another job elsewhere.

Maria's phone rang. The display showed 7:41 a.m. It was Carlos.

"I'm on the train; I'm exhausted," he said.

"How far are you?" Maria asked.

"I'm at Santa Eugenia. I should be home in 30 minutes or so, 45 maybe."

Those were Carlos's last words. Twelve hours later, his barely recognizable body was identified at a military hospital.

In the meantime, Maria had convinced herself that her husband had survived the attack. All 10 explosions occurred before Carlos's 7:41 a.m. phone call. Later, Maria learned that the clock on her phone was a few fateful minutes ahead. "I called him at 8:30 when he hadn't come home. I wondered what could have happened. There was no answer, which was odd. I thought probably the train had been delayed or something."

Shortly after, Maria Gomez left to take the two boys, ages five and eight, to kindergarten and school. She sent another text message from the car: "What's happening? Let me know." Again, there was no answer. At her son's school she heard about a train crash, but there were no details.

"The other parents were so nice. Two mothers went back home with me and the little one. They said they would take care of her if I needed to go out looking for Carlos."

By now, Maria was worried. The mothers soothed her. Her father and brother came over.

"None of us imagined at that time that Carlos might be dead. We just had to find him. There was a lot of confusion," Maria explained.

But Carlos was dead. He had been dead since 7:38, when two bombs had gone off in separate carriages of train 21435 from Alcalá de Henares to the main station of Atocha in the center of Madrid. The fatal explosions occurred just as the train pulled out of El Pozo del Tío Raimundo, a few kilometers east of Atocha. Ten bombs concealed in backpacks on four different trains were detonated by mobile phones. One hundred and ninety-one people from 17 different countries lost their lives, a number of whom commuted into the city and were immigrants who had found benefit in Spain's favorable economic climate. More than 2,000 people were injured in the blasts.[2]

That terrorist attack, which took place three days before Spanish parliamentary elections, was the worst Europe had seen since 1988, when Pan Am Flight 103 had been blown out of the sky over Lockerbie, Scotland, killing 270 people. Political commentators agreed that the Madrid bombings were a political success for the terrorists, since they had a significant effect on the elections. Contrary to the opinion polls, the Socialists won, resulting in an immediate decision to withdraw Spanish troops from Iraq.

"I'll never forget the sight of what happened here," one rescue worker told British newspaper the *Guardian* a year later, at a memorial service held at the El Pozo station where Carlos was killed. "I can still recall the smell of gunpowder smoke, how we found bodies on the platform, the head of a boy lying on a bench."[3]

Television crews arrived swiftly on the scene. Their footage shows the roof torn off one of the train carriages. A second carriage's side was ripped open. A body lay on top of a roof, blown into the air by the blast. Others lay strewn over the tracks. Sixty-seven people lost their lives here. Many bodies were so badly mutilated that DNA tests were the only means of identifying them.

Maria Gomez found Carlos late that evening. Rescue workers had discovered his wallet and ID on his body and had contacted her. She drove to the hospital with her brother and his girlfriend while her parents went in another car. By the time Maria arrived, her father had already identified Carlos, though the body had been barely recognizable.

"I said to my mother, 'Where is he?' She replied, 'He is gone.' It was like some foggy dream. I recognized his tattoo, the remains of his clothes he had on, his hands. Both his legs were missing from the knees down."

Maria's world collapsed. She had just given birth to the couple's first child, her two older children being from her former marriage. The family had only recently moved out of the city, anticipating the security of a new life away from the daily hustle and bustle. Her plans and dreams for the future died with Carlos. "It was like life just disconnected from me. I existed inside my own little space for months on end while life went on around me. I didn't care about anything. Now, it doesn't bear thinking about, but that's the way it was. It was terrible."

At the time of the attack, Spain's prime minister was José María Aznar of the People's Party. But in the parliamentary elections shortly after the bombings, Aznar's party was swept from power by José Zapatero and the Spanish Socialist Workers' Party. Many voters' confidence in Aznar was shaken by his mistaken claim that the Basque separatist group ETA (Euskadi Ta Askatasuna) was responsible for the bombings. Experts disagreed as to whether the group responsible for the Madrid attack was affiliated with al Qaeda, but it seemed clear that the blasts had been at the very least inspired by al Qaeda's ideology. In the spring of 2010, terror researcher Fernando Reinares presented new information about the terrorists' financial backers, confirming that the plan had probably been conceived, developed, and approved by al Qaeda in a Pakistani region close to the Afghan border.[4] The massacre that occurred in Madrid was another battle between radical Islamists and Western secularism.

Somewhat to her surprise, Maria found that after the attacks, her views on a number of issues aligned with Aznar's conservative party. She became a news junkie. Rather than savor quiet mornings by puttering around her home in tree-lined suburbia, she compulsively consumed the news on television, radio, and online.

"I never want to leave home again in the morning without knowing exactly what's going on," she explained.

I met Maria Gomez after reading a short newspaper article in the spring of 2007. A woman had appeared in court during the trial of the alleged Madrid bombers wearing a T-shirt printed with Kurt Westergaard's infamous cartoon. The piece piqued my curiosity, and I sought out an interview. We met less than three weeks before the bombers were sentenced.

Like the relatives of other victims, Maria had closely followed the trial. She told me about the first day in the courtroom. The victims' families had not had a chance previously to see the 28 men on trial. One woman, whose mother had been killed, began shouting at one of them: "You murderer!"

"I wanted to look them in the eye," Maria told me. "I felt the need to confront them to see if there was anything that might tell me more about what happened. But their eyes were empty; they told me nothing."

Many female relatives of victims were particularly outraged by 36-year-old defendant Rabei Osman Sayed, who in a phone conversation had bragged about planning the attack for two and a half years.

"I wanted to plan it so it would be unforgettable for everyone, including me. I was ready to blow myself up, but they stopped me," the transcript of his call read.

Spanish authorities found Osman in 2004 in Milan, where he was serving a sentence for his part in planning acts of terrorism. From 1999 until he was arrested in Italy, he had traveled throughout Europe, visiting Germany, France, Spain, and Italy, making contact with radical cells in search of potential suicide bombers. Searching his Madrid apartment, police found a computer program designed to simultaneously activate a chain of mobile phones. That same technology was used in the March bombings. According to Spanish intelligence, Osman had been an explosives expert in the Egyptian army and had served a prison sentence in Egypt for his membership in Islamic Jihad.

Osman was the first defendant to be called in the trial, but he refused to answer any questions. Maria Gomez says that at one point she made eye contact with him and was able to read his lips: "He said, 'Whore.' I could tell from the movement of his lips. I could have killed him. But I have three children to think about," Maria told me.

After the attack, Maria developed a deeper interest in Islam. When she was a child, her grandfather had been concerned about immigration into Spain from North Africa and the Middle East, and he had often told her about Spain's long history with Islam. Muslims conquered Andalusia in the eighth century and held it until 1492, when Catholic monarchs Ferdinand and Isabella reclaimed the region and forced Muslims and Jews to convert or leave the Iberian Peninsula. As a young girl, Maria had paid little heed to those stories, but now she found herself reflecting on his words. Her grandfather had feared that with the high birthrate among Muslim immigrants, parts of Spain would soon be "reconquered" by Muslims.

"I really want to understand [the terrorists], and in a way I do. Not the fact that they kill other people, of course, but we do step all over them, and I would probably be angry myself if I was one of them. But I'll never understand them fully," she said. "I don't want to bring my children up to be racists, but there is good reason to tell them about the threat of Islam. There are reasons we should be critical of Islam. Religion can be a very dangerous thing."

Maria compiled an extensive archive on her computer. One folder contained the Muhammad cartoons that had been published in *Jyllands-Posten*. Surfing the Internet one day, she found a German firm selling customized T-shirts, and she ordered a white one with a print of Westergaard's cartoon. It came to less than 20 euros, and the shirt arrived a few days later by post.

I asked her why she chose that particular image.

"Because it was the most representative of what the Islamists are all about. That drawing expressed how I felt inside my heart. It represented a piece of reality. I've had a poster of it done, too, which hangs inside my house."

On March 26, 2007, Maria dropped off her children earlier than usual at school and drove the half hour to the courtroom in Madrid. The sun was shining in a clear blue sky. So as not to call attention to herself prematurely, she was wearing a black shirt over the T-shirt.

"I felt good. I felt I would be able to show the terrorists exactly what I thought of them."

The day turned out to be more dramatic than Maria had imagined. Earlier in the proceedings, she had chosen a seat at the back of the courtroom. On this day, though, she sat up front in full view of the accused. She unbuttoned her shirt and pulled it aside, flashing Westergaard's image at the defendants on the other side of the glass cage. "I could tell from the Egyptian's face that he didn't like what he was seeing."

Several of the defendants reacted immediately, calling on their defense attorney to have Maria Gomez removed from the courtroom for offending their religious sentiments. An officer of the court informed Maria that her actions were insulting and asked that she discreetly leave the court. A secretary led Maria out. On her way out, the judge asked for her name and to speak with her in private following the day's proceedings.

The defendants watched with obvious satisfaction as she was removed. Maria was shocked. "I didn't know what to say. I was absolutely furious and started crying when we got out into the corridor. 'What is this? Don't we live in a free country? Aren't I allowed to wear whatever I want?' I asked. I felt really, really bad."

Later in the afternoon, Maria met with the judge, who made it clear to her that he would not allow her T-shirt into the courtroom, because, he said, it could be exploited by the defense to claim that the proceedings were a showcase against Islam and that the defendants were therefore not being accorded a fair trial. A similar incident had already arisen, prompted by a prosecuting attorney wearing a crucifix.

"It wasn't because I wanted to offend Muslims in general that I showed the T-shirt in court," Maria explained. "The only ones on my mind were the Egyptian and the other defendants. They were the ones I wanted to get at. I told that to the Arabic interpreter when he came out into the corridor to see the T-shirt."

On October 31, 2007, the judge ruled on the case. Twenty-one of the 28 defendants were convicted of assisting in the attack. Nineteen of those convicted were from the Middle East; three were Spanish citizens. Three were convicted of murder and received the maximum penalty of 40 years in prison. The other 18 were sentenced to less than 23 years in jail; the presumed ringleader, Rabei Osman, was acquitted, though he still had to complete his 10-year sentence in Italy.[5]

Osman's acquittal, and the fact that only three of the defendants were convicted of murder, came as a shock to Maria and the other victims' relatives. A spokesman expressed their indignation: "We are extremely surprised by the acquittals. If they didn't do it, we have to find the ones who did. Someone must have given the order."

Another response was more blunt: "I'm neither a judge nor a lawyer, but this is shameful and outrageous."

Is there indeed an Islamic ban on depicting the Prophet Muhammad, and if so, to whom does it apply? Muslims expressed various reasons for their affront at the Muhammad cartoons, both in their incarnation as a newspaper illustration and as a woman's T-shirt. Some said it was the act of depiction itself that offended them. Yet if that were the case, why didn't they react to Danish daily *Politiken*'s depiction of the Prophet in June 2005, in a cartoon that portrayed Muhammad as a psychiatric patient? Or to Gary Larson's interpretation of Muhammad and the mountain in 1994? Or to the comic strip *Mohammed's Believe It or Else*?

There have been many other pictures of the Prophet. Indeed, religious historians inform us of a long tradition within Islam of depicting Muhammad. "In the past, and still today, pictures of the Prophet Muhammad have been produced, and are still produced, by Muslim artists for Muslim patrons," wrote Oleg Grabar, a leading expert on Islamic art, in the *New Republic*. In Grabar's view, nothing in Islamic law unequivocally prohibits images of the Prophet. Although historically a majority has condemned depiction, the spectrum of opinion had always been broad, and until recently, posters had been freely available in Iran, for example, depicting the young Muhammad in a sensual pose.

Some imams in the Middle East explained that even simple knowledge of the cartoons' existence was offensive, since it could suggest to some Muslims that they could question their religion. Forbidding such cartoons was thus not about the need to protect the religious sensitivity of the individual; it was more a matter of trying to prevent them from inspiring Muslims to break with their community of faith and demand free exercise of religion and free speech. The cartoons were a challenge to the religious powers that be and their interpretive monopoly.

The well-known Saudi cleric and TV preacher Muhammad Al-Munajid, speaking on Al Jazeera, made that point clearly:

> The problem is that they want to open a debate on whether Islam is true or not, and on whether Judaism and Christianity are false or not. In other words, they want to open up everything for debate. That's it. It begins with freedom of thought, it continues with freedom of speech, and it ends up with freedom of belief.

Having said goodbye to Maria Gomez, I ambled beneath the shady trees toward Sofia Reina Museum to look at *Guernica*, the painting whose twisted images of carnage and chaos have become an icon for the torment of war.

The Madrid bombings may not have wrought such total destruction on the Spanish capital as the German and Italian air strikes did on the Basque town of Guernica in 1937, but eyewitness descriptions of the bloodbath of that March day inevitably bring to mind the horrors depicted in Picasso's painting.

I walked on toward the Atocha station where the four trains had been headed. Here, on the third anniversary of the attack, Spain's royal couple had inaugurated a memorial to the victims: a cylinder of glass, 11 meters tall, engraved inside with thousands of messages sent from around the world in the days following the attack to express sorrow, condolences, and support. Below ground level, underneath the wide boulevard in front of the station, is a stark, blue room illuminated only by streetlights above. Visitors can look up inside the cylinder and study the messages.

I thought about Maria Gomez and what she had told me. To her, Kurt Westergaard's depiction of the Prophet represented in some way what she and others bereaved by the attacks had endured. It was not an image that invited intellectual or moral analysis; to her, it was simply true. A group of Muslims had murdered her husband and destroyed her life. In their own words, their actions had been motivated by their religion—by the words and life of the Prophet as represented in the Koran. To Maria, those facts were indisputable, and they meant that criticizing Islam was a fair and reasonable response.

Is it really inappropriate to engage in pointed but nonviolent criticism of violent Islam? Philippe Val, editor of the French satirical magazine *Charlie Hebdo*, asked of the uproar at the cartoons' publication, "What kind of civilization is this if we cannot mock and satirize those who blow up trains and planes and indiscriminately murder innocent people?"

A courtroom may not be the appropriate place for protest, but the interaction between Maria and her husband's presumed murderers is quite relevant to the Cartoon Crisis and to the broader issues it has raised about tolerance and the distinction between words and actions. After all, who was the victim and who was the perpetrator on that March day in a Madrid courtroom?

Who had the right to feel most violated—a woman who had lost her husband or the men who had orchestrated his death?

Maria's small protest brings to mind the adage "The pen is mightier than the sword." Should it not be considered a mark of civilization that in the face of barbaric violence, we respond only with a cartoonist's pencil and a T-shirt?

3. From Moscow to Muhammad

I divide all works of world literature into those authorized and those written without authorization.

—*Osip Mandelstam*

As Maria Gomez waited in vain for her husband in Madrid on the morning of March 11, 2004, I was at the airport in Copenhagen, on my way to Moscow. An election was scheduled in Russia on Sunday, March 14, the same day that the Spanish parliamentary elections were to take place. Covering that vote was to be my farewell to Russia, and to my job as *Jyllands-Posten*'s Moscow correspondent, a position I had held since 1999. It was also the last stop in my roaming existence as a foreign correspondent based in Moscow and Washington.

The most memorable experience had been the Soviet Union's dramatic collapse in 1991. Each day had been dizzy with new events. Issues long taboo lost all sanctity, and dogmas long accepted were torn away. People who had spent years in prison camps as enemies of the state were elected to high office. Televised debates had people glued to the screen. For someone like me, who had been closely involved with some of the country's dissidents, it was a euphoric experience to watch the communist regime crumble into the ocean like a latter-day Atlantis, although for millions of innocent people, events grew nightmarish when the dissolution of the Soviet Union robbed them of their savings. Revolutions are overwhelming.

I was surprised by what I felt to be a moral dilemma when the Soviet Union collapsed. I had thought I approved of separatist

29

movements. It seemed to me self-evident that every nation that had been forced into the Soviet Union (or any other empire) should be allowed its freedom. But I discovered a darker side to those nationalist movements. As I traveled through the ruins of the empire, covering armed conflicts and ethnic clashes in Nagorno-Karabakh, Abkhazia, Georgia, Moldova, South Ossetia, North Ossetia, Ingushetia, Tatarstan, and Chechnya, it became evident that the leaders of many of those movements looked on human rights as basically reserved for people from ethnic groups they approved of. People from other groups were to be reduced to second-class citizens, driven away, or even killed.

I discussed the issue with Sergei Kovalev,[1] who, following the death of Nobel laureate Andrei Sakharov in 1989, had become the moral leader of the Russian human rights movement. Kovalev had spent seven years in labor camps and three years in internal exile for anti-Soviet agitation; he had since been elected to the Russian parliament, where he chaired the committee on human rights. Kovalev had been a true dissident, and he was a remarkable and dedicated activist. During the first war in Chechnya, in the early 1990s, Kovalev traveled to Grozny and remained there for the duration of the Russian offensive, which for all intents and purposes leveled the city. Nevertheless, he told me he opposed the idea of a right to self-determination through secession.

Kovalev argued that demands for the establishment of new states more often than not end in bloodshed, and any state founded on principles of ethnicity begets citizens of varying classes. Thus, the principle of national self-determination contradicts human rights. There is no universally accepted definition of a people or a nation, Kovalev said, so it is virtually impossible to identify a group that has an unambiguous right to national self-determination in any case. If it were up to Kovalev, states would be joined together rather than split apart; he saw the European Union as a model for the rest of the world.

"If we accept the right of national self-determination, we open the gate to an essentially infinite process of allowing politicians and careerists free rein. It is one thing for a people to feel its rights are violated," Kovalev explained. "It is quite another to have greedy political figures with presidential aspirations eyeing their old pal in the neighbor state who has already made it to the top. Whenever an ethnic group breaks away, a new minority will appear which wants to break away from those who already have done so."

The important thing, Kovalev told me, was to ensure the rights of the individual as a foundation for cultural, religious, and ethnic diversity. Developments in the Balkans and some places in the former Soviet Union had shown, he said, how wrong things could go if national self-determination was accorded more importance than respect for the rights of the individual. There should be only one standard, worldwide: the Universal Declaration of Human Rights, the document that served as an inspiration to Soviet dissidents. I often think back on my discussion with Kovalev, for it came to seem increasingly relevant. It threw a critical light on the notions of parallel societies with special rights, the politics of identity, and the idea of ethnic, cultural, and religious separatism, whether in the Caucasus, in the Balkans, or in Copenhagen.

I had left Denmark in 1990; 14 years later, I was heading back home to start a new life. I had put off the decision to move back several times, for fear I would die of boredom in a country wholly lacking in the kind of world-shaking news that I had been used to covering, from the Kremlin and the White House. But I felt an increasing unease at merely observing other people's lives and their societies in which they lived without having any kind of responsibility. Even though I was fluent in Russian, had family and friends in the country, and was very fond of the place, I felt that I merely stood on the sidelines observing and was not in any real sense part of the society. Any opinion I cared to entertain involved no personal suffering. The stories I covered had no consequences for me personally. I had begun to ask myself whether the meaning of my life really consisted of flitting about the world, entering the lives of complete strangers, and talking to them about life's ups and downs only never to see them again.

In the autumn of 2001, things came to a head. Following 9/11, I went to Tadzhikistan in central Asia to try to get into Afghanistan and cover the American assault that everyone was expecting. On my return to Moscow, I began to have problems sleeping. I would wake at night stricken by anxiety. Often, I would find myself gripped by panic; the fear of death worked its way into every cell of my body. In the daytime, I would find myself staring vacantly into a computer for 30 minutes or more, drained of energy and ideas.

At the time, I often traveled to Chechnya, and Afghanistan was certainly neither better nor worse. Yet for some reason, I found the place highly unpleasant. It wasn't just that four of the journalists with whom I had traveled had been murdered by the Taliban during a visit to the frontline. It appalled me to see how the Afghans could switch sides in an armed conflict so casually. One day, they would be fighting for the Taliban; the next, they were on the other side of the line. Their loyalty was for sale to the highest bidder. Given the country's recent history, that might not have been surprising, but to me it resonated with the cynicism I wrestled with in my daily work as a journalist.

Moreover, I missed working on a team. Being a correspondent meant you were your own boss; there were no long, time-wasting meetings. You got to travel the world and talk to people in all walks of life; you learned to take care of yourself and to write about anything, from tiny hunter communities in Siberia to big-time international politics. You could grow, professionally and personally. But you were alone. The first few years, I was out conquering Russia, and my appetite for that self-contradictory—at once both repugnant and tantalizing—country and its people was huge. But with time, I felt lonely.

So I had accepted the job of culture editor at *Jyllands-Posten*. It meant I was once again part of a community, everyone pulling together to make the best possible newspaper they knew how. Bearing in mind where I was coming from, with my long experience as a correspondent, it seemed obvious to me that I should endeavor to internationalize the paper's cultural coverage. When I started the job in the spring of 2004, I wrote the following to my staff:

> *Jyllands-Posten* calls itself Denmark's international newspaper, and this is something that will be reflected in its culture section to a much greater extent than previously. During the years and decades to come, we are going to find the world at large edging closer, ceaselessly breaching national borders. The challenge for the cultural section of *Jyllands-Posten* will be to stand our readers in good stead so that they may be equipped to meet the world of tomorrow.

I would have to say that in that I succeeded. *Jyllands-Posten* would indeed live up to its self-image as Denmark's international newspaper, though in quite a different way from what I had ever envisaged.

When I took the job, I felt there were two major stories in the world: One was the collapse of Soviet communism and the reforms of Chinese communism, which meant roughly 3 billion people were now integrating into a global market economy dominated by the United States. The second was the interface between Islam and the West in the wake of 9/11. Both stories fit neatly in the category "globalization" and as such would clearly occupy many column inches in the culture section.

Hardly had I settled into my office on Copenhagen's famous Kongens Nytorv Square before Islam critic Ibn Warraq's international bestseller *Why I Am Not a Muslim* appeared in Danish translation. I interviewed him. He warned Europe against compromising the rule of law, equality of the sexes, equality before the law, the separation of church and state, freedom of speech, and the right of religious free exercise. "What we risk," he said, "is the Islamization of democracy instead of democratization of Islam."

Warraq, who hails from Pakistan, but who as a child was sent to public school in England, stressed what he considered to be the great strength of Western society: its ability to level not only criticism but also self-criticism. It means, he said, that errors can be corrected, power cannot be exerted arbitrarily, and authority can be challenged. For that reason, he found it puzzling that so many on the political left were reluctant to criticize oppression elsewhere in the world. In Warraq's view, they failed to distinguish between justifiable criticism of rights violations in the Islamic world and the need to combat racism and intolerance toward immigrants in Western societies. Many of the issues Warraq mentioned pointed forward to the debate that would follow publication of the Muhammad cartoons.

In my first week on the job, I also reviewed Israeli writer Amos Oz's little collection of essays, *How to Cure a Fanatic*. That was another book that would later help me gain perspective. In it, he coined a new slogan—Make Peace, Not Love—and claimed (tongue firmly in cheek) that 9/11 was actually Osama bin Laden's declaration of love. Bin Laden cared so much about us that he wanted to turn us into Muslims and make us all better humans, redeeming us from such worldly evils as democracy, freedom of speech, materialism, and scantily clad women. Oz wrote:

> The essence of fanaticism lies in the desire to force other people to change: the common inclination to improve your neighbor, mend your spouse, engineer your child,

or straighten up your brother, rather than let them be. The fanatic is a most unselfish creature. The fanatic is a great altruist. . . . He wants to save your soul, he wants to redeem you, he wants to liberate you from sin, from error, from smoking, from your faith or from your faithlessness, he wants to improve your eating habits, or to cure you of your drinking or your voting habits.[2]

Oz was skeptical about what he saw as European naiveté. Europeans, he claimed, consider all conflict basically to derive from misunderstandings that can be cleared up if only the conflicting parties sit down and talk to each other for a sufficient length of time. And indeed, the Cartoon Crisis was all about misunderstandings and the kind of naiveté Oz mocked.

Skimming through *Jyllands-Posten*'s weekly culture magazine *Kulturweekend* from the spring of 2004, when I began my work as editor, through to publication of the Muhammad cartoons in September 2005, I found many stories about Islam. The subject interested me, but my knowledge of the debate that was going on in Europe about Islam, Muslims, and immigration was limited. That limitation became painfully apparent on November 2, 2004, when the Dutch filmmaker and writer Theo van Gogh was murdered by a young Muslim in Amsterdam. That afternoon, I received a call from one of *Jyllands-Posten*'s former interns, who was in the Netherlands working on his journalism thesis. He had interviewed van Gogh the previous day and gave me first option on the piece, quite possibly van Gogh's last interview.

I had no idea who van Gogh was; and for that reason, I was unable to see the story. An unknown filmmaker murdered by a Muslim; so what? I turned him down. It was an enormous blunder. Our competitors at the daily *Politiken* grabbed the interview, and I realized not only that my knowledge about Islam was insufficient, but also that I knew far too little about the kind of violence and intimidation that was going on in the West in the name of Islam.

In the few weeks before we published those fateful cartoons, the Danish media were full of stories that together frame the context of the debate that would rapidly explode.

On Sunday, September 11, 2005, four years after the 9/11 strikes, *Jyllands-Posten* carried a major piece on the front page of its Insight section about a research project carried out by Dr. Tina Magaard of the University of Aarhus, which compared concepts of the enemy and images of violence in the central texts of 10 religions.

Dr. Magaard concluded:

> There is no doubt that Islamic terrorists are able to find passages in the Koran, hadith, and the biographies of Muhammad which they may use as arguments in favor of performing acts of terrorism against civilians. In Islam, terror is from the outset a legitimate concept and on occasion an obligation. The texts of Islam depart significantly from those of the other religions; to a much greater degree they encourage violence and aggression. This is an issue that has long been taboo in scholarship about Islam. Some imams have claimed that the Koran forbids the killing of innocent civilians, but this is not the case. There are a number of passages in the Islamic texts in which it is quite apparent that the killing of civilian infidels is permitted.[3]

Imam Ahmad Abu Laban, who would come to play a significant role during the Crisis, reacted angrily to Magaard's research, condemning her as "stupid, prejudiced, and dishonest." He accused her of misusing the scriptures to launch an attack on the Muslim community and claimed that she was out to promote misconceptions of the Prophet and of Islam in general.

But during his trial in the summer of 2005, Theo van Gogh's murderer, 27-year-old Mohammad Bouyeri, gave a very different account. His court statement was a spine-chilling document that confirmed that at least some Muslims do interpret the holy scriptures of Islam in such a way as to justify violence. Bouyeri rejected all speculation that he had felt discriminated against as a representative of an ethnic minority, or offended by van Gogh referring to Muslims as "goat-fuckers." Turning to van Gogh's mother, Bouyeri said the following:

> You should know that I acted out of my own conviction and not because I hated your son for being Dutch or for having offended me as a Moroccan. I never felt offended. And I did not know your son. I cannot accuse him of being a hypocrite. I know he was not, and I know that he was true to his own personal conviction. So the whole story about me feeling offended as a Moroccan or because he had insulted me is nonsense. I acted on the basis of my belief. What is more, I said that I would have done exactly the same thing if it had been my own father or brother. So there is no reason to accuse me of being sentimental. And I can assure you that if one day I should be released, I will do exactly the same over again. As for your criticism, perhaps you mean Muslims when you say Moroccans. I do not blame you for that, for the same law that demands that I cut the throat of anyone who offends Allah and his Prophet says that I must not reside in this country. Or at least not in a country that goes in for freedom of speech, as the prosecution calls it.[4]

Shortly after the story on Tina Magaard's research, Danish police announced that a Danish-Moroccan binational, Said Mansour, had been detained on a charge of inciting terrorism. At Mansour's home, police had found a CD that included texts in tribute to Theo van Gogh's murderer, referring to the passages of the Koran that Tina Magaard had highlighted. Mansour had preached hatred of the infidel for some 20 years, becoming a source of inspiration for terror cells operating out of Denmark.[5]

Ten days before the Muhammad cartoons appeared, a Danish comedian, Frank Hvam, mused about the limits of humor in an age of religious fundamentalism and terror. Rejecting the idea that any-one could dictate what he was allowed to be funny about, Hvam nevertheless had to admit that a little self-censor had wormed its way inside his own mind.

> You can do comedy about the fact that we find it accept-able to kill animals and eat them but not to have sex with them. If I was a pig and someone gave me the choice of being killed and eaten or getting shagged once in a while, I'm pretty sure I know what I'd go for. People get so worked up about that kind of thing being talked about in public. I'm not saying this because of any personal urge to go out and shag the first goat I meet. I just find it interesting to explore why you're not allowed to fool around with a chicken when it's perfectly acceptable to tear its head off and eat it.[6]

Clearly Frank Hvam is not a man to respect a taboo, but he had found himself making an exception in the case of Islam.

> I realized that I wouldn't have the guts to mock the Koran on television. For me, this was a frustrating discovery, because I was brought up to believe that we all have the right to say whatever we want. I find it hugely provok-ing that there are people who are threatening enough to make me keep my mouth shut. I don't want to whip up sentiment or anything, but I do want to make the point that we all should have the right to express ourselves on whatever stage we choose, though at the same time we should respect the stage of others. You're not going to get me running into a mosque, yelling and screaming and ridiculing Islam. That's just not something I can permit myself to do. But I do insist on the right to get up on my own stage in front of a paying audience and say things that mock Muslims, Christians, and chicken farmers if that's what I want to do.

By way of conclusion for what was in every sense a remarkable interview, Frank Hvam laid out his philosophy of humor, its essence, and its purpose. It was similar to the approach of many of our newspaper's cartoonists. "When you venture out as a comedian into that rather provocative borderland, it's not just because you want to provoke," Hvam said. "You do it because you want to discover truths, explore the point at which it starts to hurt, reveal hypocrisy. Why mustn't we eat each other? Why mustn't we go to bed with our sister? Why mustn't we kill each other or steal? Nothing is fixed."

The immediate issue that led to my commissioning the Muhammad cartoons was Kåre Bluitgen's children's book on the life of the Prophet. Bluitgen, at the time 46, had trained as a teacher and spent years as an activist working for the rights of oppressed peoples in the Third World. He lived among immigrants in Copenhagen's Nørrebro district and had on more than one occasion sharply criticized his peers on the left, whom he considered to be naive about the intolerance and oppression he saw within the Muslim community in his own neighborhood.

At a party in the summer of 2005, Bluitgen ran into a reporter he knew from the press agency Ritzaus Bureau.[7] Bluitgen confided his problems in finding someone willing to illustrate a manuscript he had written about the Muslim prophet. Three illustrators, he said, had already turned him down for fear of violent reprisal. The journalist found the story interesting, and a couple of months later got in touch with Bluitgen to find out how the project was proceeding. In the meantime, Bluitgen had found someone willing to illustrate his biography, but that person insisted on remaining anonymous.

Ritzaus Bureau ran a story about Bluitgen's difficulties in finding an illustrator to depict Muhammad on Friday, September 16. Like most Danish papers, *Jyllands-Posten* carried the story the next day: "Illustrators Balk at Depicting Muhammad" was the headline. The following Monday, our managing editor, Jørn Mikkelsen, called me to discuss an idea that had been suggested at an editorial meeting over the weekend. To carry the Bluitgen story further, and to explore whether Danish cartoonists really did self-censor when it came to depicting Muhammad, we should invite them to draw the Prophet.

Already a debate was forming. On the one hand were people who felt the fuss about self-censorship was exaggerated; no Muslim would ever think of demanding that Europeans submit themselves to Islamic dogma, and anyway, depicting the Prophet was not at all prohibited, so it was nonsense. On the other hand were people who insisted that such fears were real, and self-censorship absolutely existed: many Europeans were showing Islam special consideration, since they were afraid of becoming targets of violence.[8]

By proposing a practical demonstration—Show, Don't Tell, a time-honored journalistic recipe—we would allow readers to form their own impressions. I liked the idea. I told Jørn Mikkelsen that I had just been in touch with Claus Seidel, chairman of the Danish cartoonists' society, and would ask him for help with the names of some cartoonists. When Seidel got back to me with a positive response and sent me a list of the society's members, I sat down at the computer that same evening and wrote the following:

> Dear cartoonist,
>
> We write to you following last week's debate about depiction of the Prophet Muhammad and freedom of speech resulting from the children's book by Kåre Bluitgen. It appears that several illustrators declined to depict Muhammad for fear of reprisal. *Jyllands-Posten* is on the side of freedom of speech. We would therefore like to invite you to draw Muhammad as you see him. The results of your work will be published in the newspaper this coming weekend.

I look forward to hearing from you.

Yours,

Flemming Rose

Culture Editor, *Jyllands-Posten*

Having added that the paper would be paying a symbolic fee of 800 kroner, I printed 40 copies of the letter, fetched a stack of envelopes and a sheet of stamps, and began addressing and stamping by hand. When done, I put the whole lot in a plastic shopping bag, cycled to the post office on Købmagergade, and deposited them in the postbox shortly before 9:00 in the evening, in time for next-day delivery.

After that, I gave the project no thought for several days. The idea was that the drawings would appear in the Sunday issue's Insight section, since various deadlines meant we wouldn't be able to use them in the Friday Culture section that I edited. But toward the end of the week, I received word from Jørn Mikkelsen that the project had been put on hold, since there was now apparently some doubt about Kåre Bluitgen's claim, and also some disagreement among staff members about the viability of the project.

At this point, I think I should raise the question of why I picked cartoonists, not illustrators. With hindsight, some people claimed that illustrations would not have been nearly as provocative or offensive as caricatures or cartoons. I'm far from certain about that claim. The question of what certain groups might consider offensive is a rather unpredictable matter. There was Burger King's ice-cream cone that was shaped like the Arabic word for Allah. There was the television commercial for a hair product with the slogan "A new religion for hair." There was the question of the crucifix on Inter Milan's soccer jerseys. Few of us in our wildest imagination would consider those things potentially offensive to religious sentiments.

I wanted to find people who habitually expressed themselves in images; I didn't care whether the drawings were realistic, abstract, satirical, expressionistic, impressionistic, or anything else. That was indeed apparent in the cartoons that we received. They differed greatly from one another, both in the way in which they represented Muhammad—in fact, only four or five drawings actually portrayed the Prophet and thereby violated the alleged ban on depiction—and with regard to whom the satire attacked. Many were not directed toward Islam and the Prophet at all.[9]

Three days after my invitation to the Danish cartoonists, I received an email from Claus Seidel, the chairman of the Danish cartoonists' society, wanting to know what the response had been like. My invitation, he said, was becoming the subject of lively debate within the cartoonist community. "One of the arguments against has been a certain apprehension about landing on an anti-Islam bandwagon and appearing to be opposed to immigration," he wrote. "No one wants to be a part of that. I hope you can see that point! Can you outline the angle you'll be taking in the article? Feel free to call!"

Jørn Villumsen of *Politiken* was one of the cartoonists who declined the invitation. The reason, he said, was partly because he didn't have enough time and partly because he didn't want to violate the Islamic ban on depicting the Prophet:

> Let those who believe in Muhammad have their image of him in peace. Why should we interfere? When I'm photographing and meet people who don't want their picture taken, I respect that. That's why I don't think this is about freedom of speech at all; it's about pissing on people who have another belief, something they hold dear. It seems to me to be a confrontation cooked up by the press for no reason whatsoever. Call me again when this has more substance.

That same week, I received an email from Annette Carlsen, who shared a studio with several members of the cartoonists' society. Carlsen wrote that she was receptive to the idea, but she noted that the cartoon genre was by nature satirical and therefore more provocative than any illustration in a children's book. For that reason, she wanted to get an idea of the context in which her drawing would appear. "I would like to see what sort of text you have in mind to accompany the drawings," she wrote.

I wrote the piece on Wednesday, September 28, two days before the cartoons were due to be published. I read it over the phone to the paper's editor-in-chief, Carsten Juste, who approved it. The actual page presenting the drawings had already been laid out to allow my article to be slotted in the middle.

> The comedian Frank Hvam recently admitted that he "wouldn't have the guts to mock the Koran on television." An illustrator commissioned to depict the Prophet Muhammad for a children's book wishes to remain anonymous. The same is true of the translators of a collection of essays critical of Islam. A leading museum of art removes an exhibited work for fear of Muslim reaction. The current theater season embraces three satirical plays attacking U.S. President George W. Bush, yet not one concerning Osama bin Laden and his allies. In a meeting with Prime Minister Anders Fogh Rasmussen, an imam urges the government to exert its influence on Danish media in order to ensure a more positive image of Islam.

> The above examples are cause for concern, whether or not the fear that is felt is justified. The fact is that it exists, and it spawns self-censorship. What we are seeing is an intimidation of the public space. Artists, writers, illustrators, translators, and performers are skirting around today's most significant cultural encounter: between Islam and the secular, Western societies rooted in Christianity.

> Modern secular society is rejected by some Muslims. By insisting on particular consideration for their religious sentiment they demand a place apart. This is incompatible

with secular democracy, in which the individual must be prepared to suffer scorn, mockery, and ridicule. That may not always be a pretty sight. And it doesn't mean that religious sentiment should be mocked at any price. But all that is beside the point.

It is no coincidence that people living in totalitarian societies often end up in jail for telling jokes or portraying dictators in a critical light. Usually in such cases reference is made to public feeling having been offended. It has not come to that here in Denmark, but the examples cited show that we are on a slippery slope; no one can predict where self-censorship will end.

Therefore *Jyllands-Posten* has invited members of the Danish society of cartoonists to depict Muhammad as they envisage him. Of some forty who were invited, twelve responded. Their drawings are published here, signed with the cartoonists' real names.

I then cited the names of the 12 cartoonists, before concluding:

Only twenty-five of the forty invited are active, and some of those who are active are subject to noncompetition clauses. A few have offered reasons for their declining to take part. Others have referred to pressures of work, while others still have refrained from responding at all.[10]

One of those to whom I sent the piece was Lars Refn, who of all the 12 cartoonists was the most critical toward *Jyllands-Posten*, though that was in no way obvious from our correspondence. His reaction to my article was simply, "That's how it is!" In other words, he was supportive. As for the idea itself, Refn wrote: "Thanks for your invitation regarding a cartoon on the subject 'Muhammad and freedom of speech.' It will be a pleasure for me to send you a submission by noon on Friday."

By this time, Kåre Bluitgen's claim that artists invited to illustrate his children's book had been censoring themselves had been substantiated. The illustrator who finally took on the job had explained in the Danish daily *Information* that he insisted on anonymity because he feared for his safety. "I'm truly vexed by the fact that I'm afraid to step forward, and I know how stupid it is to yield to that kind of fanaticism," he explained. "I don't have this picture of the great specter of Islam knocking on the door all of a sudden, but I am afraid of being accosted on the street and getting beaten up or worse."

In January 2006, shortly before the issue exploded onto the global stage, the same anonymous illustrator expounded on his motives in the weekly *Weekendavisen*:

> When the publishers offered me the job, the editor brought it to my attention that illustrating the story would in certain areas of the Muslim community be considered controversial, since there was a tradition for interpreting the Koran in such a way that it was forbidden to depict Muhammad. Like so many other people in Denmark, I knew nothing about it at that time, and had the editor not mentioned it to me I would have just gone ahead with it like any other job. It was a book I really wanted to illustrate, because I found there to be something very picturesque and intriguing about the whole universe in which the story takes place, but I was of two minds. Would I be jeopardizing my own safety and that of my family, or was this concern an Islamophobic overreaction?[11]

The illustrator pointed to three events that made him frightened of releasing his name: the fatwa against Salman Rushdie, the murder of Theo van Gogh, and a violent attack on an associate professor affiliated with the Carsten Niebuhr Institute at the University of Copenhagen in the autumn of 2004. (The professor in question had been accosted outside Copenhagen's Tivoli Gardens by three young Muslims who pushed him into a car and beat him up, warning him to refrain from reciting verses of the Koran in his university lectures.)

The anonymous illustrator confirmed Kåre Bluitgen's claim that three other illustrators had been too worried to take on the work. That claim was also confirmed by Bluitgen's editor at Copenhagen publishers Høst & Søn. Moreover, apparently another illustrator had originally taken on the project, also insisting on anonymity; but ignoring Kåre Bluitgen's explicit instructions, the illustrator in question had systematically portrayed Muhammad from behind. His depiction was an attempt to sidestep the issue of showing the Prophet's face.

"He turned up, and all fifteen of his drawings had Muhammad with his back to the reader, despite our clear agreement. So we had to drop the whole thing and start from scratch," Bluitgen explained.

According to Bluitgen, that first illustrator had contacted the Center for Contemporary Middle East Studies at the University of Southern Denmark to ask how dangerous the work might prove to be. The center had said there would be little danger for a non-Muslim Dane to draw Muhammad. Paradoxically, one imam who was later to become a leading figure in the campaign against *Jyllands-Posten* also declared the whole issue to be a non-starter. Abdul Wahid Pedersen told the Danish daily *Information* that the ban on Muslims depicting the Prophet simply did not apply to non-Muslims: "We cannot as Muslims interfere in the actions of others."

That's a very interesting statement, because as events emerged, it became clear that in this instance Muslims absolutely did want to interfere in the actions of non-Muslims, even in countries in which Islamic law was not in force. In the spring of 2006, I visited the Islam scholar Bernard Lewis at his home near Princeton University in New Jersey, and he emphasized that very issue, noting that it was new: Muslims were now demanding that non-Muslims, in non-Muslim countries, should adhere to Islamic precepts.

"I have been unable to find even one example discussing non-Muslims having insulted the Prophet in a non-Muslim country. So all this trouble about non-Muslims offending the Prophet in non-Muslim societies is a completely new phenomenon without any basis in Islamic history or case law," the then 90-year-old scholar commented.

When I asked him how that was to be understood, Lewis replied:

> I don't think anyone would say as much, but there seems to be an underlying assumption that Europe is now a part of the Islamic world or at least is becoming as such. It is in a state in which a country can be categorized as neither infidel nor Muslim, a state in which it is populated by infidels and governed by infidels, yet has made a treaty with the Islamic state. This was the case in some countries in Europe bordering the Ottoman Empire. But it's odd inasmuch as Europe has a long tradition of insulting the Prophet, and that has never before triggered this kind of reaction, because what the infidels do in their own lands is basically no business of Islamic law.[12]

Although Bluitgen's book provided ample documentation of the kind of self-censorship that had motivated the project, *Jyllands-Posten* was still reticent about publishing the cartoons. But a number of other issues convinced managing editor Jørn Mikkelsen and me of the need to run the piece. Comedian Frank Hvam, swayed by the fear of violence, had already voiced reservations about challenging Muslim limits in the same way as he regularly challenged those of other groups in the society. Translation of Somali-born Dutch parliamentarian Ayaan Hirsi Ali's 2004 collection of essays, *De maagdenkooi*, into a number of European languages had given rise to fears of reprisal among translators and publishers alike. (The book had been published in Danish under the title *Jeg anklager* (*I Accuse*) by Jyllands-Postens Forlag in the autumn of 2005.) According to the author's agent, several European translators had insisted on anonymity, unwilling to lend their names to a book signed by Hirsi Ali, who lived in hiding, watched over by body-guards around the clock. Without the author's approval, the book's anonymous Finnish translator had even removed a controversial statement concerning the Prophet, whom Ali had referred to in an interview as a "tyrant" and a "pervert."[13]

Yet another example of self-censorship, to which I referred in my piece accompanying the cartoons, was an episode that took place at London's Tate Britain gallery in mid-September 2005. One of British conceptual art's foremost figures, 84-year-old John Latham, had opened a retrospective, including a work titled *God Is Great*. That piece was composed of a thick glass panel in which were embedded cut-up copies of the Bible, the Talmud, and the Koran. The piece had originated in reaction to the Gulf War in 1991. The idea of presenting the holy books mounted and project-ing from the stable, transparent background, said Latham, was to show that religions originate from the same source. The written text was vulnerable, and the use of the word "God" by institution-alized religion was infected with prejudice, a state of affairs that Latham considered to be dangerous. Latham explained:

> The pieces that I'm calling *God Is Great* are there to indi-cate that underneath the theologies is a real source from which they are all extruded, if one is talking about the physical character of them, or emanated if they are in a kind of spiritual sense. People do know a source that they experience and they call this person Allah or God or Jehovah, or whatever it is that they call this source. And that's got to lose its sectarian characteristics.[14]

Although Latham and the Tate Britain curator agreed that the piece was central to the retrospective, the gallery's director, Ste-phen Deuchar, decided to remove it just before the show opened after two scholars of Islam warned there was a risk that the piece would be construed as an affront to the Koran. "We didn't want

John Latham's work to be misrepresented and given a political dimension he didn't intend," he explained to the *Observer*.[15]

Curiously, given that the Bible and the Talmud were accorded the same treatment as the Koran, no one bothered to ask why Deuchar had not also consulted experts on Christian and Jewish beliefs. It was as though a silent consensus existed that British Muslims were so utterly unpredictable and so dangerous that they should be treated in the manner of small children. Or perhaps they were seen as wild animals not to be taunted at any price. Both standpoints seemed crassly offensive and discriminating.

Latham was furious at the gallery's decision. He demanded that *God Is Great* be removed from the Tate's permanent exhibition and returned to him. "Tate Britain have shown cowardice over this. I think it's a daft thing to do because if they want to help the militants, this is the way to do it," he hit out in the *Observer*.

According to Tate Britain director Deuchar, staff members at the gallery were afraid of attack by Islamic extremists, a fear founded not on specific information, but on the general climate in the wake of terror bombings in the London underground system on July 7, 2005.[16] Shami Chakrabarti, the director of the civil liberties organization Liberty, commented:

> I'm concerned about the signal this sends at a time when we see free speech quite significantly under threat. I think that after 7 July we need this kind of artistic expression and political expression and discourse and disagreement more than ever, which is why this is worrying. Is three holy books in a piece of glass going to incite controversy? Frankly, whether it does or doesn't, controversy is what we have in a flourishing democracy.

Had I researched the issue more thoroughly, I would have found many more examples of self-censorship and demands to shut down free speech in the months before we published the cartoons. Here are just six:

1. In December 2004, the Museum of World Culture in Gothenburg, Sweden, opened an exhibition titled *No Name Fever: AIDS in the Age of Globalization*, in which Algerian-born artist Louzla Darabi exhibited a work titled *Scène d'amour*. It shows a reclining woman, legs apart, having sex with a man in a standing position whose face cannot be seen. The woman is clearly enjoying the act. At the top of the painting, the opening verse of the Koran is written in Arabic:

> In the name of God, Most Gracious, Most Merciful
>
> Praise be to God, the Cherisher and Sustainer of the Worlds
>
> Most Gracious, Most Merciful
>
> Master of the Day of Judgment
>
> Thee do we worship, and Thine aid we seek
>
> Show us the straight way
>
> The way of those on whom Thou hast bestowed Thy Grace, those whose portion is not wrath, and who go not astray.

According to Darabi, there was a tradition among Muslims in her home country of Algeria whereby man and wife would address God by quoting the verse before lovemaking. She explained that her painting demonstrated the tie between love and faith and that carnal love could also provide a way into a spiritual world. At the same time, she emphasized the point that the work could be viewed as being critical of the patriarchal society and violence against women, as well as challenging a widespread taboo in the Muslim world: women's sexual pleasure.[17]

During January, the museum received some 700 emails from offended Muslims complaining about the work and wanting it removed. Some of those emails contained threats, referencing the murder of Dutch filmmaker Theo van Gogh in 2004. "You and your disgusting work will set Muslims in Sweden alight. Learn from Holland! The biggest superpower in the world cannot protect itself, so the question is how you are going to protect yourself," warned one.

In January 2005, less than three weeks after the exhibition opened, the museum removed the work. Interviewed by *Jyllands-Posten*, Museum Director Jette Sandahl explained:

> Freedom is conditional on the freedom of others. We have no right to offend one another. You don't have the right to say what you want about other people. The rights and freedom of the Other are integral to the philosophy of law. . . . We're not looking to offend our visitors.

"Isn't that censorship?" she was asked.[18]

"I can see where you're going," she said, "but we show a lot of extremely offensive stuff here, and we are not a fearful gallery. But once in a while you have to take account of the sensibilities of your audience."

The logic of Sandahl's account was flawed to say the least. Either you reserved the right to offend or else you did not. One should not, as the director of a public museum, distinguish between those whom it's OK to offend and those whom you do your best to placate. It was obvious that in this case, preferential treatment was being given to a selected minority, either out of fear or to show consideration. Moreover, the idea that if you say something that might be construed as offensive, you somehow restrict the liberty of others is nonsense.

2. In the summer of 2005, Britain's Labor government proposed a bill criminalizing, to an unprecedented extent, speech deemed critical of religion. Salman Rushdie and comedian Rowan Atkinson responded in a public letter to the home secretary:

> We understand, as we have previously stated, that the government's intentions are to plug a loophole and protect Muslims specifically in the way that others are protected

under racial legislation. But a law which draws a wide brief in order to protect a specific instance seems misguided from its outset. . . . It will inevitably aggravate tensions amongst the various faiths, clog up the courts, and induce censorship in our artistic, broadcasting, and publishing establishments. It will also, we fear, create a climate in which expression is constrained for those who might wish to criticize some of the palpable ills associated with religious hierarchies, while encouraging those who want to use the courts and media for self-aggrandizement.[19]

3. In the autumn of 2005, a group of Muslim activists demonstrated in Saint-Genis-Pouilly, a small French town on the border of Switzerland. The local cultural center had decided to stage a reading of Voltaire's 1741 satire *Fanaticism, or Mahomet the Prophet*. The activists wanted it canceled. The mayor refused. But on the evening of the performance, riot police were deployed to keep the peace. Demonstrators set fire to a car, and isolated scuffling occurred.[20]

4. In the autumn of 2005, London's Barbican Theatre decided to remove a scene involving the burning of the Koran from Christopher Marlowe's classic 1587 play *Tamburlaine the Great*. Theatergoers were also spared several of the play's references to the Prophet Muhammad. The theater's directors explained that they feared an uncut version of the play might inflame passions in the tense social climate following the London terror attacks of July 7, 2005. However, that blatant instance of self-censorship was quickly denounced by patrons, literary scholars, and some Muslims.[21]

5. On September 13, 2005, the European Court of Human Rights issued a ruling regarding a novel by a professor of Turkish history, Abdullah Riza Ergüven. *Yasak Tümceler* (*The Forbidden Phrases*) portrayed the Prophet Muhammad as a historical figure whose holy words were in some cases inspired in "a surge of exultation" while in the arms of his young bride Aisha. "God's messenger broke the fast with sexual intercourse after dinner and before

prayer," Ergüven wrote. "Muhammad did not forbid sexual intercourse with a dead person or a living animal."

The Turkish penal code forbids insults against "God, religion, the Prophet and the Holy Book." In May 1996, Ergüven was sentenced to two years' imprisonment, later reduced to a fine. The European Court of Human Rights upheld the ruling, on the grounds that Ergüven's book had contained "an abusive attack on the Prophet of Islam" and that "believers could legitimately feel that certain passages of the book in question constituted an unwarranted and offensive attack on them."[22] In my view, the decision was a shocking step backward, part of an alarming tendency among European institutions to approve restrictions on free speech because of religious or cultural sensibilities.

6. Following the London terror attacks in July 2005, Danish Prime Minister Anders Fogh Rasmussen and two of his government ministers scheduled a meeting with a number of imams, representatives of Muslim associations, and elected politicians of Muslim background. They planned to discuss how to prevent radicalization and terror. Even before it was held, the meeting was controversial: members of the Danish parliament claimed that the government was lending credibility to imams who in several cases directly opposed Muslim integration into Danish society.

After the meeting, two of the imams said they had used the occasion to ask the prime minister to curb the Danish press.[23] Those unambiguous appeals to the government to take action against criticism of Islam created even more uproar.

I could go on. Examples of self-censorship, intimidation, and pressure exerted by governments and interest groups on free speech were legion, both before and after we published the cartoons. Most involved Islam, though there were some examples relating to Christians, Sikhs, Hindus, and others.

Many chose to pretend such activity wasn't happening. It seemed to be too uncomfortable to think about. But that was how I perceived the context in which the Muhammad cartoons were published in the autumn of 2005. I linked it to the specter of Orwellian thoughtcrime, and with my experiences in the Soviet Union, where telling jokes deemed to be defamatory of the Soviet state had the risk of three years or more in a forced-labor camp. (After the death of Stalin in 1953, at least 300,000 prisoners who had been sentenced for telling jokes were released from forced-labor camps, according to historian Roy Medvedev. He does not include those who died in the camps.)[24]

Other people gave greater weight to other factors—particularly the continuing public debate on immigration, which many felt had turned into a smear campaign against Muslims. A number of incidents were cited. Shortly before the cartoons appeared, Denmark's minister of culture, Brian Mikkelsen, spoke out against what he called "a medieval Muslim culture." On his webpage, a member of the right-wing populist Danish People's Party published a series of articles in September 2005 in which Muslims were likened to cancer cells and said they would never be integrated into Danish society. Many viewed that action as part of a government movement to collaborate with the Danish People's Party in curbing Muslim immigration.

The Muhammad cartoons were thus also seen as part of a campaign against Muslims. That was not the case. As I saw it, there were two reasons to publish the cartoons: first, to highlight self-censorship and its effect on cultural life and second, to fight the fears that underlay self-censorship. The more frequently the taboo was challenged, I thought, the more difficult it would be to maintain intimidation.

So what was in the drawings?

In the debate that followed publication of the cartoons, the diversity that they expressed seemed to get lost in the deluge of commentary. Everything was about Kurt Westergaard's drawing of the Prophet with a bomb in his turban. That shortsightedness meant that important points were being missed. Things became even more confused when some of the first death threats were aimed at two cartoonists whose images of Muhammad few considered controversial. One had drawn a sandal-clad Muhammad walking in the desert with his donkey. It was a neutral image that could easily have appeared in an illustrated biography of the life of the Prophet. The second had shown a Copenhagen schoolboy named Muhammad wearing the jersey of the local soccer club Frem, on which was printed the word *Frem-tiden* (the Future). That Muhammad, who clearly had nothing to do with the Muslim prophet, stood pointing at a passage in Persian that had been chalked on a blackboard, which translates as "The editorial staff of *Jyllands-Posten* are a bunch of reactionary provocateurs." So the cartoonist was directing his satire at my colleagues and me, rather than at the Muslim prophet and Islam.

Two other cartoons targeted Kåre Bluitgen, who had been unable to find illustrators for his book. One showed Bluitgen sporting a turban containing an orange on which the words "PR Stunt" are written. That plays on the Danish phrase *at få en appelsin i turbanen* ("to receive an orange in one's turban"), meaning to have a windfall or a stroke of luck. The second showed Bluitgen and six other individuals in a police lineup, along with a witness, who on being asked to identify Muhammad, says, "Hmm . . . I'm not able to recognize him." Muhammad himself is thus not depicted. But among those in the lineup is Pia Kjærsgaard, leader of the Danish People's Party and the country's most forceful political voice against immigration and Islam.

A fifth cartoon shows a cartoonist in a cold sweat, secretively working on a drawing of Muhammad. The cartoon sticks closely to the story line regarding Bluitgen's difficulties in finding an illustrator. A sixth consists of a semi-abstract portrayal of Muhammad, with a nose, one eye, and a mouth, the face wreathed with a green crescent and partially covered by a star, symbolic of many flags and organizations in the Muslim world. A seventh portrays the Prophet, bearded, in sandals and traditional dress. He has a neutral expression on his face and a pair of horns protruding from his turban. Is that feature a reference to Moses, who is often depicted with horns in Danish churches? Is the artist alluding to the devil, or to mythological portrayals of the horned god as representative of fertility, body, sexuality, enjoyment and sorrow, life and death? Or do the horns more generally play on the fear of confronting Islamic taboos that formed the point of departure for my invitation to the cartoonists' society? If the horns indeed were intended to allude to something dangerous and aggressive, it was certainly at odds with the Prophet's neutral and quite open facial expression.

The eighth cartoon shows the Prophet in an aggressive stance, saber raised. He is flanked by two women clad in *niqabs*, only their wide-open eyes visible through the eye openings, while the eyes of Muhammad himself are censored by an equivalent black bar, a reference to the Islamic ban on depiction. The women at his side appear somewhat fearful, an allusion perhaps to the lack of equality between the sexes in Islamic countries.

The ninth cartoon consists of five identical women in headscarves, all with the Islamic crescent and star, along with a rhyme about the subjugation of women, which says roughly (I am grateful to a *Wikipedia* contributor for this suggestion), "Prophet, you crazy bloke! Keeping women under yoke!" The artist responsible for the work, Erik Abild Sørensen, died in the spring of 2008 at the age of 89. When I wrote of his death on my blog, comments poured in from triumphant Muslims. One person wrote: "Allah is great, Allah is great. May Allah burn him in hell for all eternity."

The 10th cartoon portrays Muhammad or Allah in heaven, receiving suicide bombers who want to be admitted into paradise. However, God or his prophet responds, "Stop, stop, we've run out of virgins!"

The 11th cartoon shows two sword-wielding Muslims charging forward, apparently eager to seek out Danish illustrators who have violated the ban on depiction of the Prophet. Muhammad, however, tells them to calm down, thus appearing as a man of peace: "Take it easy, friends. At the end of the day, it's just a drawing by a Danish infidel. . . ."

Then, finally, there is Kurt Westergaard's much-debated drawing of the Prophet with a bomb in his turban. I base much of the following on Jens-Martin Eriksen and semiotician Frederik Stjernfeldt's excellent analysis of it in their book, *Adskillelsens politik* (*The Politics of Separation*).[25]

Westergaard's drawing was denounced by many for stereotyping and demonizing Muslims; parallels were made with anti-Semitic caricatures in Germany in the 1930s. Critics claimed that the cartoon denounced all Muslims as terrorists. In Eriksen and Stjernfeldt's view, however, such interpretation is unfounded. The drawing comprises three elements: a naturalistic portrait of a bearded man with a calm and neutral expression; a stylized bomb with a lit fuse; and finally the Shahadah, the Islamic creed, inscribed on the bomb in Arabic: "There is no God but Allah, and Muhammad is his messenger." The drawing does not say whether the bomb has been placed in Muhammad's turban with the intention of killing Muhammad, or whether he intends to deploy it.

It depicts Muhammad as representative of Islam, in the same way as images of Jesus refer to Christianity, as pictures of Karl Marx refer to Marxism, and as Uncle Sam to the United States.

Taking the further step to claim that the Muhammad figure not only refers to Islam but also to all Muslims is far from valid. In contrast to the anti-Semitic caricatures of prewar Germany, Westergaard's drawing includes no generalizing feature that may be taken to be true of an entire community of believers. Portraying Karl Marx with blood on his hands, the crucified Christ holding a glass of beer, or the Christian God armed with a bomb does not mean you think that all Marxists are bloodthirsty murderers or that all Christians are drunkards or terrorists. So Westergaard's stylized bomb may refer to the specific Muslims who do commit acts of violence in the name of their religion, just as a drawing of Christ armed with a bomb might refer to small groups of

Christians who have defended attacks on abortion clinics in the United States. Nothing in the cartoon can reasonably be claimed to stereotype Muslims. Westergaard's cartoon differs significantly from the German anti-Semitic caricatures, all of which are heavily marked by racial stereotypes, such as the hooked nose, greed, the Jewish star, and the notion of the eternal Jew, signifying that a drawing is to be understood as referring to an entire group. The claim is: all Jews are like that. That is not at all the case with Westergaard's cartoon, which does not single out and attack a particular group within society, but a religious doctrine.

Mikkel Bøgh, art historian and rector of the School of Visual Arts at Copenhagen's Royal Danish Academy of Fine Arts, also feels that the juxtaposition of Muhammad and the bomb can be interpreted on several levels.[26] Are we meant to infer that the Prophet represents Islam and that Islam is a warrior religion? Or is the idea rather that the image of the Prophet is being destroyed by terrorists who commit acts of violence in his name? Is the cartoon saying that Muhammad is oblivious to the fighting going on in his name, since his expression is neutral, even vacant, and he appears unable to see the bomb that is about to blow him to pieces? Or are we to understand from the drawing that Islam as a religion is self-destructive?

Astonishingly, many of Westergaard's critics insisted that the cartoon was unambiguous and could be interpreted in only one way. Those critics (a number of whom had never laid eyes on Westergaard's cartoon or any of the other published drawings) were in no doubt that it portrayed all followers of Muhammad as terrorists and suicide bombers. Others insisted that it could be read only as saying that Muhammad himself was a terrorist.

The explosive sense of affront and outrage arising from the cartoons raises the question of what prompts us to assign such destructive force to a simple drawing. Why do images seem to possess more power than words? That is a question addressed by American art scholar W. J. T. Mitchell in his book *What Do Pictures Want?*[27]

Mitchell says images have always been potent and threatening. In the Christian story, Adam and Eve were created in the image of God, and God banished them from paradise when they showed themselves to be disobedient, defaming God's image as it was reflected in their own being. When God decided to give his chosen people a new chance, he did so on the condition that the Israelites obeyed his laws, and by the first of those, he forbade the making of images. "You shall not make for yourself an idol, whether in the form of anything that is in heaven above, or that is on the earth beneath, or that is in the water under the earth." That commandment is accorded greater treatment in the Old Testament than all the others put together, and it is punishable by death.

With any offensive image, the greater the efforts to destroy or damage it, the more vivid it becomes. The physical image may be destroyed, yet the perception of it lives on in memory, tales, and imagination. Mitchell believes that images, in the manner of wild animals, are untamable, refusing to defer to man's attempts to control or forbid them. "My point is that the (futile) effort to destroy the offending image is invariably counter-productive; it is a battle with a phantom or specter that only makes the offending image stronger," he says.[28]

This observation clearly applies to the Muhammad cartoons, since those who felt offended by the images and wanted them banned and destroyed were instrumental in their being spread throughout the world.

In Mitchell's view, images in themselves say nothing. Only we make them come alive, reading meaning into them, becoming angry because of them, or finding joy. Their message is defined by the beholder and whatever context he or she cares to construct. The claim is supported by the fact that offensive images are notoriously unstable artifacts.[29] Images that a hundred years ago were considered pornographic, disgusting, or blasphemous may in our day be deemed to be great works of art: think of two of French impressionist Édouard Manet's most prominent works, *Le déjeuner sur l'herbe* (*Luncheon on the Grass*) and *Olympia*, both slammed as vulgar and immoral when first exhibited in Paris.[30]

Thus, it is not Kurt Westergaard's depiction of the Prophet with a bomb in his turban that stirs up feeling, but the beholder's verbalization of what he or she sees. In some instances, that verbalization happens to be "Muhammad is a terrorist" or "All Muslims are terrorists"—regardless of the fact that it was not Westergaard's intention to draw such an image, and despite closer analysis of the image revealing that it appears to provide no immediate basis for such an interpretation.

Is art entitled to be transgressive?[31] Is it a privileged zone in which the individual has the right to say things not normally tolerated, and is Westergaard's cartoon art? The argument is sometimes deployed to distinguish between Salman Rushdie's *The Satanic Verses* and the Muhammad cartoons: Rushdie's novel is a work of art, whereas the cartoons are vulgar doodles devoid of aesthetic value. But is art somehow special? Some people highlight art's ability to express messages and impressions differently, to transgress borders and break down taboos, allowing audiences to see, experience, and understand the familiar reality of the world in new ways, thereby paving the way for new insight. Art's "estrangement" ability serves to break the automatic, routine experience of reality and is therefore particularly valuable.

Another line of defense of art's right to offend rests on the so-called canonic alibi, claiming that transgressive art is part of a tradition and should be understood in light of references to previous works.

That view is relevant to the Muhammad debate insofar as it makes clear that the cartoons were partly created in a context in which the breaking of taboos is considered to be progressive rather than intended to offend or attack a religious minority. Artists such as Robert Mapplethorpe and Andres Serrano were a source of uproar in the United States in 1989, triggering reactions that bring to mind those following the Muhammad cartoons. The difference, however, is that whereas criticism of Mapplethorpe and Serrano issued mostly from the Christian right, the attacks on the Muhammad cartoons primarily came from the progressive left.

In 1989, the American art photographer Robert Mapplethorpe's sensational exhibition *Robert Mapplethorpe: The Perfect Moment* was removed from the program of Washington's Corcoran Gallery of Art three weeks before it was due to open.[32] The gallery feared that its funding from the National Endowment for the Arts would be withdrawn because of the homosexual and sadomasochistic subjects of Mapplethorpe's work. The Corcoran's self-censorship occurred in the shadow of another scandal that took place in 1989, when conservative members of Congress, launching a campaign against public funding of offensive art, took issue with *Piss Christ*, an image by Haitian-Cuban photographer Andres Serrano.[33] *Piss Christ* showed a plastic crucifix immersed in urine, and one gallery where it was shown had secured public funding for its exhibition; Serrano himself had received $15,000 for his work.

The ensuing debate again illustrated that opinions about what can be deemed offensive differ greatly. Interest in Serrano's work (and its market value) skyrocketed. One Catholic nun defended *Piss Christ* on theological grounds: she believed it highlighted the way modern society regards Christ and the Gospels.

In 1999, an exhibition titled *Sensation: Young British Artists from the Saatchi Collection* opened at London's Royal Academy and the Brooklyn Museum of Modern Art in New York. One image, by Marcus Harvey, showed child murderer Myra Hindley. The mother of one of Hindley's victims demanded the work be removed because it offended her, and Hindley herself wrote to the gallery from her prison cell, asking that it be removed because it would cause grief both to the families of the children she had murdered and to those suffering as a result of similar crimes. The work remained on exhibition; the gallery suffered several smashed windows.

In New York, the Hindley piece went largely unnoticed.[34] But another of the 110 works on exhibition created a media storm. Chris Ofili's *The Holy Virgin Mary* depicted the Virgin Mary as a black Madonna adorned with resin-covered lumps of elephant dung and surrounded by images of female genitalia cut from pornographic magazines.[35] New York Mayor Rudy Giuliani, who like the artist himself was a Catholic, threatened to cut off the city's $7 million annual support to the museum unless the work was removed. Every politician in New York appeared to feel the need to take a stand.

Ofili himself believed the aggressive reactions had little to do with his work, but were fired by political agendas. In an interview, he explained that the elephant dung was a reference to his African heritage. The elephant and its excrement were symbols of power and fertility. African art had a long tradition of using dung expressively, and as such, there was nothing at all offensive about it.

"There's something incredibly simple but incredibly basic about it. It attracts a multitude of meanings and interpretations," Ofili said to the *New York Times*. "I don't feel as though I have to defend it. The people who are attacking this painting are attacking their own interpretation, not mine. You never know what's going to offend people," he added.

No one had predicted that Harvey's and Ofili's works specifically would become objects of outrage. Some considered Damien Hirst's *This Little Piggy Went to Market*, consisting of a dead pig in formaldehyde, to be the work most likely to cause affront and had anticipated the wrath of animal rights activists, but as it turned out, it got few reactions.[36] Moreover, the exhibition revealed that even in countries rooted in the same culture, opinions as to what is offensive can differ markedly. The intentions of the artist were not determinative of what a specific work communicated, and— as Ofili pointed out—it was not the image itself that caused offense, but the critics' (and not the artist's) interpretation of it.

For W. J. T. Mitchell, it is often the language we use to represent an image that defines whether or not it is considered offensive. People who have never laid eyes on Ofili's image of the Virgin Mary, but have heard it referred to as *Madonna with Elephant Dung*, classify it as offensive, although in reality the piece, according to Mitchell, appears quite harmless: unobtrusive, gentle, and innocent. The noun "dung" provokes the offense and gives rise to the conclusion that the painting is disrespectful. As with Andres Serrano's *Piss Christ*, the title of the work establishes a mental context, and that, rather than its actual properties, is the true source of offense. If Serrano had called his work *Christ Bathed in Light*, most likely it would not have attracted the kind of attention it did.

From all these cases—Manet, Ofili, Serrano, Mapplethorpe, and many others—we see that the propensity of an image to cause offense is not a fixed characteristic. It emerges socially out of the interaction between individuals, institutions, and events past and present. And different images do not cause offense in the same way. Some offend the beholder; some offend the person depicted. Some images offend because they pour scorn on something people perceive as valuable, others because they glorify something people think of as contemptible. Thus, the glorification of Muhammad among Muslims may be perceived as offensive to those whose kin have been killed in Muhammad's name. That was clearly the sentiment of Maria Gomez after her husband had been killed in the Madrid bombings of 2004 by terrorists in the name of Islam.

Mitchell does not believe in using legislation to curtail offensive images in the broad sense, only in contexts in which people are forced to look at images they would otherwise choose not to see. Citizens, he says, have the right not to have offensive images thrown up in their face, while they simultaneously have the right to see images that others find offensive. The right to show offensive images is therefore above all a matter of context rather than content, of the setting in which an image appears rather than what it shows: basically, it's about where, when, and to whom.[37]

Opening my email on the morning of September 30, 2005, I read the first reactions to the cartoons. With one exception, they were positive.

"Thanks for a superb initiative printing the Face of Muhammad in JP today," one reader wrote. "Features of this nature make us appreciate our newspaper even more than we did before. The piece illustrates what satire really can do. Many of the cartoons were so funny they had me laughing out loud, without their in any way presenting a negative picture of Islam."

Another commented: "Not used to writing in—but my word, these cartoons are brilliant! Moving, incisive, hilarious! Looking forward to reactions the next few days, they will come, surely! Fantastic."

Then one mildly negative reaction, from a Muslim: "Don't play with religion. In Denmark there is room for all of us. We live in Denmark, so we should accept Danish rules. We need to hear and write about the positive sides of our lives."

During the course of the day, I also received a phone call from a store owner in Brøndby, west of Copenhagen. He criticized the cartoons and informed me that they had been the subject of discussion at his mosque, with widespread support for a boycott of *Jyllands-Posten*. I explained to him our reason for publishing the cartoons, and that I felt they in no way overstepped the generally accepted approach to satire in Denmark. I pointed out that my article on the same page emphasized that Muslims should receive the same treatment as Christians, Buddhists, Hindus, Jews, and other believers and nonbelievers. By putting Islam on the same footing as other faiths, the cartoons integrated Muslims into a Danish satirical tradition, since we were thereby considering them as equals in the society rather than outsiders. They were inclusive rather than exclusive of the Muslim community in Denmark. During the months that followed, I reiterated that argument in media all over the world, as well as in public discussions, to the extent that eventually I could reel it off in my sleep, like the chorus of some pop song.

On the afternoon of September 30, 2005, I went out into the city to meet with an old friend from Washington, D.C., who happened to be visiting Copenhagen. We sat at a sidewalk café on Kongens Nytorv enjoying the autumn sun. I mentioned in passing that we had just published some cartoons that had given rise to a few reactions from readers. We carried on chatting about Danish domestic policy and what was going on in the United States and Russia, a passion shared by us both. At that point, I was more interested in what stories were going to run in the days that followed than what had been in the paper that morning. I had no idea what the coming months and years had in store.

4. The Infamous Ability of Humans to Adapt

According to the Danish Security and Intelligence Service (PET), Kurt Westergaard was to be murdered in his home on a quiet residential street in a suburb of Aarhus, Denmark's second-largest city.

"I imagine it was going to be with something from the kitchen drawer," said Kurt Westergaard drily. "It wouldn't have been a pretty sight, I'm sure."[1]

He looked like what he was: a hippie grandfather in a black-velvet jacket, a red scarf, turquoise socks, red-checked shirt, and sneakers. Having spent eight months in hiding, he and his wife Gitte were back home in their tidy row house in Viby, Jutland. It was a November evening in 2007, and they were sitting outside on the patio under the eaves that Gitte had just finished fixing when PET called. A group of radical Muslims were planning to assassinate her husband. The group had blueprints of the house and had been watching it for some time. The couple was given a few hours to pack before being whisked off to safe houses—a series of holiday cabins, hotels, and apartments.

By now, Kurt was convinced he would be living with police protection for the rest of his life. He was 73 years old: "Too old to be scared," he commented. PET had turned the house into a small fortress. There were closed-circuit television cameras everywhere; the windows were bulletproof; and a safe room had been installed, with an alarm that, if activated, would bring police help within two minutes.

The safe room probably saved Kurt Westergaard's life on New Year's Day in 2010, when an attempt was made on his life. A 28-year-old man of Somali origin forced entry into the artist's home at around 10:00 p.m., while Westergaard and his 5-year-old granddaughter were home alone. The girl's parents had gone to a movie, and Gitte was holidaying abroad. Westergaard and the child, whose leg was in a cast following a recent accident, had been watching *The Wizard of Oz* and reading a book. Suddenly, all hell broke loose.

"I'd just been to the bathroom and was on my way back into the living room when there was a series of tremendous blows against the glass door leading into the garden," Westergaard recalled when I visited him again in the spring of 2010. By now, security had been further tightened, and guards were permanently staked out in a container unit put up alongside the house.

According to PET, Westergaard's attacker and potential assassin was linked to the al Shabaab terror movement in Somalia.[2] He had arrived in Aarhus by train from Copenhagen that same evening. From the train station, he had taken a taxi to Westergaard's home and had asked to be dropped off at the end of the road. The driver later recalled his customer saying that he had been there before and could find his own way. He crossed a public lawn, went around to the back of the house, and climbed over the gate. He carried a bag containing an axe and a knife. He used the axe to smash his way into the living room where Westergaard's grandchild was lying on the sofa with her broken leg. Westergaard himself retreated to the safe room—the bathroom from where he had just come.

"I had to make a quick decision," Westgaard recalled. Should I confront him and risk being killed in front of my grandchild? Or should I go back into the safe room and hit the police alarm? I chose the latter," he explained, "remembering that PET had told us that those kinds of terrorists only go for whomever they think has offended Islam, leaving their families alone. Fortunately, it turned out to be true, but I was very, very scared."

His axe-wielding would-be assassin launched himself at the door of the bathroom, chopping wildly and screaming: "I'm going to kill you!" and "Revenge." Then, as the flashing blue lights of police vehicles appeared in the street outside, he turned and took flight with the words, "I'll be back." At first, Westergaard thought others must be involved, so violent was the commotion. On his way out, the attacker smashed a television and a computer. Westergaard's grandchild had begun screaming when the attacker forced his way inside. Now, Westergaard assured her that she needn't be frightened. Confronted by police on the street outside, Westergaard's attacker hurled his axe at an officer and started waving his knife. Police responded by shooting him in his right leg and left hand; they then overpowered and arrested him. He was charged with attempted murder and terrorism.

The artist was among the country's most likely targets for a terrorist attack, and he had been under PET protection for two years. Yet a man who was under surveillance on suspicion of being involved in a terrorist network had succeeded in gaining entry to his home and carrying out an attempt on his life. Westergaard and his wife declined to go into hiding again; they resigned themselves to a life in which they would be shadowed by armed police wherever they went. However, the attack so alarmed Westergaard's hairdresser that she refused to cut his hair. Out of concern for the safety of its staff, a major auction house declined to sell a watercolor Westergaard had painted to support Haitian earthquake victims. Not wishing to be the cause of undue concern among his colleagues, Westergaard decided to resign his freelance position at *Jyllands-Posten* in the summer of 2010.

Even the first evening I spoke with Westergaard and his wife, two years before that attack, they told me that Gitte had been asked to stay away from her job at a local kindergarten on the grounds that her presence compromised the safety of the staff and children. Kurt had been informed by the Hotel Radisson in Aarhus that they no longer wished him to stay there: guests had begun to recognize him, and he was bad for business.

When PET made that first phone call in November 2007, Westergaard knew that his life was about to change drastically. Only close family were informed about their situation. PET wanted to give the impression that the couple was still living in the house so any potential attackers could be apprehended if and when they should strike. The mailbox was emptied regularly. The lights in the house turned on and off automatically, and surveillance equipment was installed. The couple had to leave their car behind, which was parked outside the house and moved every so often.

The Westergaards celebrated Gitte's birthday as usual on December 14, 2007, coming home the day before to decorate the house for Christmas; they even put up and trimmed a tree. Fifty guests were invited, and Gitte served a buffet of traditional Christmas fare accompanied by wine, beer, and schnapps. No one noticed anything was amiss. Armed intelligence agents were staked out in a shed in the back garden and kept a sharp eye on proceedings with a camera mounted in a birdhouse.

"Afterward, we took everything down again, stayed the night in the house, and moved back out to our secret hideaway on the coast the next day," Gitte Westergaard recalled.

To begin with, it was all very Hollywood. Kurt Westergaard remembers how one agent, who drove them to their first hideaway, reminded him of Al Pacino in the movie *Serpico*. They drove a circuitous route, throwing out red herrings along the way, and generally acted like they do in the movies. As time progressed, however, and no solution to their plight ensued, the mood sank. The sense of not being in control of one's life became a source of distress.

"I felt like I'd been hit by this tremendous exhaustion. We would sit around in deserted holiday areas out of season with no one around and nothing to do," Westergaard explained.

One cool spring day in 2008, Kurt and Gitte Westergaard were being moved yet again, this time closer to family and friends: a hotel apartment in Fredensgade in the center of Aarhus. As they retrieved their luggage from the car, two couples of Middle Eastern appearance passed by on the other side of the street. One of the men recognized Kurt.

"May you burn in hell!" he shouted.

"Can we talk about it now or should we wait until we meet there?" Westergaard quipped. He had always had a sharp, sometimes bracing, sense of humor. But the upshot of that involuntary encounter was that Kurt and Gitte had to put their luggage back in the car and return to their previous city.

Throughout his tribulations, Kurt Westergaard has never doubted his feelings about religion: "I'm an atheist, and I can only say that the reactions to my drawing have made me stronger in my faith." Confronted by criticism and charges that he was to blame for the violence and deaths that occurred during the Cartoon Crisis, Westergaard had an anecdote he liked to recount about his favorite artist, Pablo Picasso. During World War II, Picasso ran into a German officer. When the German officer figured out whom he was talking to, he said,

"Oh, you are the one who created *Guernica*?" referring to the famous painting of the German bombing of a Basque town by that name in 1937.

Picasso paused for a second and replied, "No, it wasn't me, it was you."

Kurt Westergaard had always been a storyteller as a child. Kurt's father ran a grocery store in the village of Døstrup in North Jutland. With the whole village as customers, having a son who went round making up stories about people often proved to be a strain.

"Much later, I discovered there was a synonym for lies—imagination. That changed my whole perspective."

As the son of the village shopkeeper, it was imperative that he maintain friendly relationships with everyone. Causing trouble and fighting with the other children were out of the question, and the subject of religion was particularly charged. With religion came taboos: sex, the body, tales of sin and perdition, devoutness and piety, heaven and hell. Neither of Westergaard's parents was strongly religious; he refers to them as "culturally enlightened" Christians. But as the shopkeeper's son, he was forced to attend Sunday school out of deference to his father's customers. The school was run by the so-called Inner Mission, a pious, 19th-century revivalist movement that had arisen as a reaction to the rational approach to Christianity that had issued from the Enlightenment.

"Nowadays we'd call them fundamentalists," Westergaard muses. "If you did certain things you were damned—swearing, using dirty words, thoughts about sexuality. If, like me, you had a lively imagination and were branded a liar, there was a lot of anger. I felt unable to navigate my way around in my imagination without running into the fear of God that the teaching instilled in us."

Westergaard found himself gazing up at a blue sky one day after Sunday school, thinking: there's a long way to heaven, but Satan is just beneath my feet. "The way I was taught, religion was all about hell rather than God, damnation rather than salvation."

In 1951, Kurt Westergaard began attending a high school in the town of Randers. In the summer months, he lived at home with his parents, cycling the first seven kilometers from the village to Hobro, and then taking the train. During the winter, he had his own room in student housing. A teacher introduced him to the so-called cultural radicals, a liberal intellectual movement that in many senses was to transform modern Denmark. Poul Henningsen's texts in particular sparked Westergaard's interest: his defiance of Nazism, his rejection of bourgeois conservatism, his dismissal of the religiously infected sexual morals of the day.

"All the authorities I had felt to be so oppressive in my childhood were brought tumbling to the ground one by one," he explained. "Poul Henningsen bemoaned what he called the infamous ability of humans to adapt. He let fly at it all: morals, architecture, religion, nationalism."

Westergaard wanted to study art; his parents talked him out of it. Instead, his father suggested he become a teacher. He did, and gradually he became more interested in subjects involving storytelling: history, geography, and art. Toward the end of the 1960s, he developed an interest in teaching children with learning difficulties, ending up heading a school for severely handicapped children for 25 years. Much of his work consisted of devising teaching materials for children with handicaps. A major challenge was to establish low-readability, age-relevant materials capable of capturing the attention of the older pupils. During that time, Westergaard illustrated some 120 books. "It wasn't great art. It was all about creating a straightforward and unambiguous form of expression that could be easily understood and that we could apply in our teaching."

In 1982, Westergaard joined *Jyllands-Posten* as a freelance cartoonist, his work in a smaller paper having been noticed by one of the editors. His contributions became a regular feature. It was a dream come true: "It was a huge luxury to be able to sit on my own and concentrate on my drawing. At the school, I was used to being interrupted all the time, so for me it was marvelous. I've never regretted taking the plunge."

Westergaard points to three artists in particular as exemplary Danish cartoonists in the 20th century: Hans Bendix, Arne Ungermann, and Bo Bojesen. Bendix was a master of the immediate, spontaneous expression, his work always shaped with a lightness of touch that on occasion gave the impression that his pencil strokes had been sprinkled casually onto the paper. Ungermann was an intellectual artist, whose drawings often accompanied lengthy texts. Bojesen's satire manifested his detailed scrutiny of the society in which he lived.

"When it comes to satire, I've always been inclined toward a sharpness of expression, which probably can be seen in my Muhammad cartoon," Westergaard said. "There's a saying along the lines of 'While humor laughs and irony smiles, there's nothing funny at all about satire.'"

Working for *Jyllands-Posten* in the 1980s, Kurt Westergaard sensed that certain themes would be better left alone. He remembers three in particular: U.S. President Ronald Reagan, naked women, and the apartheid regime in South Africa. "That was beyond me completely. Why the hell shouldn't we make fun of South Africa?"

Readers reacted strongly to some of Westergaard's cartoons. One depicted a crucified Jesus with dollar signs in his eyes; it illustrated an article on organized religion's pragmatic stance on money matters. Letters to the editor accused Westergaard of blasphemy. On another occasion, he illustrated a piece on the Israeli–Palestinian conflict with a cartoon equipping a Palestinian with the Star of David. A few years later, and on the same theme, Westergaard delivered an image of a Palestinian fenced inside the Star of David, peering through barbed wire. Another showed the Star of David with a bomb attached to it—reminiscent now of his depiction of Muhammad in 2005. On that occasion, he received an indignant phone call from Arne Melchior, a prominent member of Jewish society in Denmark who was also a member of the Danish parliament. Reactions from readers were angry and plentiful, though no death threats were received.

"Melchior dressed me down and lectured me about the symbol being of such significance for Jews that it could not be turned 180 degrees in a satirical cartoon," Melchior said. "I pointed out that it was just a drawing. I said it was a pity if the drawing had offended people, but I had to insist on my right to visualize the content of an article, even if it offended some people."

It was a line of reasoning Westergaard maintained as fundamental to his work. Although describing his relationship to religion as "untroubled," he has always reserved the right to mock any kind of religious malfeasance or misbehavior:

> In that way, I'm immensely satisfied with my drawing of Muhammad, though I do have a rather ambivalent relationship to it. On the one hand, I can see all the trouble it's caused. On the other, I genuinely feel that I've expressed myself in a way that has found resonance. I'm glad I did it so late in life. It stands now as the culmination of my work. "You succeeded," I think to myself. "You kept going. And now there's a small price to pay."

The drawing was done on September 21, 2005, the same day that he and other members of the Danish cartoonists' society received my letter inviting them to depict Muhammad as they saw him. Westergaard liked the idea. It was a perfect opportunity to target people who exploit religious faith in order to legitimize violence and spread fear:

> The idea came to me immediately. The bomb is an age-old symbol of terrorism, and I thought if I use the Arabic inscription from the Islamic creed I'd be able to make the point clear that Islam is the terrorists' spiritual ammunition. It proceeded from there. It took maybe an hour, all told. It was just another day at the office, really.

Westergaard did not immediately see his drawing as being particularly controversial in any way. "My feeling was, it was on the button—a bit severe, perhaps, but the creative process had been smooth. You get an idea and then do a drawing right away. It was just like you want it to be. I felt it all hung together very well."

From his own family, however, he is well aware that different cultural codes can lead to misunderstandings. In February 2006,

Westergaard was visiting his son and his Peruvian daughter-in-law in the United States. He had been sitting in the garden sketching, portraying the couple's two little girls with wings, making them look as though they were floating in the air. His son's wife was aghast when she saw what he was doing. To her, the wings of angels portended that the children soon would die. Westergaard erased them. It was an incident that took place in the middle of the violent reactions to his cartoon in the Middle East and other Muslim countries. "I was sitting out by the pool," he said, "and could see that the television was on in the living room. I saw the Danish flag and went inside to see what was going on. As it happened, there were riots, and Danish embassies had been burned to the ground. I was shocked."

Westergaard admits that it was hard to comprehend exactly what was going on. None of it, however, gave him second thoughts as to the wisdom of his drawing:

> I can't see myself being responsible for the fact that certain despicable regimes in the Muslim world, which are unable to fulfill the basic needs of their peoples, send them out into the streets to work off their aggression on cartoons that a newspaper has published in some far-off country. Every time my drawing has sparked off threats and violence, it makes me more defiant. As I see it, I did a job. I'm entitled to my opinion, and what I expressed in the drawing is true.

Although Westergaard's cartoon triggered strong reactions in the Islamic world, and many Muslims felt that it touched a sore spot, Ekmeleddin Ihsanoglu, secretary general of the Organization for the Islamic Conference (OIC), which weighed in with an international campaign against Westergaard's drawing and Denmark in general, acknowledged that extremist ideas have spawned acts of terrorism that have indeed been perpetrated in the name of Islam.

"We do not have the luxury of blaming others for our own problems. It is high time we addressed our national and regional problems with courage, sincerity and openness," Ihsanoglu stated. He stressed the need to combat poverty, illiteracy, and corruption in the Muslim world, saying that "when these issues are not addressed properly by legitimate means, they are used as an excuse to push for extreme ideas."[3]

At the Muslim World Congress in Mecca in December 2005, Saudi Arabia's King Abdullah likewise deplored the way extremists had hijacked Islam. "It bleeds the heart of a believer to see how this glorious civilization has fallen from the height of glory to the ravine of frailty, and how its thoughts have been hijacked by devilish and criminal gangs that spread havoc on earth," he said.[4]

As a youth seeking to rebel against oppressive religious and cultural norms, Westergaard was inspired by Poul Henningsen's denunciation of "the infamous ability of humans to adapt." He understood that view as a critique of inaction, of the passive acceptance of injustice that had been a widespread attitude in Denmark during the 1930s, following the rise to power of Adolf Hitler in Germany and his National Socialists' initial moves to exert pressure on Germany's neighbors. In fact, Denmark witnessed several crises that foreshadowed the attempts of totalitarian regimes and movements to restrict the Muhammad cartoons. The first of such cases concerned one of Westergaard's own idols, the artist Hans Bendix, who together with the multitalented Poul Henningsen and other critics of Hitler's new regime, began publishing the first anti-Nazi journal to appear in Danish.

Aandehullet (Breathing Hole) was the name of the new publication, and it carried in its first issue an article by Bendix that attacked the fawning Danish media's appeasement of the Nazis. Most Danish institutions at the time upheld a distinction between supporting free speech in domestic politics but maintaining strict neutrality abroad, particularly with countries stronger and wealthier than tiny Denmark. Bendix called that distinction "cowardly and stupid." That kind of appeasement was to surface again during the Cartoon Crisis, when three of Denmark's former ministers of foreign affairs took it upon themselves to lecture their compatriots on diplomacy, and the European Union's commissioner for foreign affairs Javier Solana assured Middle Eastern potentates that publication of the Muhammad cartoons would not be repeated. The question of who had equipped him with such a mandate on behalf of the citizens of the EU was unclear.

Aandehullet brimmed with satirical drawings and caricatures skewering Hitler, National Socialism, and its supporters. And after only three issues, Hans Bendix was summoned to the office of the prime minister, who threatened to remove him from his full-time job on the Social Democrat Party newspaper unless *Aandehullet* was shut down.[5] Bendix did so, and Denmark's first caricature crisis thus ended in victory for those who believed that free speech should bow to pressure from foreign powers and those who wished to appease them.

It was a pattern that repeated during the Cartoon Crisis, though pressure in that instance came from rather different quarters: the Organization of the Islamic Conference, Muslim countries' ambassadors in Denmark, Islamic clergy in Denmark and abroad, three former Danish foreign ministers (Mogens Lykketoft, Niels Helveg-Petersen, and Uffe Ellemann-Jensen), and various retired Danish diplomats, as well as parts of the media and much of the business community.

The parallel with the 1930s gained particular salience following the attempt to assassinate Kurt Westergaard in January 2010, when critics of Westergaard and *Jyllands-Posten* declared outright that Westergaard and *JP* had invited the attack. Hans Bendix and Poul Henningsen had provoked the wrath of the Nazis in exactly the same way in 1935, the year after *Aandehullet* closed. A pamphlet of drawings by Bendix triggered an eight-hour debate in parliament after Nazi mouthpiece *Der Völkische Beobachter* denounced one of the cartoons, which showed Hitler washing blood from his hands beneath the heading "Dolfuss in memoriam—the latter-day Pontius Pilate." (Austrian leader Engelbert Dolfuss was murdered by Nazi agents in 1934, though Hitler denied any connection with the murder.) Bendix was sharply criticized from both sides of the chamber, which deplored the detrimental effects the cartoon could have on Danish exports. Prime Minister Stauning ended the session with a warning to the press against poking fun at foreign leaders.[6]

In the spring of 1933, another cartoon crisis descended on Denmark. On April 30, Copenhagen daily *Berlingske Tidende* published a caricature by Norwegian newspaper artist Ragnvald Blix, which triggered a crisis between Denmark and Germany. It depicted Hitler in the company of Gestapo founder Hermann Göring and Nazi propaganda head Joseph Goebbels with a text reading, "That happy-go-lucky Austrian attitude is anti-national, but how do we throw people in jail for being nice?"

A week after the drawing appeared, the paper's correspondent in Berlin received a visit at home from five uniformed men and two in civilian clothes; they displayed a copy of the paper with the cartoon and searched the house. Later that same year, a German advertiser and hotel owner in Hamburg lodged a complaint with the Ministry of Foreign Affairs in Berlin on the grounds that his guests had on several occasions expressed their dissatisfaction with the *Berlingske Tidende*'s cartoons. The Danish foreign office reacted promptly, approaching the paper's chief editor with criticism against Blix. From then on, many of Blix's cartoons were shelved.[7]

In 1938 came a third cartoon crisis, this time with Copenhagen daily *Ekstra Bladet* cast as the bad guy. Niels Spott—a pseudonym of Arvid Møller—repeatedly incurred the wrath of the German ambassador on account of his scathing satires of Hitler and his henchmen. Former foreign minister Erik Scavenius was head of the board of the publishers of *Ekstra Bladet*. He was incensed in particular by one of Spott's cartoons that showed a barber being led away by a Gestapo officer after attempting to use a curling iron on Hitler's hair. According to Scavenius, that was a blatant case of scorn, mockery, and ridicule of a foreign leader; he had made it quite clear on several occasions that he would not accept his paper's publishing cartoons that poked fun at the Führer. Indeed, Section 107 of the criminal code expressly prohibited personal insults to leaders of foreign governments. However, as *Ekstra Bladet*'s legendary editor Ole Cavling noted in his diary, Scavenius "was never the slightest bit bothered about even the most vicious caricature targeting the British."[8] Niels Spott was removed from *Ekstra Bladet*'s back page, and the paper's foreign coverage was placed under Scavenius's direct control.

Poul Henningsen was a free-speech fundamentalist, who had little time for lamentations about offense to religious sentiments, retorting that the world would be a better place if reason, rather than religion, could be protected. Many of the discussions in which he became involved proved relevant to the Cartoon Crisis. He emphasized the importance of distinguishing between words and actions and pointed out that the more a society asks its citizens to accept common norms and values, the more crucial it becomes to maintain unrestricted freedom of speech. In the tense climate of impending war, Poul Henningsen—the man who would later inspire Kurt Westergaard—was impressively unyielding in his insistence that free speech should be permitted to people whose opinions he did not share, be they anti-Semites and racists, Nazis, or communists working to establish a Soviet regime in Denmark. He adhered to English writer George Orwell's notion that freedom makes sense only if it involves the right to tell people what they don't want to hear.

Henningsen excoriated the prudish narrow-mindedness he found so typical of Denmark, castigating religion and calling for sexual freedom. Throughout the Nazi occupation of Denmark, he aimed the sting of his merciless criticism at National Socialists and the Danish establishment who sought to appease them. After the war, he spoke out against those who called for a ban on National Socialist parties, and he was appalled that so few voices protested the McCarthy persecution of freethinkers in the United States. In Henningsen's view, dictatorships and democracies both impose limits on individual liberties. Both systems prohibit theft, speeding, and tax evasion; total, uninhibited freedom exists in neither framework. The crucial distinction between open and oppressive societies consists in unconditional freedom of speech.

"It is in the most vital interests of democracy that political freedom is seen to be absolute, since this is the only way in which the population may develop the antidotes necessary to combat mindless extremism," Henningsen wrote, just months after the Nazis capitulated in the spring of 1945:

> If we tamper with free speech and the freedom of ideas, we undermine the only defenses we have to protect the democratic system of government by the people. If we do not believe that the people as a whole will choose democracy, what right have we to enforce it upon them and still call ourselves democrats?[9]

Henningsen could have been talking about the 21st century, when calls are made to ban Islamic parties, such as Hizb-ut-Tahrir, which struggle to abolish democracy and establish theocratic rule. It is also pertinent to a current Europe-wide trend that is especially worrying: increasing support for legislation aimed at criminalizing speech that is deemed to be "inciting religious hatred."

The modern dispute regarding the boundaries of free speech began with the Nuremberg trials of 1945–1946, in which 24 Nazis stood accused for their roles in the genocide of World War II. The trials established clear ties between the Nazis' mobilization of the media, which in words and pictures had demonized and blackened the character of the Jews, and the subsequent Holocaust.

Julius Streicher, former editor of the anti-Semitic tabloid *Der Stürmer*, was among those the tribunal condemned to death.

The judgment against him ran:

> In his speeches and articles, week after week, month after month, he infected the German mind with the virus of anti-Semitism and incited the German people to active persecution. . . . Streicher's incitement to murder and extermination at the time when Jews in the East were being killed under the most horrible conditions clearly constitutes persecution on political and racial grounds in connection with war crimes as defined by the Charter, and constitutes a crime against humanity.[10]

In that understanding of the origin of the Holocaust, the racist propaganda of the Nazis resulted in the extermination of the Jews. Without extensive freedom of speech in the Weimar Republic of the 1920s and 1930s, the Nazis would never have been able to carry out their hateful attacks on the Jewish community and may never have risen to power at all; the Holocaust could have been avoided. If evil words beget evil deeds, then forbidding evil words will lead to fewer evil deeds. It is a logic that has no empirical basis; yet that argument continues to drive advocates of wide-reaching constraints on the freedom of speech.

Nazi Germany was ruled by a tyranny of silence. As in the Soviet Union, or in George Orwell's masterful novel *1984*, the verbal hygiene of the totalitarian state was designed to ensure the development of the ideal society. Banning mention of certain things meant they would cease to exist; language (or in this case, silence) became an instrument for creating the world in one's own image. Thus blinded by Soviet ideology, even Party Secretary Mikhail Gorbachev was at first unable to grasp what was happening as national separatist movements rose up to eventually condemn the Soviet Union to history's scrap heap.[11]

In the pre-Nazi Weimar Republic, insulting communities of faith—Protestant, Catholic, or Jew—was a punishable offense, commanding up to three years' imprisonment. Incitement to class warfare or acts of violence toward other social classes was also prohibited by law. The Jewish community often sought the protection of that law to defend itself against anti-Semites, who countered, occasionally with success, with the claim that their attacks on Jews were not incitements to class hatred but were instead aimed at the Jewish "race," thus not an offense.

Leading Nazis, such as Joseph Goebbels, Theodor Fritsch, and Julius Streicher were all prosecuted by the Weimar Republic for their anti-Semitic speech. Streicher served two prison sentences. But those court cases served as an effective public-relations machinery for his efforts. The more charges he faced, the greater became the admiration of his supporters. On the occasions on which he was sent to jail, Streicher was accompanied on his way by hundreds of sympathizers in what looked like his triumphal entry into martyrdom. In 1930, he was greeted by thousands of fans outside the prison, among them Hitler himself. The German courts became an important platform for Streicher's campaign against the Jews.[12]

Aryeh Neier, who fled the Nazis with his parents in 1939 and later became a well-known human-rights activist in the United States, invoked the wrath of many when in 1977, as leader of the civil rights organization the American Civil Liberties Union (ACLU), he defended the right of a group of Nazi sympathizers to march on the Illinois town of Skokie, home to many East European immigrants who had survived the Holocaust. Years later, Neier reflected that the ACLU's argument for defending even Nazis' freedom of speech had come to be widely supported in the United States. He felt that was because after they won the right to demonstrate, the Nazis failed to gain much attention, and the movement died soon afterward. The story serves as one illustration of the fact that the most effective means of combating Nazism was to defend the freedom of speech of the Nazis themselves.

"I could not bring myself to advocate freedom of speech in Skokie if I did not believe that the chances are best for preventing a repetition of the Holocaust in a society where every incursion on freedom is resisted," Neier wrote in his book *Defending My Enemy*.[13] Neier points to several examples during the Weimar Republic when efforts to restrict the free speech of the Nazis were counterproductive. In 1925, Adolf Hitler was prohibited by Bavarian authorities from speaking in public. The Nazis reacted by producing a poster of Hitler, with his lips sealed with tape on which was written, "Alone among 2 billion people of the world, he is not allowed to speak in Germany." That propaganda image so enhanced Hitler's popularity that the authorities felt obliged to lift the ban.

The widely touted claim that hate speech against the Jews was a primary cause of the Holocaust has no empirical support. In fact, one might as well argue that what paved the way for the Holocaust was the ban on hate speech, insofar as it handed Streicher and other Nazis a glorious opportunity to bait the Jewish community in the bully pulpit of the courtroom. For supporters of democratization of the Weimar Republic, a far more effective strategy would have been to address Nazi propaganda in free and open public debate. But in Europe between the wars, confidence in free speech was running low.

What the Weimar government failed to do was to safeguard its society against political violence, particularly politically motivated murders. Those who spoke out against Hitler and his supporters were not protected or defended; instead, they were abandoned to the mercy of Nazi violence, and in that climate, many elected to remain silent. Streicher's and other Nazis' Jew-baiting occurred in a society with no real freedom of speech, thus no possibility to counter the witch-hunt against the Jewish community. As Neier wrote, the history of the Weimar Republic "does not support the views of those who say that the Nazis must be forbidden to express their views. The lesson of Germany in the 1920s is that a free society cannot be established and maintained if it will not act vigorously and forcefully to punish political violence." He continued: "Violence is the antithesis of speech. Through speech, we try to persuade others with the force of our ideas. Violence, on the other hand, terrorizes with the force of arms. It shuts off opposing points of view."[14]

That is the core issue. Words might offend or shock, but they can be countered in kind. Words are a democracy's way of dealing with conflict.

Agnès Callamard, executive director of the human rights organization Article 19, made a speech in 2006 that confronted that issue. She pointed out that constraints imposed on free speech with the intention of safeguarding minorities against hatred more often than not resulted in the most controversial voices of the minority being either silenced or imprisoned. "Experience shows that restrictions on freedom of expression rarely protect us from abuses, extremism, or racism," she said. "They are usually and effectively used to muzzle opposition and dissenting voices, silence minorities, and reinforce the dominant political, social, and moral discourse and ideology."[15]

As Neier wrote in the quarterly *Index on Censorship*, "Freedom of speech itself serves as the best antidote to the poisonous doctrines of those who try to promote hate."[16] And yet, 14 European nations have laws criminalizing Holocaust denial, and many more have adopted legislation against speech inciting hatred.

On December 10, 2005, International Human Rights Day, I took part in a panel discussion organized by Amnesty International and the Danish Institute of Human Rights under the banner "Victims of Free Speech." That title was not intended as a joke. A number of those who took part believed that the Muhammad cartoons had left in their wake a trail of victims: the victims of free speech.

I found myself wondering for whom the human rights community would take up the cudgels next—victims of the welfare

85

state, perhaps, or of liberal democracy? Victims of free education? Of gender equality? Or maybe even victims of religious freedom? When I suggested during the debate that by and large, in a society based on the rule of law, there could only be victims of crime, and that the idea that we could discuss "victims" of citizens who were exerting their statutory rights was therefore nonsense, I was answered with anger. An official representative of the Danish Union of Journalists branded the 12 Muhammad artists as "useful idiots for *Jyllands-Posten*." At the time, several of the artists had been forced into hiding by death threats, but even their own professional organization didn't mention their plight.

I pointed out that "victims of free speech" in the West—if we were to use that phrase—had to be those who had been murdered or exposed to violence because of their speech: people like Ayaan Hirsi Ali, Theo van Gogh, and Salman Rushdie. Five years on, we might add names such as Seyran Ates of Germany, Robert Redeker of France, Ehsan Jami of the Netherlands, Shabana Rehman of Norway, Lars Vilks of Sweden, and Kurt Westergaard of Denmark, as well as many other Europeans. But that opinion was loudly booed by the progressive audience.

When I expanded the list of "victims of free speech" by adding dissident voices in dictatorships and others persecuted by totalitarian regimes, I was told that those were not victims of free speech, but of the arbitrary powers of the totalitarian state. Clearly, the audience and most of the panel wished to limit the business of "victims of free speech" to people who had taken offense to the drawings published by *Jyllands-Posten*. It was amazing to me that Amnesty International, the Danish Institute for Human Rights, the writers association PEN, and a former Danish minister of justice who also appeared on the panel apparently had lost all sense of proportion and had completely failed to distinguish between words and deeds.

In addition to his opinion that free speech was the best way to fight racist ideology, Poul Henningsen, the Danish author and freethinker, also opposed public decency laws that banned erotic literature and pornography. On that he won: Denmark became the first country in the world to lift a ban on pornography in the late 1960s. And although he was a Conservative, Denmark's justice minister Knud Thestrup, who lifted the ban, had a very similar argument to Henningsen's: the state should not dictate the morals of the individual, nor should it decide what he or she should have the right to read.

Henningsen also argued that law is temporary, a passing convention that at any time could be superseded by a new reality. Exiled Russian writer Aleksandr Solzhenitsyn provided a prominent example some four decades later: when communism collapsed, Solzhenitsyn returned to Russia, was honored by the state, and saw his work republished after having been banned for almost 30 years. Václav Havel was elected president of a democratic Czech Republic after multiple terms of imprisonment. Nelson Mandela is a third example, and the shifting constraints on permitted speech aren't only a feature of dictatorships. The West features countless examples, as more liberal views of sex have prevailed. Vladimir Nabokov's novel *Lolita* was banned in France and Great Britain; John Steinbeck's *The Grapes of Wrath* was banned for a while in California. D. H. Lawrence's *Lady Chatterley's Lover*, James Joyce's *Ulysses*, Allen Ginsberg's *Howl*, William S. Burroughs's *Naked Lunch*, and almost everything by Henry Miller are examples of works subjected to censorship in the United States on the grounds of alleged pornographic content. By 2010, all were freely available, many hailed as major world literature.[17]

That change raises an interesting issue. On many occasions, proponents of a ban on an erotic book will claim that it is an inferior work, filth rather than literature, and that a ban is therefore a reasonable course of action. By contrast, opponents of a ban often say that it is a work of literature; it is art; it is a good book; and it should therefore not be banned. One of my predecessors as culture editor of *Jyllands-Posten*, the literary critic Jens Kruuse, defended a novel by Agnar Mykle from censorship in 1957 by employing that line of reasoning: "A writer may concern himself with issues deemed indecent by the law in such a way as to raise them up out of the realm of indecency and onto a higher level."[18]

In other words, artistically acceptable speech should be granted wider freedom than speech the literary elite did not much care for. Thus, Norway's Supreme Court acquitted Mykle on all charges of pornography because of the artistic merits of his book. But while Mykle's supporters were still celebrating their victory at a famous Oslo watering hole, the same court ruled in favor of confiscating and banning U.S. writer Henry Miller's autobiographical novel *Sexus*, on the grounds that the work was pornographic and devoid of artistic quality. Half a century later, literary experts would be inclined to highlight Miller's art to the detriment of Mykle's.[19]

Anders Heger, a Norwegian publisher and author of a biography on Agner Mykle, believes that those cases continue to resonate today, when fundamental issues of tolerance and freedom within a democracy have been rendered topical by the Rushdie case and the Cartoon Crisis:

> In legal, literary, and ideological terms, they are linked by the same principle, which says that freedom is more significant for such thoughts as are deemed 'worthy' than those which are not. Put differently: what I find to be art must be protected, and I am indifferent to all else.

Heger calls that a pitiful corruption of Voltaire: "I agree with what you say, and I will defend it regardless of what it may cost others."[20]

On February 1, 2006, as the protests, violence, and boycotts of what had become the Cartoon Crisis gained momentum by the hour, I received an email from a colleague at one of the major Copenhagen dailies. She wrote as follows:

> Dear Flemming Rose,
>
> I'll make this brief: I'm very proud of having been brought up in a country that prides itself on its broad-mindedness, tolerance, openness, and enlightenment. Therefore, I'm mortified and ashamed to have to share this country and this line of work with *Jyllands-Posten*, whose Muhammad cartoons to the best of my convictions are borne by the exact opposite: embarrassing ignorance, intolerance, lack of respect and distasteful arrogance. As a journalist I will always seek to protect and fight for the right of individuals to speak freely. But to drape oneself in the mantle of free speech in order to publish a series of contemptuous depictions of other people's religion is in my opinion downright shameful. We shudder now at Nazi depictions of the Jews prior to and during World War II. In the future we will also shudder at *Jyllands-Posten*'s depiction of an entire world religion.

Point taken. The sender had clearly turned up the volume on her politically correct indignation, which mirrored a widely held myth that European Muslims were the Jews of our time. *Jyllands-Posten*, so the story goes, had published cartoons demonizing Muslims in exactly the same way as Julius Streicher had done in *Der Stürmer* before the extermination of the Jews in the Holocaust of World War II. One could almost hear the marching feet and Nazi anthems in the distance, and imagine how my accomplices and I were busily constructing the gas chambers after having prepared the ground with our hateful propaganda.

German writer and Nobel laureate Günter Grass echoed that view in an interview with the Portuguese magazine *Visao*, when he said the Muhammad drawings "are reminiscent of those published in the famous Nazi tabloid, *Der Stürmer*. They published anti-Semitic caricatures in the same style."[21] Grass added that our decision to publish the drawings had been a calculated provocation and that we had been warned that they would be perceived as offensive. Grass does not read Danish, and he was not present during any of the meetings at which the decision to publish was made, so one could be tempted to ask him which critical sources exactly had prompted his conclusion. Indeed, one would have to be unusually illiterate in picture analysis to be able to see any kind of similarity at all between the Muhammad cartoons and the anti-Semitic caricatures of *Der Stürmer*.

European Muslims, too, paralleled their situation with the plight of the Jews in the Germany of the 1930s. That deliberate cultivation of the role of victim is part of a contemporary grievance culture that I feel is poisonous to integration and equality in a democratic society. In many cases, Islam and Muslims were actually given special treatment. A number of European countries have adopted legislation specifically created to protect Muslims and Islam against mockery. One British government minister insisted on referring to acts of terrorism committed by Muslims in the name of their religion as "anti-Islamic activity."[22] The BBC similarly stopped using the expression "Islamic terrorists" following a complaint lodged by the Muslim Council of Britain.[23] Muslim organizations took on a partner role for governments throughout Europe and received public funding. Prayer rooms were established in many workplaces and in public institutions. Kindergartens and schools served halal food, and public swimming pools separated men and women at certain times of the day, all to accommodate Muslim demands. The archbishop of Canterbury and scholars of Islam supported the introduction of elements of Islamic law in the European systems of justice.[24]

The situation of the German Jews following Hitler's takeover of power in January 1933 was dramatically different. Jews were interned in concentration camps and hardly a week passed without street violence targeting the Jewish community. Jewish shops and businesses were vandalized; the general public was urged to boycott them; and numerous Jewish people were openly murdered on the streets. In the years that followed, Jews were barred from taking on positions as lawyers, doctors, and journalists. Jews were unable to use public hospitals; they were prohibited from working in the public sector; and after the age of 14, they lost the right to public education. Public parks, beaches, and seaside hotels were closed to Jews. Street benches and seats on trains and on busses were marked so that Jews and Germans remained separated. The Nuremberg Laws of 1935 deprived Jews of citizenship rights; marriage between German citizens and Jews was forbidden, as was extramarital sex with Jews. Less than two years after the Nazis took power, some 50,000 Jews, amounting to 10 percent of the Jewish population, had fled Germany. When war broke out, fewer than 100,000 remained. Violence against the Jews permeated society from top to bottom, staged by the authorities.[25] The Jews were subhuman. All of those measures involved not merely words, but actions discriminating against and sanctioning persecution of the Jewish community.

Victor Klemperer, professor of literature and a prominent scholar of the French Enlightenment, himself Jewish, noted in his diary as early as the spring of 1933, "No one breathes freely, no word is free, neither printed nor spoken."[26]

I find it astonishing that even intelligent people can bring themselves to parallel the plight of the Jews before World War II with the situation of Muslims in the 21st century. Such statements must result from extreme ignorance, irrational hatred of one's own civilization, or a guilt complex that fills the air with ghosts. Claims from Muslim spokesmen to the effect that an anti-Muslim storm is brewing over Europe and will end in Muslims, like the Jews before them, being sent to the gas chambers are rarely countered directly as the nonsense they are.

Of course, there is no lack of examples of Muslims being subjected to discrimination and demonization, and that indeed should be fought.

However, at the beginning of the new millennium, European Muslims enjoy all the same rights as all other citizens of Europe; in some cases, they are even afforded preferential treatment compared with representatives of other minorities. By contrast, the Jews enduring German Nazism of the 1930s were systematically deprived of the rights enjoyed by all other citizens of the Third Reich. The real issue about Muslims and civil rights is that many Muslims who enjoy the freedom of civil liberties in Europe are often prevented from doing so within their own Muslim communities. That is especially true of women, homosexuals, and those who have renounced their faith.

Kurt Westergaard's drawing of Muhammad caused offense, though not always of the kind associated with riots in the Islamic world. In February 2006, a 72-year-old Iranian standing outside the Danish embassy in Tehran identified the insult suffered by his government. That hired revolutionary had not set eyes on Westergaard's cartoon before instructing Iranian students to hurl Molotov cocktails at the embassy. Later, when he met with that man in his house outside Tehran, Danish television journalist Karsten Kjær showed him the infamous drawing.

The elderly demonstrator was explaining that someone had told him the Prophet had been insulted and that he was to organize a demonstration. He duly followed orders, though he had never seen the offending drawing. On being shown the image that allegedly incensed 1 billion Muslims, the man smiled into his beard and with a gleam in his eye put his astonishment—or was it affront?—into words:

"He looks more like a Sikh than a Persian."[27]

Not a word about the bomb in the turban.

5. The Pathway to God

For you don't count the dead
When God's on your side.

—*Bob Dylan*

A much repeated claim by Muslim spokesmen around the world at the height of the Cartoon Crisis was that 1.3 billion Muslims had been offended by the 12 drawings. No doubt, many did indeed feel they had suffered an affront, regardless of whether or not they had seen the drawings. Likewise, no doubt, many people of Muslim background were offended at being cited in support of that view when no one had bothered to ask them about it. Such manipulation of Muslim opinion actually prompted several ex-Muslims living in European countries to step forward publicly and insist on their right of apostasy—the rejection of their former religion—which in some Muslim countries was (and is) deemed a "crime" punishable by death.[1]

One of those who certainly did take offense at the Muhammad cartoons—on his own behalf, as well as that of his cobelievers—was a young man from Tunisia. So offended was he that according to Danish police he took it upon himself to try to murder Kurt Westergaard, who at the time was 72 years old. That young man was Karim Sørensen. He had come to Denmark in 2000 and had married a Danish woman he had met in his hometown of Sousse, a popular holiday destination on the Tunisian coast. Some seven years later, he was apprehended by police in the early hours of Tuesday, February 12, 2008, in a suburb of Denmark's second-largest city Aarhus. According to the charges brought against him, he had conspired with two others—a Danish citizen of Moroccan descent and a Tunisian—to kill Kurt Westergaard at his home. The intended method was strangulation.

A search of Karim's home yielded a pistol and two axes, as well as a note on a calendar detailing a route to Kurt Westergaard's address. One of the two Tunisians proved to have a large sum of money in his apartment. According to his wife, that money was for a car, most likely to be used by the assassins to escape through Europe after the attack. The Danish citizen was released without charges, but the two Tunisians were administratively expelled from the country—a decision their lawyers appealed, claiming that their clients risked being subjected to torture should they be returned to Tunisia.[2]

I wanted to interview Karim for *Jyllands-Posten*, and I contacted his lawyer. To my surprise, Karim accepted the opportunity to convince Danish readers that he had never planned to kill Kurt Westergaard. When I called the Danish Security and Intelligence Service (PET) to arrange a time for the interview, the agents' first reaction was that my request was an April Fool's joke. The evening before the interview, a PET agent telephoned me to ask me to come much earlier than already agreed, and to get off the train at a different station where he would pick me up and drive me the rest of the way. The same agent called me again as I sat on the train for Køge, half an hour south of Copenhagen. He told me where his car was parked; its make, color, and license plate number; and what he was wearing, black pants and a black jacket. I found him immediately. When I got in the car, he tried to talk me out of doing the interview.

I politely declined, and we set off for Køge. On the way, the agent told me that our meeting had been moved for security reasons from the remand center to a local police station. He explained that Karim and I would be placed at each side of a wide table that would impede physical contact. We would be escorted in and out of the room through different doors. Should anything untoward happen, I was to follow the PET agent. Two others would take care of Karim. When we arrived at the station, the PET agent went through the layout of the building with me, explaining which way we would exit the building should an emergency occur.

The room was bare. It had a table in the middle, with a chair on each side. Against one wall was a swivel chair on which the PET agent sat while the two police officers remained standing behind Karim. The windows were covered by a transparent material that blocked the sun's glare. I took out my tape recorder and note-book. Karim was a short, burly young man, nimble on his feet, and obviously in good physical shape. He had close-cropped hair and a little goatee that reminded me of the French soccer player Zinedine Zidane. His teeth were astonishingly white. We shook hands. He was wearing a sky-blue sweatshirt with a hood, jeans, and blue plastic sandals.

Initially, the atmosphere was a little tense, but soon I felt Karim relax. He seemed smart: open and reflective, rather than introvert-ed or fanatical. He readily answered all my questions and showed no sign of anger or desperation about his situation. It crossed my mind that he could have been one of my pupils when I had taught Danish to immigrants years ago—a model student whom I would have promoted as an example to the others.

Karim had declared himself not guilty of all charges and had told the press that he had no idea who Kurt Westergaard was or where he lived, a claim police later disproved. Now, he told me his story, beginning with his parents' unhappy marriage. His father was more or less an alcoholic, whose drinking binges were accompanied by domestic violence. One such attack on his wife resulted in Karim being born two months premature.

The father was a mechanic, and the mother, a decorator. Karim told me his mother had been forced into the marriage, though she saw it as a chance to get away from her family who treated her like a slave. But the couple divorced when Karim was a year old, and he grew up with his mother. She was poor, without regular work, and eked out a living doing occasional jobs. Money was so tight they often went without food. And they were regularly forced into hiding when Karim's father would come round to try to take back his son. They found peace only when the father was arrested in Morocco with 20 kilos of cocaine in his car.

Karim did well at school. No one in the family was particularly religious, and they seldom went to the mosque. Karim wanted to be an astronaut. As an adolescent, he began to take part in combat sports, and he became fascinated by Eastern mysticism and the Eastern religions' focus on discipline and self-control. He felt doubtful of his future in Tunisia. Around him, he saw a society that was corrupt and rigidly hierarchical. Without money and the right connections, he had no hope of advancement. He became a leading practitioner of shootfighting—a blend of Thai boxing and wrestling—hoping that it might become his ticket to a better life outside of Tunisia.

One day, his mother came home and told him her boss had refused to pay her the money she was owed. Karim decided to leave the country. He wanted to be able to support his mother financially. A friend told him about the French Foreign Legion; Karim's combat prowess would help him get in, and after five years' service he could request French citizenship. But while Karim was getting together the paperwork for his application, he met a Danish woman from Aarhus who was on holiday in Sousse. She fell in love with him, visited him several times, and tried to talk him out of joining the Foreign Legion, inviting him instead to Denmark for Christmas and the New Year. They married. Karim took his wife's surname and was granted a work permit in Denmark. His wife said that if he found a job, it would cancel out her right to social welfare benefits so instead, he took Danish lessons and joined a shootfighting club in Aarhus.

"I thought: what am I good at? The answer was combat sports. So I thought I'd give it a go as a career and then try to get started as a security guard when I was finished with language school. I really wanted to be a bodyguard."

Karim found work as a doorman at a nightclub in Aarhus and slid into the criminal world. He began drinking and smoking pot, spending less time in the gym. He and his wife divorced. His boss told him that with his French and Arabic, he could get a job as a bodyguard for Saudi princes traveling to Germany and Switzerland. But when war broke out in Iraq, the security firm that employed him ceased all activities in Europe and moved to Iraq. During that time, Karim was convicted for fighting outside the nightclub where he worked. He had attacked an aggressive guest and received 60 days in an open prison. The blot on his record made it difficult to get another steady job.

Karim moved in with another woman, a single mother with a small child. He felt bad about living off her. In the summer of 2005, they went to Tunisia to visit Karim's mother. Here, he struggled to put an end to his drug abuse and instead turned to religion. He prayed five times a day. After returning to Denmark, he began attending the mosque in the concrete-block Gellerup area west of Aarhus, where a number of radicalized Muslims lived— among them a former Guantánamo prisoner, Slimane Hadj Abderrahmane; the Moroccan Athmane Meheri, who was later expelled from the country for his part in a terrorist-related bank robbery; and Syrian-born Abu Rached el-Halabi, who according to Spanish police had connections with the 2004 Madrid bombers. The mosque's spiritual leader was Sheik Raed Hlayhel, a Palestinian imam who had studied in the Saudi city of Medina.[3]

"I wanted to use religion to find discipline in my life. I remember when I was a boy, how I looked up to those who prayed and attended mosque," Karim explained.

Raed Hlayhel first drew attention to himself with a Friday sermon in February 2005, when he recommended that women be completely covered from head to toe. That was, he said, "a divine order." He also warned against women going to hairdressers and using strong perfume. "Women," he said, "can be Satan's instrument against men." Later, during the Cartoon Crisis, he claimed that *Jyllands-Posten* was driven by a Jewish conspiracy against Islam; in the spring of 2006, Hlayhel opined that people like Kurt Westergaard would never be pardoned by Muslims, and the threat of being killed for his blasphemous drawing would be with him for the rest of his life.

In one of his last Friday sermons before leaving Denmark for good in the autumn of 2006, Hlayhel issued a thinly veiled threat against those who might be tempted to reprint Westergaard's drawing or to commit any similar form of blasphemy. Karim witnessed that sermon:

> We have Allah on our side, and he who has Allah on his side cannot be overcome. We love death and will sacrifice ourselves before the feet of Allah's messenger. Abstain therefore from repeating this tragedy, for it will then become your own tragedy and that of the entire world.

In that environment, Karim—lonely, frustrated, and impressionable—found a new identity that raised him above the infidels among whom he lived and by whom he felt humiliated. He looked up to Raed Hlayhel, considered him his spiritual adviser, and an authoritative scholar of Islam. "He is a wise man. He understands what is going on in our time. He senses how things should be. He is a modern man," Karim told me as he related how he turned to Islam.

He rejected the notion that Hlayhel harbored radical views:

> A lot of people think his views are extreme, but it's not true. I once asked him about 9/11 and the London bombings in 2005, and he said it was wrong to kill innocent people. He referred to verses in the Koran and hadith where there are rules on how to behave in war. He said killing innocent people was forbidden and that you were not to lay a hand on children, women, old men, and those who did not carry arms. Buildings and nature are not to be destroyed either. He said the attacks had damaged Muslims as well as non-Muslims.

During his religious radicalization, Karim's relationship collapsed. For a short while, he moved in with a girl he had known before, only to run into another dead end. Eventually, he decided to move to Copenhagen and start afresh. "I just wanted to get away; I wanted out of where I was, smoking pot and getting stoned."

In the capital, he ran into an Afghan who was involved in a group of radical Muslims, several of whom would be arrested in 2007 and charged with planning acts of terrorism on Danish soil. (Karim's Afghan friend would be sentenced to 7 years in prison, to be followed by deportation; the ringleader, a Dane of Pakistani origin, received 12 years. He had trained in a camp in the northern part of Pakistan's Waziristan region, where al Qaeda had set up its new headquarters.) Karim moved in with another acquaintance and began attending the controversial mosque at Heimdalsgade in Copenhagen's multiethnic Nørrebro district, a mosque frequented by a number of figures convicted of terrorism.

"I didn't really know anyone. I took on a few odd jobs to begin with, but otherwise I just sat around waiting for something to do. While I was waiting, I started going to the mosque."

I pulled out a copy of the page containing the Muhammad cartoons as published in *Jyllands-Posten* and ask Karim if he would mind commenting on them. "Sure, why not?" he said. He told me he had seen the drawings just after they were published on September 30, 2005, though he added untruthfully that he had only seen them once. (Police later revealed that the cartoons had been saved on Karim's computer and had been viewed a number of times.)

"I thought, what's all this about? Drawings making fun of the Prophet. I didn't understand what was going on and couldn't see anything constructive about it at all," Karim told me, describing his first reactions to the drawings. He was, he said, annoyed and angered. "It can't be right that you can offend people like that. If the drawings were done to defend freedom of speech, they shouldn't have insulted people's feelings. The least you could have done afterward was apologize."

Karim compared publication of the Muhammad cartoons with burning the Danish flag. "*Jyllands-Posten* was well aware that the drawings were going to offend a lot of people," he said. "I think you did it to provoke and cause trouble. It said to Muslims: this is how we see your religion, and they saw that as a provocation. The drawings could have been done in a different way, more balanced and constructive."

"How do you see Kurt Westergaard's drawing?" I asked.

"It says Muslims only think about bombing other people," Karim replied. "Muslims all over the world see a head that's meant to be the Prophet, and a bomb, and they think the Prophet's head is going to be blown off. I'm almost a hundred percent sure that's what most Muslims think. In a way," Karim continued, "I can understand that an old man like him does a drawing like that when the only things he sees in the media about Islam and Muslims are violence and bombings. So he thinks, 'Right, that's what Muslims are like, and the Prophet is the source of their actions,' but the Prophet wasn't like that at all."

"What would you say to Kurt Westergaard if he were sitting here instead of me?"

"I would tell him I'm sorry his life and mine have been ruined. Maybe I'd encourage him to read about the Prophet. A lot of people in the West have had a wrong picture of the Prophet through history."

"Is there anything you regret?"

"I regret a little bit hanging out with people with extremist opinions. I don't regret it as a person, but it's the reason I'm where I am now. It was my way of finding out what's right and what's wrong," he explained. "I believe you have to find things out for yourself and not shut yourself off. I wanted to study things for myself and investigate the various thoughts and ideas that are found in Islam. Because of that, I'm sitting here now."

Karim Sørensen left Denmark in August 2008 with his wife, a Somali. The police were reluctant to charge him with planning to murder Kurt Westergaard, so initially they settled on expelling him to Tunisia, his country of citizenship. However, the Danish authorities were unable to send him back because, according to human rights organizations, Karim risked being subjected to torture in Tunisia. Thus, he was accorded so-called tolerated residence in Denmark, with restrictions on his freedom of movement. Thus, it was not until August that Karim agreed to be escorted to Copenhagen Airport and to sign a document that he would never set foot in Denmark again. He was flown to Syria, from where he went on to an unknown Arab country. In 2009, his wife gave birth to their first child—in Denmark.

Karim Sørensen's story was in many ways typical of many young men of Muslim background who went to Europe seeking the good life. Their dream involved getting an education, enjoying newfound freedoms, and finding a good job that would allow them to look after families who had remained behind. But when the dream collided with reality, the new life proved problematic, plans went askew, and choices made along the way barred the path to integrating into the wider community, Karim Sørensen ran into an identity crisis. Who am I? Why can't I find a job? Why do my relationships always fall apart? Karim found his answer in Islam.

But it was not the Islam he knew from his home culture in Tunisia, and on which almost all social institutions in his home country were based. The Islam he chose was a revolutionary identity that saw itself in opposition to the society that Karim had come to join. It was an identity that suddenly transformed him from loser to winner, from patsy to foe. Karim's new identity needed to be brandished;[4] and what act more actively demonstrates his belief than cutting the throat of someone who had defamed the Muslim prophet? In the eyes of Karim Sørensen's radical cobelievers, he would become a hero, a certified good Muslim, if he killed Kurt Westergaard.

To me, Karim Sørensen did not seem like the kind of person who harbored especially dark thoughts or who was predisposed to killing old men. All he wanted was to get a grip on his life, to regain his crumbling self-confidence, and to amount to something. The radical imams and the community of the mosque were able to deliver that, but the price was his rejecting any compromise between Islam and the society that surrounded him. His hope was that it would make him a winner. Instead, he ended up, in the words of German author-poet Hans Magnus Enzensberger, "the radical loser."[5]

6. Aftershock I

Late in the afternoon of Tuesday, October 27, 2009, I received a phone call from the Danish Security and Intelligence Service (PET). I was in my office struggling with a leading article for the next day's paper. The words weren't flowing as I wanted them to, but nevertheless the piece was almost done when the phone rang. A familiar voice on the other end told me two men had been arrested by the Federal Bureau of Investigation (FBI) in Chicago, thereby foiling an imminent attack on *Jyllands-Posten* that had specifically targeted Kurt Westergaard and me. The PET agent refused to go into details but suggested we meet as soon as possible so he and his colleagues could brief me on the situation and discuss measures for my safety. We agreed on the following morning at my home.

I had hardly put the phone down when it rang again. This time it was Bloomberg News in New York wanting a comment on the story that was now on its way around the globe, since the FBI had apparently released information about a thwarted terror attack against Denmark.

In the days that followed, I was bombarded with phone calls and text messages from reporters near and far, but I had nothing to add. What are you supposed to say when a studio anchor asks how it feels to have terrorists planning to kill you? It wasn't an amusing thought, but I had not suffered physically; there had been no angry Muslim appearing out of nowhere; no sudden cry of "Allahu akbar"; no flailing axe as Kurt Westergaard had been subjected to only two months before. It was all somewhat hypothetical, and the drama of the situation to a large extent hinged on my own imagination.

I took note of PET's information, turned my phone to mute, and went back to work. Because of the unexpected interruption that afternoon, I was forced to reschedule a meeting with a colleague, so we met up later over coffee. I played the whole thing down: just another day at the office.

I had been incensed the first time some lunatic put a price on my head; there was a rush of adrenaline. But with time, it became apparent that those threats came mostly from rather impulsive individuals with neither the patience nor the intellectual where-withal to carry them through, and I had become more detached and rational about it. Not that it didn't bother me, because it did, but I simply realized that keeping a cool head was to my own advantage, as well as that of my family and colleagues.

When I returned from coffee, I called managing editor Jørn Mikkelsen. I didn't think we could publish the next day without a leading article on the Chicago arrests. Jørn agreed but felt that under the circumstances, someone else should do the piece. Still, I offered to write up a draft and sat down to begin. We ran the article the next day.[1]

> Terror, threats and intimidation are weapons used to change behavior, to make people act in accordance with the wishes of the terrorists. . . . Those responsible for threats and planned attacks against *Jyllands-Posten* are dissatisfied with the publication of the Muhammad cartoons. They have demanded the drawings be banned, and they have sought to intimidate the Danish public. Regrettably, albeit perhaps understandably from a psychological point of view, some people have identified this newspaper as responsible for the threat of terror that has been issued against our nation. They are misguided. Nothing can justify the use of violence or threats against citizens practicing their statutory rights. We would do well to keep this in mind—for the sake of liberty and security.

We know from history that if we submit to terror and threats, what we do not get is less terror and fewer threats. What we get is more terror and more threats. When an individual, media, or society submits to intimidation, the message it sends to the terrorist is that his despicable and contemptible actions work. The most effective weapon we have against threats of terror is therefore to show that we do not intend to succumb; we do not intend to sell out the principles that are the foundation of our liberty and welfare. In that way we make it clear to those who wish to put an end to freedom of speech that no matter what they do, no matter how much they intimidate, we shall continue to do as we always have done, even to the extent of "scorn, mockery and ridicule."

The article concluded:

What poses the greatest threat to our liberty is "insult fundamentalism." It presupposes that feeling insulted is accompanied by a special right to react with violence, and it runs all the way through our era's multiple efforts to impose restrictions on free speech. The time is now ripe to reject this.

Before going home that evening, I had given the paper a short interview and had phoned my children. One of them was sitting at home watching the television news and was rather worried; my other child took things easier. My wife Natasha was away taking a course and hadn't heard the news at all. Fortunately, she was more interested in my reading through her paper on project management, which she was to present a few days later.

Before leaving the office at about 8:30 p.m., I printed out copies of the indictments against the two men who had been apprehended in Chicago: an American and a Canadian, both of Pakistani origin. Following dinner, I sat down to study the FBI's summary of the case against the American, David Headley.[2]

He had visited Denmark on two occasions in 2009, with the aim of planning a terrorist attack on *Jyllands-Posten*, and he had already purchased a third ticket to Copenhagen for late October 2009. When apprehended at Chicago's O'Hare International Airport, he had been about to board a flight to Philadelphia; from there, he had intended to travel to Pakistan to meet up with a known terrorist leader in northern Waziristan, a mountainous tribal region bordering Afghanistan that is often referred to as the headquarters of international terrorism. Most likely, Headley was going to finalize details of the strike against Denmark.

Who was this David Headley?[3] He was born in Washington, D.C., in 1960 as Daood Sayed Gilani. His father, who died in 2008, was a Pakistani radio broadcaster, diplomat, music scholar, and poet who worked for Radio Pakistan for 40 years. Serrill Headley, David's mother, came from a small town outside Philadelphia and moved to the U.S. capital in the 1950s to take a secretarial job at the Pakistani embassy. She met her future husband, and the couple left the United States in 1960 with their newborn son, Daood, to take up residence in Pakistan.

For Serrill Headley, the move was an enormous culture shock. She found it difficult to come to terms with the role of women in Pakistani society. The marriage fell apart, and following a court case in which she lost custody of her two children—Daood and his younger sister—she returned to the United States in the 1970s. "In Pakistan, men own the children. Women have no rights," she later commented in an interview.

In 1973, Serrill Headley purchased a bar in Philadelphia, which she promptly named the Khyber Pass, turning the place into a popular music venue with hippie décor. At that time, Daood was attending a military school for children of the elite in Pakistan's Punjab Province. Here, he befriended Tahawwur Rana, whose acquaintance he renewed many years later in Chicago in connection with the plans against *Jyllands-Posten* and scheduled terror attacks in India. Rana was arrested in Chicago two weeks after David

Headley was apprehended. Whereas Rana did well in school, Daood had difficulty concentrating on academic work. He often failed in mathematics and preferred sports to homework.

In the summer of 1977, Pakistani President Zulfikar Ali Bhutto was ousted in a military coup and later executed. Power was seized by General Muhammad Zia-ul-Haq, a brutal dictator who initiated the country's all-encompassing Islamification. Those developments were a source of concern for Headley's mother, who, with the help of her former husband, managed to convince the 17-year-old Daood to move to Philadelphia, where he gained admittance to the Valley Forge Military Academy and College.

Daood dropped out after a single semester. Later, he made an unsuccessful bid to become an accountant. According to the *Philadelphia Inquirer*, the young man was appalled at seeing his mother selling hard liquor behind a bar and generally behaving rather differently from women at home in Pakistan. Serrill Headley later handed the business over to her son. She died in 2008 at the age of 68.

After an upbringing characterized by discipline and limited contact with the opposite sex, Headley made up for all the things he'd missed in a big way. In the 1980s, he became addicted to drugs and piloted the bar into financial ruin until it was finally sold. When his mother moved to New York, he went with her, opening two video stores in Manhattan. There were regular trips to Pakistan, where he made use of his contacts to smuggle heroin into the United States. In 1988, he was arrested by U.S. narcotics officers at Frankfurt Airport while carrying two kilos of heroin. Opting to cooperate, he ended up with a relatively short four-year prison sentence after leading some of his regular customers into the arms of the police.

In 1997, he was apprehended a second time for the same offense, once again electing to cooperate with authorities by informing on those to whom he was selling. This time, he received 15 months in prison, whereas his partner was sentenced to 10 years.

Headley was released with the approval of the Drug Enforcement Agency after serving only six months. In late 2001, Headley's lawyer and the prosecutor requested that the parole period following Headley's release (which was supposed to extend until 2004) should be annulled. The request was accepted. Less than two months later, with America still licking its wounds in the wake of 9/11, Headley traveled to Pakistan, where by his own account he paid his first visit to a training camp run by the terror organization Lashkar-e-Taiba (LeT).

LeT, "Army of the Pure," was set up in the early 1990s as the military wing of Islamist movement Markaz-ad-Dawa-wal-Irshad, which in the early 1980s had recruited soldiers to oppose the Soviet occupying forces in Afghanistan.[4] LeT received funding from, and was trained by, the Pakistani military intelligence agency Inter-Services Intelligence, in return for carrying out attacks and acts of terror against Hindus in Jammu and Kashmir, Indian provinces to which Pakistan laid claim.

According to Husain Haqqani, Pakistan's ambassador to the United States and a former scholar at Washington's Carnegie Endowment for International Peace, the organization later received funding from Saudi Arabia and formulated as its aim the gathering of all countries in the region of Pakistan into a single theocratic state devoted to Wahhabism, a radical version of Islam that has inspired a number of modern terror organizations, as well as forming the religious basis of the Saudi regime.[5] LeT ran schools, hospitals, farms, markets, and entire housing areas. But in 2002, the United States termed it a terror organization, and it was subsequently banned by Pakistani authorities—although experts cautioned that it continued to enjoy widespread support in the Pakistani intelligence agency.

David Headley's first sojourn in a LeT training camp was a three-week introduction to the organization's ideological universe. During the two years that followed, Headley took part in four training sessions, lasting from three weeks to three months.

He learned to operate firearms and grenades and was trained in hand-to-hand combat, survival techniques, surveillance, and counterespionage.

Now a member of LeT, Headley moved to Chicago sometime around 2005 with his Pakistani wife and their four children. They rented an apartment that had been vacant since the death of its previous occupant. In order to conceal his tracks, Headley did not change the name of the tenant on the lease. He repeated the trick for his mobile phone. Headley spoke both English and Urdu without an accent and was able to move seamlessly between the two cultures. Those abilities made him attractive to Islamic terror groups, yet Headley was conflicted. Though he idealized the strict Islamic lifestyle, he continued an affair with a non-Muslim woman in New York.

"'Infidels.' He would use words like that," his first American wife told the *Philadelphia Inquirer* in the autumn of 2009. "When he would see an Indian person in the street, he used to spit, spit in the street to make a point. I guess he was torn between two cultures. I think he liked both. He didn't know how to blend them."

According to the FBI, Headley first traveled to Denmark in January 2009. By that time, he had changed his name from Daood Sayed Gilani to David Coleman Headley, in order to be able to travel more easily through post-9/11 security. Claiming to be representing a company called First World Immigration Services that was planning an advertising campaign, he managed to meet with advertising salespeople in the *Jyllands-Posten* offices in both Copenhagen and Aarhus. He then flew to Pakistan, where he met with representatives of LeT and with Ilyas Kashmiri, a notorious terrorist leader holed up in northern Waziristan.

Subsequently, the FBI investigation turned up evidence that Headley had already discussed a possible terror attack against *Jyllands-Posten*. In October 2008, he had met with a member of LeT who urged him to begin planning as soon as possible. At about the same time, he vented his anger at the Muhammad drawings in an Internet forum for former pupils of the cadet college in Punjab that he had attended in the 1970s. "Call me old-fashioned," he wrote on October 29, 2008, "but I feel disposed towards violence for the offending parties."

Headley flew to Denmark for the second time in July 2009. According to the FBI, he met with an al Qaeda cell in the United Kingdom, which he had contacted via Kashmiri. That cell would carry out the attack. Kashmiri had suggested two possible plans of attack. Headley could drive a truckful of explosives into the *Jyllands-Posten* building, or a group of warriors could force their way in, murder indiscriminately, and then throw the headless bodies out the windows so as to gain maximum exposure. But according to page seven of the FBI report:

> Headley declared that he had suggested that the operation against the newspaper be reduced from an attack on the building as a whole to the liquidation of the paper's culture editor, Flemming Rose, and Kurt Westergaard, the artist who had depicted the Prophet Muhammad with a bomb in his turban, because Headley felt they were directly responsible for the drawings.

How did that make me feel? By that time, four years after the cartoons were published, I was well aware that I was a potential target for people's violent feelings on the subject, and it was definitely an unpleasant thought. Still, I felt almost relieved that Headley had decided to target me rather than innocent citizens who had nothing to do with the whole business, other than perhaps being employed by the newspaper that had published the drawings. Kurt Westergaard and I had chosen to take full part in the debate about the cartoons. And although it was absurd that a newspaper editor and a cartoonist should have to consider the risk of violence and murder for printing a drawing, even early on we were both quite aware of the possible consequences.

The nightmare scenario was that random people would be kidnapped or killed in retaliation for the drawings, and that the media and the general public would subsequently hold the newspaper responsible. That was something I would never be able to accept. Yet that scenario, and the sense that the threat of terror suddenly had become unpleasantly real, had a major effect. It was a principal factor in the paper's decision not to republish Westergaard's drawing following the news of Headley's terror plot and the attempt on Westergaard's life in January 2010.

The newspaper claimed that since most people were by now familiar with the cartoon, there was no need to reprint it every time we mentioned the Cartoon Crisis. That argument was by no means watertight. As one critic noted, articles on President Obama would often be accompanied by pictures even though our readers clearly knew what he looked like, and pieces on 9/11 were usually accompanied by dramatic images of the Twin Towers. Those images were far more ingrained in the public mind than Westergaard's drawing. The truth was that one attack motivated explicitly by the cartoons had already occurred: a strike against the Danish embassy in Islamabad in June 2008, which cost the lives of six people.[6] And now the terrorist circles responsible for the Islamabad attack had been linked to Headley and his plans for an attack in Denmark.

When I met with PET on the morning of October 28, 2009, I had been awake for several hours and had run almost 20 kilometers to rid my body of adrenaline. Mostly, I was worried about whether David Headley had found out where I lived. PET had evidence that he had tried to do so but thought he had failed. That was a relief.

Was I scared? Not really. Was I angry? Not really. I had become used to keeping alert, being watchful of who sat down next to me on the bus, who was standing around when I left a building. In cafés and restaurants, I always sat facing the door. I was on my guard against anyone behaving oddly or who didn't seem to fit in, but I was also determined to lead as normal a life as possible. I had a running dialogue with myself: If you let this get to you and stop doing things you want, then they've already won.

At first, local terror experts failed to take David Headley and his plans to strike at Denmark seriously. He was an American, a family man, of mature age: surely, he could not be some hot-headed jihadi. That impression shifted as more information was released. Headley had played a major role in planning LeT's attack in Mumbai in November 2008, when 10 terrorists turned the city into a war zone for more than two days, killing 166 and injuring more than 300.

His American identity meant that Headley could operate freely; he opened an office in the name of the company First World Immigration Services and traveled to Mumbai repeatedly over a two-year period to carry out intelligence work for LeT, including camera footage of the selected targets around the city and the best landing area for the terrorists' dinghy. The detailed nature of Headley's intelligence activities during those two years made it difficult to write him off as an amateur.

When Headley's groundwork for the Mumbai attack was complete, he turned his attention to *Jyllands-Posten*. The method was the same: espionage carried out under the cover of representing First World Immigration Services. He gathered information and video footage, which he then forwarded to those who were to carry out the attack: hideouts, cafés, routes, and distances, so people unfamiliar with Copenhagen could get an idea of buildings and locations and find their way around. But apparently, by the spring of 2009, LeT's interest in the project was waning. The operation was laid aside indefinitely, in favor of renewed strikes against India.

Headley was determined to carry out the attack on *Jyllands-Posten* and continued planning it with Abdur Rehman Hashim, an old acquaintance from Headley's days at cadet college in Punjab. Hashim was by now a retired major of the Pakistani armed forces and had links to LeT and to Ilyas Kashmiri,[7] who had allied himself with al Qaeda sometime in 2005. According to official American sources in Chicago cited by the Copenhagen daily *Politiken*, plans for the attack on *Jyllands-Posten* were in their final stages when Headley was apprehended.

The day after the FBI and PET released the news of Headley's terror plot, I received an email from the chief editor of *Die Welt* asking me to write a piece for that newspaper under the headline "Was It Worth It?"

"Do I regret that *Jyllands-Posten* published the Muhammad cartoons?" I wrote.

> I think that is a misguided description of what's at stake; it's like asking a rape victim whether she regrets having worn a short skirt when she went out on Friday night. In Denmark, putting on a short skirt to go out dancing is not an invitation to rape. Similarly, publishing cartoons ridiculing people who bomb airplanes, trains, and buildings in the name of religion is not an invitation to terror and violence. Religious satire is a lawful and quite normal activity. What kind of civilization do we have in Europe if we are to do without humor and the right to ridicule terrorists?

There is nothing wrong with criticizing Westergaard, his drawings, or the whole cartoon project. You can call the images childish, tasteless, and unnecessarily provocative; you can say they're done by a second-rate artist, an attention-seeking amateur or worse—that's what free and open discussion means. But it is absolutely deplorable that some people blamed Westergaard, or our newspaper, for the terrorist threats on Danish targets. There is a big difference between a blasphemous drawing—"a crime without a victim," as Salman Rushdie called it—and violent terror.

When the crisis was at its peak, in February 2006, I was asked by Danmarks Radio, the country's leading public-service media, how many bombs had to go off before *Jyllands-Posten* would apologize. Implicit in that question was the view that the newspaper and I would be to blame if there were a terrorist attack. It was by no means an uncommon charge. In letters to the editor and at public discussions, I was continually being asked how I could sleep at night, being responsible for the deaths of innocent people. Certain individuals demanded my resignation in the interest of domestic security and Denmark's reputation in the international community. Danish and foreign media habitually stated that the drawings had incited riots and killings. In September 2007, the *New York Times* wrote that the cartoons had "incited violent and even deadly protests in other countries."[8]

That is dangerous logic, popular among fanatics who equate blasphemy and terror and widespread in countries like Pakistan, Iran, and Saudi Arabia, where both are crimes punishable by death. It is a reverse logic that involves evaluating speech on the basis of the reactions it generates, without considering whether those reactions are proportionate or reasonable, or whether the speech is legal or meaningful. Basically, it amounts to giving people who feel like reacting with violence a free hand to decide whether a speech incites terror.

Kenan Malik, author of an excellent book on the lessons of the Rushdie affair,[9] has analyzed that sort of equation among those who held the author of *The Satanic Verses* responsible for deaths that occurred in protests against it. In Malik's view, none of us can control or determine the reactions of others to what we say. And words or images cannot in themselves cause any action. The individual has to assume responsibility for what he or she does. Fanatics and racists, of course, are influenced by fanatical and racist speech, but the responsibility for turning speech into actions is entirely their own. Legislation against hate speech blurs the distinction between word and actions, only undermining our understanding of the nature of human actions and moral responsibility.

Shooting the messenger is an old habit. During the Cold War, dissidents were often accused of destabilizing East–West relations via their appeals to the West to put pressure on Soviet client regimes. They got in the way of doing business. According to a Danish newspaper editor, one Danish diplomat told him in the 1980s that it would be disastrous for Europe if too many figures like Polish trade union leader Lech Walesa were to appear in the Eastern Bloc. Walesa and his Solidarity movement, who forced the Polish regime to the negotiation table and played a vital role in the peaceful and civilized transition to democracy in Poland, were demanding freedom and self-determination, but that he viewed as a threat to peace and stability in Europe. It was grotesque, but I had often seen that attitude.

Was it reasonable to blame *Jyllands-Posten* for rioting and other violence, four months or even four years after the paper published the cartoons? What exactly was the connection between the drawings and the murder of civilians in Libya, Afghanistan, Lebanon, Pakistan, and Nigeria? The paper was under pressure, but it often accepted that logic far too quickly. When asked if we would have published the drawings had we known they would lead to violence and killings, the answer was always no. But that response meant that we effectively handed the job of editing the newspaper to fanatics and terrorists thousands of kilometers away.

It goes without saying that no drawing is worth the life of a human being, yet many Muslims firmly believed that Kurt Westergaard and I deserved to die. Seemingly, they were of the opinion that a cartoon could justify a killing. Danish comedian Anders Matthesen came perilously close to subscribing to that logic in early February 2006, at a time when several of the cartoonists involved had been forced into hiding following death threats, and *Jyllands-Posten*'s offices in Copenhagen and Aarhus had been evacuated because of bomb scares. Matthesen believed that the newspaper and the drawings themselves were to blame for the trouble that had ensued, since violence in his opinion was a natural reaction to affront and only to be expected.

"Try going out on the street. Find a biker and tell him he's a fat bastard!" the comedian commented in *Politiken*.[10]

"You're perfectly entitled, but in the real world you're going to get your head kicked in for that kind of thing. Those who did the drawings must be fucking stupid," he added.

Funny? Well, considering Matthesen had otherwise made an entire career out of poking fun at others and the things they believed in, the logic at least seemed rather warped—quite apart from the fact that he seemed to be equating Muslims with violent criminals.

What Matthesen and those who agreed with him were purposely overlooking in their eagerness to appease violent Islamists was this: people like David Headley, LeT, al Qaeda, and the millions who supported them claimed that *Jyllands-Posten* and the 12 cartoonists had defamed Islam and the Muslim prophet and not, as they repeatedly stressed, Muslims themselves. The drawings were blasphemous, an affront to the Prophet, not to the feelings of individuals, and blasphemy was punishable by death.

The Islamists not only had an issue with me, Westergaard, and *Jyllands-Posten*; they also believed parliamentary democracy was blasphemous, that the separation of church and state, freedom of speech and religion, equality of the sexes, and the right to life of homosexuals should never be accepted by Muslim believers. All those issues were an affront to their faith.

The Cartoon Crisis forced Kurt Westergaard to reflect on his upbringing in a restrictive religious environment. Years later, the opportunity to get back at religion using satire came as a release, yet his drawing of Muhammad with a bomb in his turban almost cost him his life. It made him famous too. Kurt Westergaard was a walking piece of history. Fame—or notoriety—and the hassle of navigating daily life became a serious test of his ability to deal with inner feelings of narcissism and vanity that perhaps would prove to be beyond his control.

The Muhammad cartoons led Karim Sørensen onto a perilous sidetrack to his efforts to discover himself and gain control of his life. The decisions he made would make it difficult for him ever to realize the dreams he had taken with him when he immigrated to Denmark.

I too felt prompted by the Cartoon Crisis to delve into questions of my own identity: who I was, what had made me the person I had become, what kinds of experiences had directed my life and left their mark.

I grew up in the Copenhagen suburbs, in Kastrup, close to the city's international airport. My parents were relatively young when I came into the world. My father drove a taxi and had a milk round, while my mother worked as an office assistant. My youngest brother had just been born when my father left us to move in with a teenager whom he later married and had children with. For a while after that, we drifted from place to place, often unsure of whether we would have roof over our heads the following week. All the while, my mother kept knocking on the doors of housing offices and other public authorities to secure us a permanent place to live.

One of my brothers and I were eventually placed with foster parents in the town of Fredensborg, where we were mostly left to our own devices. Our youngest brother was put in a children's home. As well as trying to find a home for us, my mother had to hold down a job: her father had cut her off completely. In August 1963, my mother's brothers contacted the Copenhagen tabloid *Ekstra Bladet* in the hope of starting an outcry about our plight.

Victor Andreasen, a legendary figure in Danish newspaper history, had just become chief editor. He wanted to make the paper more relevant to people's daily lives—starting with the housing shortage, which hadn't yet made the news. Andreasen called in his culture editor, Rachel Bæklund. She went to Copenhagen's Central Station to meet with my mother, who sat waiting with me and one of my younger brothers. "That story turned out to be my biggest break as a journalist," Bæklund, age 91, recalled in the spring of 2010. "Everyone was talking about it."

On Monday, September 2, 1963, *Ekstra Bladet* began a series of articles titled "Are You Sleeping Well, Mr. Housing Minister?"— a quote from Rachel Bæklund's story about the homeless single mother and her three children. Most of the front page was devoted to a photo of me and my younger brother with the caption "Mommy, when can we have somewhere to live?"

The piece created a major stir. In the six months or so that followed, Rachel Bæklund put my mother up in her home, accompanied her to the local housing offices, and eventually celebrated when she was allocated a two-room apartment in Kastrup, and my mother could once again unite her children. Shortly after, I began school, and we all embarked on a new life. My father was rarely mentioned.

I did reasonably well at school, socially and academically, although homework became problematic when I hit adolescence. My life revolved around soccer; although I entered college in 1979, studying Russian, all I wanted to be was a professional soccer player. (I had been selected to take part in the national junior competition, so that wasn't just a flight of fancy.) I was influenced by hippie culture and went around with long hair, an Afghan coat, cotton shirts from India, and cowboy boots. For a while, I smoked a fair amount of pot and despised materialism and status symbols. Religion wasn't an issue either at home or at school, but I studied transcendental meditation for a while, and then a new, Scandinavian form of meditation known as Acem Meditation.

That discipline had no ready-made, ritualized answers, but an awareness of the complexities of human psychological processes, coupled with the notion that integrity in human relations was essential to personal growth and self-awareness. Tolerance was a key concept, and so was becoming one's own confidant, and learning to be close with whatever it was that made you restless, depressed, or aggressive. Meditation meant that I became more interested in addressing my own psychological limitations and their negative effects on my life, and I was less concerned with the ideas of political revolution and social and economic upheavals that captured so many of my generation. My subsequent interest in politics and society grew out of my efforts to understand how internal and external freedoms were related.

In 1982, while I was still studying Russian in college, I began working as an interpreter for the Danish Refugee Council. Two years later, I started working for that organization as a language teacher, and I held the job until 1990, when I was appointed *Berlingske Tidende*'s first Moscow correspondent. The language school embraced an enormous spectrum of colleagues, and each day was a new journey into foreign cultures. I discovered that the lack of liberty I had seen in the Soviet Union was also a feature of life elsewhere. I saw too how easy it was for a foreigner to feel like an outsider in Denmark: the homogeneity of the culture and the population meant that the slightest accent or the tiniest physical feature revealed you to be foreign. It wasn't that the Danes disliked foreigners particularly, but they weren't used to living alongside people from other cultures.

The Soviet émigrés I met had refused to succumb to the lies and the tyranny of silence laid down by their dictatorship. They were idealists, yet the regime seemed to fear them more than it feared foreign armies because they undermined the West's Kissinger-style realpolitik engagement with the Soviet Union. They attacked it as a betrayal of the founding principles of democracy embodied in the Universal Declaration of Human Rights of 1948, a document they revered. They were people who went to jail with their heads held high, with a sense of dignity and devotion to what they believed in. Of course, they also had flaws, but they possessed a moral clarity I found inspiring.

When the Cartoon Crisis was at its peak, and condemnation of *Jyllands-Posten* seemed unyielding, I found myself thinking about the dissidents I had held in such esteem throughout my adult life. Not that I in any way sought to compare my own situation with theirs. There were many obvious differences. *Jyllands-Posten* was a leading newspaper, free of threats or censorship from despotic officials, operating in a country that was tolerant and democratic. But I saw that the dissidents had maintained their standpoints regardless of what people were saying, and with no thought for the personal price they might have to pay. It was a lesson, I thought, on the principle of sticking up for what you thought was right.

I realized that I couldn't imagine any worse fate than succumbing to intimidation and mouthing opinions I did not really hold. It didn't matter whether the intimidation issued from politically correct Social Democrats branding me a racist, or from religious fanatics who put a price on my head. If the reasoning behind the Muhammad cartoons made sense in my mind—if it was in sync with my own personal values, and if no one had managed to shift my opinion through rational argument—then it didn't matter whether a majority disagreed with me. To retain my self-respect and my dignity, I had to stand fast.

From then on, living with threats and constant surveillance by intelligence agents was easy enough.

The drawings were published on September 30, 2005. They exploded on the global scene as a political issue in late January and early February 2006. In between, I was doing two jobs: one as culture editor and the other as explainer and defender of the cartoons in the public debate at home and abroad. As the months passed, that second job began to take up more of my time. During the autumn, there were growing calls for the drawings to be retracted, and for the paper to apologize and announce that it would never again publish similar drawings. There were demonstrations, protest petitions, letters to the editor, articles, discussions on radio and TV, and pubic debates. The public prosecutor began investigating whether a case could be brought against the paper for blasphemy or racism.

120

In mid-October, I was given the first taste of the international dimension into which the issue was to develop when I learned that ambassadors of 11 Muslim countries had written to Prime Minister Anders Fogh Rasmussen calling for a meeting to discuss the cartoons and urging him to take measures against *Jyllands-Posten*.[11] Later, the Organization of the Islamic Conference joined the debate with an official complaint about the persecution of Muslims in Denmark, and in November, the issue of the drawings was brought before the United Nations high commissioner for human rights, Louise Arbour, who expressed sympathy with Muslim disgruntlement.[12]

Threats were made against the artists and editors, and I had my first meeting with the Danish intelligence agency PET concerning my security. Foreign media began reporting on the crisis. We were claimed to be leading an anti-Muslim witch hunt, and it got to the point where it looked like I devoured Muslims for breakfast, and *Jyllands-Posten* was the equivalent of a Nazi, anti-Semitic broadsheet. Misunderstandings, half-truths, and outright lies were legion. The experience was both frustrating and educational.

Besides debating with Muslims in the media and at public meetings, I also met behind closed doors with the Danish Islamic Society in December to discuss the cartoon issue at length with the society's leader, Imam Ahmad Abu Laban, and his spokesperson Ahmed Kassem. I already knew Abu Laban; as Moscow correspondent, I had done a piece on a Muslim refugee in Denmark who had gone to Chechnya to fight against the Russians. He had frequented Abu Laban's Copenhagen mosque, so I had interviewed the imam.

When we met again in December 2005, Abu Laban presented me with a book titled *Freedom of Expression in Islam*.[13] It said that according to Islamic law, blasphemy was punishable by death. But during our discussion, his opinions were not that of a rabble-rouser. Referring to the drawings as "a possible mistake," he added that their publication perhaps had been a good thing, since they had sparked a debate about religious values in Danish society, an issue he had been trying to encourage the authorities to address for years. I had no idea that Abu Laban had already dispatched a delegation to Egypt with a view to mobilizing the Muslim world against *Jyllands-Posten* and Denmark. In fact, he stressed that it was time to look forward, suggesting that our paper, a Danish university, and the Islamic Society should together organize a Muhammad Festival to frame the Prophet in a positive light.

When he had finished speaking, I placed the newspaper cutting with the cartoons on the table in front of him and explained why we had published them. The intention had not been to cause offense, but to bring into focus the question of self-censorship. I said that the dialogue and tolerance he sought could not merely involve an exchange of platitudes, but they entailed differences of opinion that could be emotionally charged. My impression was that Abu Laban wanted to find a way out of the crisis, but that he needed to demonstrate clear results to his community, so I offered to discuss the issue with him in public, on his own turf, where he and I could confront each other's views and enter into a dialogue with his community. He could talk about respect for religious sentiments, while I could talk about freedom of speech and make clear that *Jyllands-Posten* had no hidden agenda targeting Muslims in Denmark.

Abu Laban agreed to get back to me with a proposed date for the event, but I never heard from him. I did not see him again until we met two months later in a debate on the BBC's *Hardtalk* program,[14] in which he criticized Denmark for treating Muslims like schoolchildren. By that time, the cartoons had gone global, and it was pretty much impossible to turn on a TV set anywhere without hearing about what had now been dubbed the "Cartoon Crisis."

It had taken four months from the publication of the cartoons for the affair to turn into a global crisis. However, that doesn't mean that until then the cartoons had been ignored by Danish Muslims, Islamic countries, and international organizations, like the Organization of the Islamic Conference (OIC) and the Arab League. The process was influenced by coincidences, misunderstandings, and shortsighted political interests in domestic situations in several countries, but underneath were a logic and cohesion in the unfolding drama culminating in the spring of 2006 that were anything but coincidental.

Imams in Denmark, governments, commentators, and Islamic scholars in the Muslim world, the Arab League, and the OIC all agreed that cartoons of the Muslim prophet, religious satire, and criticism of Islam had to be banned on a global level. That mandate wasn't a new one. It grew out of the Rushdie affair in 1989; and since 1999, the OIC had succeeded in getting it into UN resolutions.

Two days after publication of the cartoons, representatives from mosques and Muslim associations met at the offices of the Islamic Faith Society in Copenhagen in order to work out a coordinated response to the cartoons.[15] Raed Hlayhel, a Saudi-educated imam who came to Denmark a few years earlier to receive government-financed treatment for his disabled son, was appointed chairman of a committee to protect the honor of the Prophet. The participants agreed on a plan of action that included taking *Jyllands-Posten* to court, contacting the embassies representing Islamic countries in Denmark, and contacting the media and Islamic scholars in the Muslim world.

In an interview with *Jyllands-Posten*, Hlayhel demanded an apology and a retraction of the cartoons. He also threatened the paper, referring to the killing of Dutch filmmaker Theo van Gogh. "When you see what happened in the Netherlands and you nevertheless publish the cartoons, that's stupid."

Apart from his eagerness to defend the Muslim prophet, Hlayhel had a personal bias against the paper. He and Ahmed Akkari, another imam who played a key role in the campaign, felt they had been treated badly, Hlayhel because the paper had publicized one of his controversial Friday prayers. He had lambasted women who used perfume and didn't cover their full body as "a tool of the devil." The words triggered a wave of criticism against Hlayhel. Akkari had been featured in a story where he as a teacher had talked approvingly about an attack on a Muslim girl who was targeted in the schoolyard for failing to wear a headscarf.

In mid-October 2005, a demonstration against the cartoons took place at the Town Hall Square in Copenhagen, where 2,000 to 3,000 Muslims called on the Danish government to put an end to the defamation of Islam. In a parallel development, 11 Muslim ambassadors to Denmark sent a letter to Prime Minister Anders Fogh Rasmussen complaining about what they described as "an ongoing smear campaign against Islam and Muslims in the Danish media and public." They called on the prime minister to hold *Jyllands-Posten* accountable according to the laws of the land and asked for a meeting. The letter was signed by the ambassadors from Turkey, Saudi Arabia, Iran, Pakistan, Egypt, Indonesia, Algeria, Bosnia, Libya, Morocco, and the Palestinian Authority.

The Danish prime minister responded two weeks later. He stressed that in Denmark there was freedom of expression; therefore, he couldn't interfere with the press. But he added that blasphemous and discriminating speech was forbidden, and any offended party could take his or her complaint to the courts. In light of those facts, the prime minister declined to meet the ambassadors.

Egypt was driving the campaign. In an op-ed, its ambassador to Denmark demanded "an immediate stop to insults to Islam in the Danish media and public circles." Egypt sent a letter to OIC that was almost identical to the one that the 11 ambassadors wrote to the prime minister, and through diplomatic channels, Egypt expressed its dissatisfaction with the Danish government's handling of the case, and said that it would raise the matter on an international level. Egypt made sure that the cartoons were on the agenda of the OIC summit in Mecca in December 2005. In the words of Egypt's foreign minister Ahmed Aboul Gheit, the goal was to put an end to the publication of cartoons offending Islam and to convince Europe to take all the necessary steps. That was the motive driving Egypt to take its criticism of Denmark to the UN, the Organization for Security and Co-operation in Europe, the Organisation for Economic Co-operation and Development, the European Union's foreign policy coordinator Javier Solana, and two human rights groups.

The Egyptian embassy in Copenhagen also facilitated a visit to Cairo by the Danish imams' Committee for the Defense of the Honor of the Prophet. On December 3, a delegation of five arrived in Cairo, where they met with Mohammad Sayed Tantawi, the supreme religious leader of Al-Azhar University; Ali Gomaa, Egypt's grand mufti; Amr Moussa, secretary general of the Arab League; and Muhammad Shaaban, adviser to Egypt's foreign minister and former ambassador to Denmark. The delegation justified the visit by claiming that nobody wanted to listen to them in Denmark. That wasn't the case. They had access to every media platform in Denmark, and I debated leading Muslim voices on radio, on television, and in other public forums. From the publication of the cartoons until the spring of 2006, national newspapers published more than 10,000 letters to the editor and op-eds. A significant number were contributed by Muslims. The fact is that a majority of the public listened and evaluated the arguments put forward by the imams and denounced them as a call for censorship.

The imam delegation to Cairo brought along a controversial dossier that they gave to their counterparts in Egypt. The dossier was the main source of information for the OIC and the Arab League about the life of Muslims in Denmark. It said that the Muslim faith wasn't officially recognized in Denmark. That was wrong. The dossier included offensive cartoons that were never published in *Jyllands-Posten* or any other newspaper but were presented as if they had been. One depicted the Muslim prophet as a pedophile devil; another pictured the praying Prophet being sexually assaulted from behind by a dog; and a third cartoon featured the Prophet as a pig. The latter was in fact a copy of a photo taken from the Internet showing an auto mechanic in southern

France. He had participated in a local competition on imitating a pig's scream.

The Egyptian press covered the visit and after interviewing the members of the delegation reported that the Koran was about to be censored in Denmark. The local press also claimed that *Jyllands-Posten* was owned by the government and that the government planned to finance a new documentary, *Submission Part II*, a follow-up to *Submission Part I* that was directed by the Dutch filmmaker Theo van Gogh and written by Somali-born Dutch parliamentarian and feminist Ayaan Hirsi Ali. Van Gogh was killed by a young Muslim who claimed he had defamed Islam, and Hirsi Ali was forced into hiding after the murder. All the claims in the Egyptian press were false and contributed to the Muslim world's distorted picture of the life of Muslims in Denmark. In fact, as citizens, Muslims enjoyed more rights in Denmark than in any Muslim country.

A second delegation representing the Committee for the Defense of the Honor of the Prophet traveled to Lebanon in mid-December. They were received by religious leaders and ministers, among them the grand mufti of Lebanon and the leader of the Shia Muslims. A member of the delegation traveled to Damascus to present his case to the grand mufti of Syria. The delegation was interviewed by Hezbollah's TV station Manar, which reported that the Danish media and politicians had initiated a campaign to insult Islam and the Muslim prophet.

The dossier with cartoons that had never been published and that distorted information about Muslims' situation in Denmark was distributed to the leaders of the Muslim world at the OIC summit on December 7–8 in Mecca, on Egypt's initiative. The summit was later perceived as a turning point in the escalation of the conflict that culminated in late January and early February 2006. In the summit's final communiqué, the OIC (in line with its lasting campaign in the UN) demanded a universal criminalization of "insult to Islam and its values" along the same lines as racism.

The UN's high commissioner for Human Rights, Louise Arbour, expressed her understanding of the demands of the Muslim world and in doing so gave her support to the pressure being exercised on Denmark. In a critical report to the UN Human Rights Commission, the UN special rapporteur on racism, racial discrimination, and related intolerance, Doudou Diéne, denounced the cartoons as "hatred of Islam."

At the newspaper, we imagined that things had calmed down by Christmas, and I left for Miami Beach in the vain hope that when I returned from my vacation, I would spend more time covering cultural life and could leave the cartoon debate behind. It turned out to be wishful thinking. The OIC summit in Mecca didn't mark the end of the conflict, quite the opposite: a month later, it lead to huge demonstrations, violent attacks on Denmark's embassies, and the boycott of Danish products across the Muslim world. The conflict moved from the corridors of government to mosques and the media and made it to the top of the domestic agenda in many countries.

Egypt wanted to use the cartoons to send a message to the West about what would happen if the United States and the EU pressed too hard for democratic change in the Middle East.[16] After 9/11, the United States was pushing for a freedom agenda for the Middle East. The thinking was that political reform, strengthening of civil society, and more open societies would, over the long haul, be the most effective way to contain the terrorist threat. To promote that process, the G-8 founded Forum for the Future. It was accompanied by similar initiatives by the EU and the United States. The forum meets once a year to debate reforms in the Arab world. It's attended by foreign ministers of the G-8 and the Middle East, and human rights activists from the region.

Forum for the Future met in Bahrain November 11–12, 2005, at a time when the Mubarak regime found itself in the middle of an election in which the Muslim Brotherhood had done pretty well. As a result of U.S. pressure, Mubarak had been forced to accept an

"Egyptian Spring" that gave more space to the opposition and to civil society activists. The Egyptian government didn't like it. The meeting in Bahrain ended in an open disagreement between the United States and the Arab ministers of foreign affairs who were in no hurry to pass democratic reforms, secure freedom of expression, or conduct free elections.[17]

In that context, the cartoons became a convenient instrument to manipulate the public and show the West that the repressive regimes in the Middle East were necessary to keep the masses under control. Denmark turned out to be an easy target. Egypt's assistant foreign minister for European affairs put it this way:

> Eighty-nine percent of the Egyptians hate the United States. Sometimes we can go against the will of the people, but we cannot do it one hundred percent of the time. Of course, we will never do something like this to the United States. We are allies, but who cares about the Danes?[18]

The grand mufti of Jerusalem made the same point: "Denmark is an easy target. A small country without any significant importance for the Arab countries. That's why nobody is concerned that the protests continue," he explained to a Danish newspaper.[19]

On January 10, 2006, a small Norwegian newspaper[20] reprinted *Jyllands-Posten*'s 12 cartoons of Muhammad as documentation for a story about cartoonists' self-censorship, but the publication was perceived as part of a plot against the Muslim world. The same day in Mecca, an imam called on an audience of 2 million on the spot and another 100 million viewers on TV who followed the imam's prayer marking the end of the pilgrimage, to oppose the alleged campaign against the Muslim prophet. The Danish embassy received hundreds of letters a day protesting the cartoons, and during the Friday prayer on January 20, imams called for a boycott of Danish goods.

The call was repeated the next day by Yusuf al-Qaradawi, the spiritual leader of the Muslim Brotherhood, on his TV show.

Qaradawi called for a boycott of Denmark and Norway if the governments of the two countries didn't put an end to the media's insult to the Prophet. The grand mufti of Saudi Arabia demanded that *Jyllands-Posten* be punished. In a few days, the call for a boycott spread like wildfire through email and text messages. The next weekend, Danish products were being taken off the shelves in Bahrain, Lebanon, Oman, Qatar, Yemen, and the United Arab Emirates.[21] The secretary general of the OIC supported the boycott because the Danish government refrained from punishing *Jyllands-Posten*. Three weeks earlier, the public prosecutor declined to initiate a criminal case against the paper because the cartoons had been published in the context of an important public debate.

Monday, January 30, 15 armed men wearing masks invaded the office of the EU in Gaza and said that all Danes and Norwegians had 48 hours to leave the area.[22] The next day, 10,000 people in Gaza demonstrated against the cartoons and burned the Danish flag together with effigies of Denmark's prime minister.

In light of the escalating international crisis and boycott of Danish companies, the prime minister tried to calm the waters. He still insisted that he wouldn't interfere with the press and its decision about the kinds of cartoons to publish, but he made it clear to the Muslim world that he himself would never depict Muhammad and other religious figures in a way that may be perceived as offensive.[23]

It didn't help. The pressure on Denmark was growing. The demand for censorship and punishment in the Muslim world triggered a republication of the cartoons in newspapers across Europe. By the end of February 2006, they had been published in at least 143 newspapers in 56 different countries around the world.[24]

Throughout the time of escalation and culmination of the conflict, religious authorities in the Muslim world played a key role. From mid-January until mid-February, they mobilized fellow believers. Yusuf al-Qaradawi called for "a day of rage" on Friday, February 3. His call was heard. After the prayer, there were demonstration in at least 13 countries, and over the next three days, Denmark's embassies in Damascus, Beirut, and Tehran were attacked and set on fire. In Beirut, one demonstrator was killed. Anger increased owing to false rumors that had been circulating between Muslims in Denmark and the Middle East that the Koran would be burned in a public place in Copenhagen.

In mid-February, encouraged by a wave of anger against the cartoons, the OIC put forward five demands to the EU: (a) the European Parliament should pass a law criminalizing Islamophobia, (b) the EU and OIC should jointly sponsor a resolution in the UN General Assembly that would call on every member state to criminalize defamation of religion and prophets, (c) the EU should commit itself to new rules for journalistic ethics, (d) new limits on freedom of expression with regard to religious symbols should be imposed, and (e) the recently reformed UN Human Rights Council should operate within new guidelines that would put banning blasphemy and mockery of religion at the top of its agenda.[25]

And how did the EU respond to that challenge to its fundamental values? Basically, it left Denmark high and dry. Only a few grasped the relationship between the cartoons and the OIC's global campaign against freedom of expression, among them the Dutch and countries from the former Eastern Bloc. A book about the Cartoon Crisis put it this way:

> Nobody among the world's proclaimed defenders of freedom and democracy—the UN, U.S., U.K. and EU—in official statements denounced the fact that lawful speech in a free country was confronted with death threats and threats of violence by religious leaders in other countries and unveiled calls for boycott from political and religious leaders in one nation after another.[26]

Javier Solana, the EU foreign policy coordinator, went especially far in accommodating the OIC. On February 2, he called OIC

Secretary General Ekmeleddin Ihsanoglu, and according to OIC's summary—Solana didn't deny it—the top EU bureaucrat's position was closer to the dictatorships in the Middle East than to the Danish government. Solana assured his counterparts in the OIC that people in Europe saw the publication of the cartoons as an unfortunate action that Europeans looked at with "resentment and disgust." Then, Solana traveled to the Middle East and at the OIC's headquarters in Jeddah, he promised that the EU would do its utmost to make sure that that kind of cartoon wouldn't be published in the future, and he didn't contradict Ihsanoglu when the OIC secretary general said that the parties had agreed to promote a UN resolution calling for the criminalization of blasphemy and defamation of religious feeling. In the words of the OIC, Solana also supported new journalistic ethics for the EU. It sounded like Solana was willing to concede to every OIC demand. After having met the religious leader of Al-Azhar University in Cairo, Solana said that the parties had discussed how to protect religious symbols.

The final reconciliation between the OIC and EU and the total sellout of freedom of expression were planned for a summit in Qatar on February 25. Solana and Austria's temporary chair of the EU were supposed to sign an agreement that committed the signatories to promote a global ban on defamation of religious sensibilities. However, Solana and his Austrian colleague never showed up in Qatar because of disagreement among the EU countries. Not everybody was willing to surrender to the OIC. That was confirmed a few days later when the EU limited itself to expressing regret that some people had perceived the cartoons as offensive.

Spain, a member of the EU, and Turkey, an applicant to the EU, signed the agreement at the summit in Qatar. The two countries and Qatar were behind the Alliance of Civilizations, a forum created to overcome mutual mistrust between the West and the Islamic world. Also present were UN Secretary General Kofi Annan and the leaders of the OIC and the Arab League. They all signed the agreement calling for a global ban on defamation of religion, a decision that if implemented would criminalize religious satire, including cartoons of the Muslim prophet.[27]

The first week of February 2006 is a blur. I can pick out images of burning embassies, furious crowds, and Danish business leaders tearful about lost jobs and markets. It was emotional, certainly, but I was nonetheless quite clear that I personally had little influence on such external events. The only things I could do was to explain and defend the paper's reasons for publishing the drawings, and to take part in the debates—on self-censorship and religious sentiment, on immigration and the treatment of minorities in our democracies, on liberal principles, globalization, and the bounds of freedom of speech. But I had already been doing all that for four months. And eventually, I lost sight of the big picture and made a couple of stupid mistakes.

It came to a head on February 8, on what turned out to be a dramatic day for *Jyllands-Posten*. Editor-in-Chief Carsten Juste spoke afterward of a sense that the earth was opening up under his feet as angry emails began pouring in that evening, and hundreds of subscribers canceled their subscriptions in protest against my comments.

I felt it too. I sat on the floor of my study late that night with my back against a bookcase, staring vacantly into space. I'd had dinner at the Hotel Kong Frederik with an old friend and colleague from my Moscow days who was in Denmark to cover the Cartoon Crisis. I had been on the phone with a couple of colleagues and, exhausted, I was thinking over the whole surreal scenario. The world had gone mad on account of 12 cartoons. I felt tears well up and run down my cheeks, a spontaneous physical reaction to accumulated stress. For weeks, I had faced, and rejected, claims that the paper and I were responsible for the deaths of innocent people; that we were vicious Muslim haters; that we had planned all that as a provocation. For months, I'd heard the most incredible comments from people I had never met and who had no idea of what I or the paper stood for. I had ignored all of it, or tried to repudiate it with facts and logical argument. But now, a new situation had arisen in which I could only give my critics the benefit of being right: I had done something stupid.

I had spent the morning at home writing a column for the paper. It was about lies and their significance, and it was inspired by a piece I'd read in the *New York Times Magazine*. From there, I went to the studios of Danish channel TV2 to be interviewed on CNN's *American Morning*. I'd been invited to comment on charges put forward by media and critics that *Jyllands-Posten* was concealing an anti-Muslim agenda. A story had appeared in the *Guardian* about an editor of *Jyllands-Posten's* Sunday edition refusing to publish satirical drawings of Jesus offered to the paper by a freelancer in 2003.[28]

"I don't think the readers of *Jyllands-Posten* will find the drawings funny. In fact, I think they would probably raise an outcry. For that reason, I won't be publishing them," the editor had apparently said in his reply to the artist in question.

Thus, *Jyllands-Posten* was accused of a hypocritical double standard. Actually, the two instances differed significantly. First, as the editor in question explained, the drawings had been of poor quality; he had made the mistake of not telling the artist that directly and instead rejected his work with reference to the possible offense it might cause to the paper's readership, which was really only a polite excuse. Second, like other papers, *Jyllands-Posten* receives submissions every day from freelancers wanting us to publish articles, illustrations, and cartoons. Third, the Muhammad cartoons were commissioned as part of a journalistic project that had been devised by the editorial board.

But such subtleties tend to fall by the wayside. So when I heard that the editors of our Sunday edition were planning to run a full page of satirical drawings the paper had published over the years—drawings that made fun of both Christians and Jews—I printed three of the drawings and took them with me to the TV2 studios. All three were by Kurt Westergaard, the man behind the cartoon of Muhammad with the bomb in his turban. One depicted Jesus on the cross with dollar signs in his eyes; another showed the Star of David with a bomb attached; a third depicted an undernourished Palestinian caught up in a barbed-wire fence in the shape of the Star of David.

When CNN asked me why the paper had rejected caricatures of Jesus, I explained that the Muhammad drawings issued from a news story about self-censorship in dealing with Islam, and, holding up Westergaard's drawings, I added, "These cartoons might also be offensive to Christians and Jews, and they were done by the same artist who did the cartoon of the Prophet with a bomb in his turban. My point is that we're not specifically trying to offend Muslims any more than anyone else."

That part of the interview was fairly uncontroversial when it ran on CNN, but on the Danish TV2 news program that evening, it was a bombshell. The impression was given that the drawings I was holding up were new, commissioned by *Jyllands-Posten* as part of the current controversy, rather than archive material the paper was printing in order to refute claims that it was pursuing an anti-Muslim vendetta. In other words, not only had we more or less deliberately offended the world's Muslims; we were now planning to repeat the stunt by targeting Christians and Jews.

I didn't watch the news that night; I was being interviewed by the American TV channel ABC. But I did notice that my phone was suddenly ringing nonstop. There were already more than a hundred messages on my answering machine from the media wanting comments.

I had also made another mistake in that CNN interview. At the time, an Iranian government newspaper had responded to the Cartoon Crisis by requesting cartoons about the Holocaust, to see whether the West would uphold the principles of free speech regarding the Nazi genocide to the same standard as it did regarding the Prophet Mohammad. The studio anchor asked me to comment, and I answered, "I can tell you that my newspaper is trying to establish a contact with that Iranian newspaper, and we would run these cartoons the same day as they would publish them."[29]

My mistake was not saying that *Jyllands-Posten* would run Holocaust cartoons, because in actual fact it had already done so only four days previously. On Saturday, February 4, 2006, we had carried a full page containing 13 examples of anti-Semitic cartoons from the Arab press. We didn't think they were funny or appropriate, or in any way comparable to religious satire, but with so many in the Muslim world in an uproar about the Muhammad cartoons, we found it relevant to show examples of satire from the Arab press so our readers could judge for themselves. Publishing something is not the same as supporting it. So we ran a cartoon from the Jordanian paper *Ad-Dustur* showing Auschwitz; instead of a swastika, the Israeli flag waved from a watchtower, accompanied by the words "Gaza Strip or Israeli death camp?" A second drawing, from *Arab News* in Saudi Arabia, depicted Israeli premier Ariel Sharon hacking children to pieces with a swastika-shaped axe. A third, taken from *Al-Watan* in Oman, showed a Jew with a swastika on his back, thrusting a Star of David sword into a bleeding Palestinian. A brief editorial comment stated:

> Unambiguously anti-Semitic drawings are not nearly as frequent in Arab newspapers as they were only a few years ago. However, they are far from rare. Since both Moses and Jesus are considered by Muslims to be prophets, and thus above criticism, caricatures portraying these two figures never occur. By contrast, anti-Jewish—and occasionally anti-Christian—cartoons are often published. Many Muslims claim that *Jyllands-Posten* "would never dare publish drawings of an anti-Semitic nature." They may now consider it done.[30]

So it wasn't the Iranian Holocaust cartoons as such that were the problem, although Editor-in-Chief Carsten Juste distanced himself from my comments. But CNN squeezed the story into a news brief that made it appear that I had announced that *Jyllands-Posten* would be working together with the Iranian government newspaper to sponsor the Holocaust competition—not what I had said at all. My mistake was making CNN's viewers privy to an editorial process that at that point in time was nobody's business but the paper's editors'.

It was clear that I was doing too many interviews. I faced a tsunami of requests for them, and it is hard for a journalist to turn another journalist down. Some, however, were bizarre. On January 29, 2006, I had taken part in a program on Al Jazeera. Denied the chance of speaking to the studio anchor beforehand, I was completely in the dark about the context in which I was to appear. All of a sudden, I was live from a studio in Copenhagen. The first thing I did was to express regret that anyone should feel offended by the drawings. I stressed that we had not set out to do so, and that scathingly satirical cartoons were a common feature of Danish newspapers. None of those comments, however, were translated into Arabic. Translation began only when I explained why *Jyllands-Posten* would not apologize for the drawings, and why every paper should have the right to publish drawings that could be construed as offensive. So my comments appeared far more confrontational than I had intended.

A few days later, I took part in a Norwegian satirical program, shaking a tambourine while the host played the guitar and sang. Then, late one Friday evening, one of the major Arab TV stations called on me at my office. The interview itself took only five minutes, but the reporter and his female assistant spent half an hour lecturing me about the indefensibility of what *Jyllands-Posten* had done. They told me how they loved their Prophet more than their own children and spouses, and that I—and the newspaper, therefore—had committed the worst form of sacrilege. For my part, I countered by saying that their statement reminded me of the Stalin era, when ordinary Soviet citizens were brainwashed into putting Stalin and the Soviet state before anything else. Those who professed to love a religious symbol more than their closest family could be talked into committing atrocities against children, spouses, and parents in the name of their faith. In my view, it was perverse.

I told them the story of the Russian teenager Pavlik Morozov, who according to Soviet propaganda had informed against his father in 1931 for opposing Stalin's policies of enforced collectivization. Testifying in court, the boy condemned his father's crime, whereupon the following exchange occurred: "But this is me, your father," exclaimed Trofim Morozov. His son turned to the judge and replied: "Indeed, he was once my father, but I no longer consider him as such. I act not as a son, but as a communist." Pavlik Morozov was hailed as a hero and an example to all Soviet children, celebrated in books and music. Statues of the boy were erected, and plays were performed, turning the unselfish child who had sacrificed his own father to the cause into his own cult. The moral of the story was that children should love the Communist Party and Stalin more than their own parents. It was twisted, yet it heavily affected a whole generation of Soviet children.

The two Egyptians shook their heads in impatient exasperation as I related the tale. The atmosphere between us was hardly one of cross-cultural understanding, but the hour was late, and we were tired.

Four months in the spotlight, and now a couple of inglorious errors of judgment, meant that I was relieved to step out of the public eye. I was burned out and decided to take a vacation.

What made me do all those interviews anyway?

I felt there had been sound journalistic reasons for publishing the Muhammad cartoons. Perhaps naively, I thought that reasoned argument would eventually put things in their proper perspective. And occasionally, I did feel it made a difference. Not all those efforts were in vain.

Also, it was in a sense exciting. Being the focus of such enormous exposure was a challenge of a magnitude that I had never before encountered. The paper was under fire, and I felt I was fighting for what I believed in, like a gladiator, cheered on or booed by the crowd.

I learned a lot from the experience, about the media and about myself. It was by no means easy to acknowledge that I had fallen foul of the kind of narcissism I so deplored in celebrities who are hungry for TV exposure and a fast ride to riches and fame. I could sense the rush of being the center of attention, but I refused to admit that it played a part in why I was so eager to appear in the media around the globe. How beguiling it is when the most influential media in the world queued up to talk to you.

But it was also an overwhelming experience. Part of me was scared and overwhelmed by all that was happening around me; throughout, I had a clear sense of being up against forces within myself that I had difficulty controlling. The taste was at once sweet and bitterly unpleasant. It seemed like the kind of thing I imagined compulsive gamblers, pyromaniacs, and serially unfaithful partners experience: allowing themselves to be seduced by their own vanity, physical urges, and a desire for excitement. They know what they are doing is wrong, but they are unable to resist the temptation.

7. Aftershock II

This fear of finding oneself in bad company is not an expression of political purity; it is an expression of a lack of self-confidence.

—*Arthur Koestler*

By not admitting that it exists, self-censorship aligns itself with lies and spiritual corruption.

—*J. M. Coetzee*

The violence, destruction, and killings that occurred during the Cartoon Crisis took place in countries without freedom of speech and religion. The conflict was much more peaceful and civilized in countries that enjoyed extensive freedom of speech and of religion. And yet, the Crisis saw renewed calls in the West for stronger protection of minority religious sentiments. Some called for new legislation: blasphemy codes, such as every country in the West once had, that severely punished speech against God. Others, as we've seen, advocated self-censorship.

Was it not completely insane to react to the issue with demands for tighter legislation to criminalize speech? Wasn't that just legitimizing the violent reactions? Closer scrutiny of the violence yields an ambiguous picture of its origins. Nigeria, a country with 150 million inhabitants, of whom just over half are Muslim, was the scene of the worst riots that occurred during the Crisis. Demonstrations against the drawings turned into mob rule. A Catholic priest and members of his community were burned to death in the province of Borno on Saturday, February 18, 2006. Three days later, acts of retaliation were carried out in another province. The number of killings varied from 150 to 165, according to local reports; some put it even higher.

In fact, the drawings were unlikely to have been the direct source of the violence. Nigerian newspapers the *Daily Independent*, *This Day*, the *Vanguard*, and the *Daily Champion* carried no mention of the drawings in their coverage of clashes, killings, vandalism, and retaliation; that omission was probably because rioting and religious violence had been rising dramatically in Nigeria since 2000, when Sharia law began to be established in several areas.[1] That is, the rioting and religious violence were not something rare and attributable to drawings in a Scandinavian newspaper that the vast majority had never set eyes on. A survey of events in the *Washington Post* in February 2006 concluded, "The cause of the latest outbursts is less the Danish cartoons than the legacy of Muslim–Christian tensions that began long before the European cartoonists caricatured the Prophet Muhammad."[2]

The same applied in other countries. In Libya's medieval city of Benghazi on February 17, protesters trashed and burned the Italian consulate. Police opened fire: 11 died, and some 50 were badly wounded. Two days before, an Italian government minister had appeared in public wearing a T-shirt printed with Kurt Westergaard's drawing. Libya was once an Italian colony, and in the view of Libyan leader Mummar el-Qaddafi, the attack on the Italian consulate was triggered by continuing hatred of the former colonial power rather than by the cartoons. A young protester later wrote on his blog that the target of the protests had been Qaddafi himself: "For us, the youth of Benghazi, this is our chance to rise up against this Pharaoh. . . . The protests are to draw attention to the plight of young people—no education, no work, no money, no opportunities."[3]

Many critics of the Muhammad cartoons and *Jyllands-Posten*'s reasons for publishing them claimed that self-censorship is a positive thing, a sign of good behavior and common sense. That claim bypasses an important distinction between self-censorship and good manners. I am a sworn devotee of good manners. Being with friendly people who do their best to make one feel comfortable, who speak nicely, don't interrupt all the time, and never act aggressively, is a pleasant experience, no question. But we decide to be well mannered of our own free will; self-censorship stems from coercion exerted by fear. The Danish illustrator who chose to remain anonymous in the context of Kåre Bluitgen's book on the life of Muhammad, thereby prompting *Jyllands-Posten* to commission the Muhammad drawings, was not declining to have his name on the front cover in order to be polite, or to show consideration, or to demonstrate modesty. He wanted to illustrate a children's book about the life of the Prophet, but he was afraid of threats and violence.[4]

The self-censorship to which I drew attention in the autumn of 2005 and identified as a problem for the European democracies became more visible in the years that followed. It became clear that the Muhammad cartoons had hit a sore spot. Self-censorship continued following the cartoons' publication; new examples, new crises, were appearing all the time.

In Sweden, conceptual artist Lars Vilks received death threats, was physically abused, and was subjected to an arson attack after he drew Muhammad with the body of a dog in 2007 and attempted to exhibit the work in order to test the boundaries of the art world. In the spring of 2010, Swedish intelligence uncovered a plot to murder him. Police sources revealed that Muslims from several countries were involved, among them an American convert calling herself "Jihad Jane."[5]

In Norway, angry Muslims protested against Oslo daily *Dagbladet*, which had published a drawing of Muhammad as a pig writing the Koran. It was a drawing that had originally been done by an Israeli woman, who in 1997 had attempted to post it in on the wall of a Palestinian store in Hebron on the occupied West Bank before being stopped by police. Her actions cost the 28-year-old Soviet immigrant two years in prison for inciting racial hatred and offending religious sentiments.[6]

In April 2010, the animated comedy program *South Park* poked mild fun at Muhammad dressed up as a bear, prompting one incensed Muslim to threaten the program's creators. In a clear instance of self-censorship, the network reacted by removing the infamous episode from subsequent airings. Their action prompted *South Park* fans on Facebook to organize an "Everybody Draw Muhammad Day": if millions drew Muhammad, the terrorists would hardly be able to kill all who in the eyes of Islamists had defamed Islam, and the threat would thus deflate. The intention was not to offend personal religious sentiments or to demonstrate disrespect for Islam, but to reiterate the First Amendment of the U.S. Constitution, which guarantees freedom of speech.[7]

The incident's initiator, cartoonist Molly Norris, would later distance herself from the idea, but others went through with it. More than 10,000 Muhammad drawings were submitted to the Facebook group, and in Pakistan, authorities blocked access to Facebook to prevent people from seeing them.

British visual artist Grayson Perry is a man well known for his provocative approach to many subjects, including religion; he has, for example, done a piece involving a teddy bear being born out of a penis in the shape of the Virgin Mary. However, Perry said in the autumn of 2007 that he was too frightened to tackle Islam:

> I've censored myself. I'm interested in religion and I've made a lot of pieces about it. With other targets you've got a better idea of who they are but Islamism is very amorphous. You don't know what the threshold is. Even what seems an innocuous image might trigger off a really violent reaction, so I just play safe all the time. The reason I haven't gone all-out attacking Islamism in my art is because I feel real fear that someone will slit my throat.[8]

In January 2006, Norway's most famous newspaper artist, Finn Graff, said he would be afraid to draw the Muslim prophet. Graff was not a man who had trouble satirizing other sensitive issues. Six months before, he had depicted two Norwegian politicians as copulating pigs, and in connection with a debate concerning

Christianity, he had drawn marching Christians clad in brown shirts, the swastikas replaced by crucifixes. He had also done a number of very controversial drawings about Israel, including depicting Menachem Begin as a concentration camp commandant looking the other way while two German shepherds devoured a prisoner.

In the summer of 2006, Graff drew Israeli leader Ehud Olmert standing on a balcony in a concentration camp, armed with a rifle, while a Palestinian lay bleeding from gunshot wounds. It was an image inspired by a scene in Steven Spielberg's Holocaust movie *Schindler's List*, in which a sadistic camp commandant picks off Jewish prisoners from his balcony for target practice. Graff's drawing prompted the Israeli ambassador to Norway to lodge a formal complaint with the Norwegian Press Association, which found that the drawing could not be considered a breach of sound press ethics. (I would have liked to have included Graff's depiction of Ehud Olmert in this book so that readers might judge for themselves, but Graff declined permission, being reluctant to be seen keeping "bad company," as he put it in an email to my publishers.)

But Graff drew the line at tackling Muhammad. That was about fear.

"When there's a certain likelihood that reactions come in the shape of threats and violence, or you risk getting your throat slit open, that's it for me," he told Norwegian paper *Magazinet*. Then— somewhat inconsistently for a man who time and again had demonstrated that he held precious little in reverence—he went on to say that he respected the ban on depiction in Islam. "So my decision is just as much about respect for the religious idea as it is based on real fear," Graff concluded.[9]

The same kind of ambiguity surfaced elsewhere. One of the directors of the 2008 Danish animation movie *Rejsen til Saturn* (*Journey to Saturn*), Thorbjørn Christoffersen, explained how the Muslim main character had been spared the scathing satire to which other characters in the movie were constantly subjected. Christoffersen told *Berlingske Tidende*:

> Unfortunately, making fun of Muslims' religion has become no-go. I do think we deliver a few blows to the Jamil character in the movie, but it's certainly true that we don't mess with his religion. It's simply too sensitive an issue, and I can't take on the responsibility for broaching that. I've a family to think about, and a place of work. I'm no fighting man, and certainly not one to relish the prospect of fanatical Muslims knocking at my door.[10]

A few days later, Thorbjørn Christoffersen and his codirector Kresten Vestbjerg Andersen expounded on their views in an interview with *Politiken*:

> My favorite part in the script is where the Danish astronauts land on Saturn and say: "We are the white Gods." It's so cool. "We come in the name of democracy and freedom of speech." We wanted to take the piss out of the conservative reality we live in. As an artist you're kind of an anarchist. You become that automatically when you're funny.[11]

From that point of view, then, the movie was mordant satire, a form of edification in reverse. When confronted with his comments on self-censorship and reluctance to turn the sting of his satire toward Islam, Christoffersen replied:

> We do stuff we know people will laugh at, however crass it might be. I mean, we're pretty crude about the Queen as a symbol of nation. But Muhammad cartoons aren't funny. If we started being critical of Jamil's religion it'd be like 'them and us,' 'Ha, ha, ha' and 'Fuck you,' that kind of thing.

At that point Christoffersen's codirector added: "The only thing we'd achieve from that would be to show disrespect, which just wouldn't be funny. It'd be the same as shooting the Queen. It'd just be totally tasteless."

The self-compromising hypocrisy of the two animators could have almost brought tears to the eyes. Those brave humorists apparently considered satire targeting religious ideas to be a much more serious offense than attacking living individuals. And the parallel drawn between religious satire and murder was revealing. Theocracies and religious fanatics could not have worded the rationale behind their worldview better or more succinctly than those two funny guys.

Grayson Perry, Finn Graff, and the directors of *Rejsen til Saturn* all subjected themselves to self-censorship. Those are merely three random examples. There were hundreds more, all over Europe, and good manners had nothing to do with it.[12] It was self-censorship governed by fear, though in some cases, the individuals involved had difficulty standing by their decision, finding it embarrassing and at odds with their self-image, thus attempting to explain it away with reference to respect for the faith of others and a reluctance to provoke. That was exactly the kind of intimidation of the public space that had given rise to our cartoon project in the first place.

Besides the issue of self-censorship, the debate following the cartoons revealed a number of fractures in European culture and self-understanding. One of those issued from an event that Europe wished to avoid repeating at all costs: the lesson learned from the Jewish Holocaust was that words could kill, and hateful words can beget hateful actions. It was widely held that if only the Weimar government had clamped down on the National Socialists' verbal persecution of the Jews in the years before Hitler's rise to power, or if the Nazis had been prevented from pursuing their propaganda of hatred following 1933, then the Holocaust would never have happened. Proponents of that view saw a parallel between unfettered freedom of speech, demonization of the Jews in Nazi propaganda, and their subsequent genocide in the concentration camps.

It was the same train of thought that prompted Denmark's then foreign minister Per Stig Møller in 2009 to warn that free speech could be abused to incite violence. "We see it today in the message being sent out by Osama bin Laden. And we saw it in Germany, where anti-Semitic rhetoric eventually led to die Endlösung [the Final Solution], by which six million Jews were killed," he wrote.[13]

Nazi propaganda played a significant role in mobilizing anti-Jewish sentiment; that is irrefutable. But to claim that the Holocaust could have been prevented if only anti-Semitic speech and Nazi propaganda had been banned is stretching a point. Let's separate out some facts here. Anti-Semitism in the Weimar Republic sparked violence and calls for Jews to be deprived of all rights. Under Nazi apartheid, Jews were excluded from German societies; their civil rights were annulled; and pogroms and the Kristallnacht occurred. During World War II, there was the Holocaust. What unites them is that at no point during those periods did freedom of speech exist unhindered in Germany.

In my view, we are generally misguided to speak of the "abuse of free speech," particularly in the case of dictatorships. Hitler's morbid, paranoid propaganda prior to the Final Solution had little to do with abusing free speech, not least because no free speech existed. No logical link exists between Hitler's propaganda in a totalitarian regime and the call for constraining freedom of speech in democratic, open societies.

I often heard it said that *Jyllands-Posten* had "abused its freedom of speech" by its decision to publish the Muhammad cartoons. Authoritarian regimes also clutch at the phrase when incarcerating dissidents. Chinese dissidents are deported to labor camps for "abusing their freedom of speech." Egyptian dissident Saad Eddin Ibrahim was imprisoned for "abusing his freedom of speech" by criticizing Egyptian president Hosni Mubarak. Murdered Russian journalist Anna Politkovskaya "abused her freedom of speech" by penning articles critical of the wars in Chechnya. If Hitler's propaganda within a totalitarian regime and activist criticism of a totalitarian regime can both be termed "abuse of freedom of speech," the phrase is clearly meaningless, insipid, and open to manipulation.

Following the Holocaust, European democracies concluded that a ban on hate speech could prevent or at least contain racist violence.[14] History provides no evidence for that reasoning. Nonetheless, legislation to that effect was passed in Germany and Austria, and it became a driving force in international human rights efforts in the decades after the war.

Following its inception in 1949, the Council of Europe took steps toward establishing the European Convention for the Protection of Human Rights, one of the world's first human-rights treaties. A European Court of Human Rights was set up to monitor and to address complaints by citizens who believed their rights had been violated. That development was quite momentous and indeed laudable. For the first time, individuals were accorded rights across national boundaries. The court was not a court of appeal. It was not empowered to nullify the ruling of courts of law at the national level, but it could order a member state to align its practice with the human rights convention in the case that it ruled in favor of a plaintiff.[15]

Since 2000, however, the constraints on free speech contained in United Nations and European conventions have become a significant instrument for grievance fundamentalists and for authoritarian regimes that use them to justify oppression of dissidents and minorities. Their use has tended to occur with particular reference to two articles: Article 20, paragraph 2, of the International Covenant on Civil and Political Rights, and Article 4 of the International Convention on the Elimination of All Forms of Racial Discrimination.[16]

The first runs as follows: "Any advocacy of national, racial or religious hatred that constitutes incitement to discrimination, hostility or violence shall be prohibited by law."[17]

The second, taking as its point of departure a rather broad definition of "racial discrimination," declares that the state "[s]hall

147

declare an offence punishable by law all dissemination of ideas based on racial superiority or hatred, incitement to racial discrimination . . . against any race or group of persons of another colour or ethnic origin." Moreover, states were obliged to prohibit organizations and propaganda activities that promoted or incited racial discrimination, just as participation in such organizations or activities was to be made punishable by law.[18]

The wording is awkward and technical, though the intention is clear: there is to be no difference in principle between saying something discriminatory and doing something discriminatory. With time, definitions of "racism" and "discrimination" widened, and the distinction between words and actions became even more blurred. In the European welfare states, that blurring of distinction coincided with the state undertaking to realize an ideal of equality that involved positive discrimination for those deemed weak or considered to be victims, and sometimes a corresponding negative discrimination of those whose personal resources were found satisfactory. As an increasing number of groups were classified as weak, it also seemed more important to protect them against speech that might be interpreted as discriminatory.

With large-scale immigration to Europe from the Islamic world, European welfare states suddenly found themselves under pressure. The gaps that emerged in cultures, religions, and lifestyles in Europe's newly diverse countries meant, on the one hand, that the welfare state had to impose demands on its new citizens to make them adapt to the norms of the society and thereby to ensure a continued community of values; while on the other hand, the state was forced to take measures against indigenous citizens who expressed discontent with the new demographic developments in language it considered discriminatory or a threat to social stability. Wide-reaching freedom of speech essentially ran against the grain of the welfare state in a multicultural society.

There were sharply divergent notions as to what was actually going on. One side insisted that free speech was under pressure:

new diversity and new sensitivities were squeezing free debate. The other side claimed that Europe was now a place in which Muslims were subject to witch-hunts and persecution. There were calls to ban mosques, minarets, and traditional Muslim clothing for women: some likened that development to the plight of the German Jews in the 1920s. So how could anyone even claim that free speech was under fire?

The fact that two such opposing views could exist side by side was a symptom of the crisis into which the welfare state had plunged. The culture of rights that had shaped the welfare state to begin with, and that had formed the basis of its steady growth for half a century, now threatened to undermine it completely. It was unable to contain the diversity and the internal disparities imposed on it by a multicultural society.[19]

We were heading for a Europe driven by fear of its own shadow, a Europe wanting to protect itself against the new reality, rather than one able to create a framework for the free interplay of its citizens. Fear was undermining freedom—both for those who feared Islam and for those who feared insulting it.

In the European welfare state—in which government reserves the right to interfere in people's lives with reference to positive values, such as human dignity, security, and social harmony—freedom is not likely to be liquidated suddenly in the manner of the brutal dictatorship, where oppression is a visible constant, and opponents are rounded up in the dead of night. Rather, it will occur gradually and without fuss.[20]

The grievance lobby in the UN, the European Union, and the human rights industry was directed by the notion that criminalization of racist utterances (so-called hate speech) would lead to racism being eradicated. They drew up a succession of reports urging member states to prosecute and punish perpetrators of hate speech to a much greater degree than before. The grievance lobby wanted the definition of racism expanded to encompass still more groups within society. They were on solid ground: the

Convention on Racial Discrimination directed that member states adopt prohibitive legislation and generally take measures to eradicate hatred. The state was to educate and reeducate its citizens, an aim that appeared at once hysterical and ominous—and about as realistic as banning snow in Greenland. Yet it won immediate favor. Sentiments, not least those offended, took on primary significance and political clout. French expert on international relations Dominique Moïsi went so far as to speak of "the geopolitics of emotion."[21] The Cartoon Crisis was one terrifying illustration of what he meant.

The ambition of the Convention on Racial Discrimination to cleanse society of bigotry accorded the state a role that, as Danish human rights lawyer Jacob Mchangama noted, appealed strongly to the political left.[22] There was something rather utopian about the project, but more seriously, it gave government free rein to introduce censorship and, paradoxically, to oppress the very human rights it had originally been conceived to protect. Those efforts to eradicate hatred and racial discrimination encompassed two specific threats to freedom of speech.

The first issued from the lack of a universally accepted definition of "hatred" in international law. Not even member states of the European Union were in accordance. Dictionary definitions of "hatred" highlight feelings of extreme antipathy or disapprobation and abhorrence. "Hate speech" is defined as utterances expressing hatred of, or intolerance toward, other social groups, particularly on the basis of race, gender, nationality, ethnicity, religion, or sexuality.[23] But intolerance and hatred toward others may, in many contexts, be quite legitimate emotions. They may surface in any of us when confronted with those who commit violence, oppress women, persecute homosexuals, or indeed in any number of contexts involving gross injustice and abuse of power. Where is the dividing line between expressing hatred, abhorrence, or antipathy within the bounds of the law and doing so in such a way that it should be prohibited? There is no clear-cut answer, which opens the field for arbitrary interpretations endangering freedom of speech.[24]

The second threat to freedom of speech arose from broadening interpretations of racism encompassing increasing numbers of social groups and types of speech. In Denmark, legislation against racial discrimination was introduced in 1939 to counter outrageous attacks on Jews, that, for example, they drank the blood of Christian children and other monstrous myths. Following the adoption of the Convention on Racial Discrimination, the scope of this so-called racism paragraph was successively widened, and sanctions tightened in 1971, 1986, and 1995, the aim being not merely to protect citizens against false accusations inciting hatred of specific groups, but increasingly to criminalize scornful and offensive speech regardless of their truth. Today, action may be taken against individuals expressing personal opinions, value judgments, and moral evaluations. After the law was widened to safeguard the sentiments of the homosexual community, a woman of Christian faith narrowly avoided conviction for publicly stating in a letter to the editor that she personally considered sex between homosexuals to be the most disgusting form of fornication.[25]

The racism card was played left, right, and center. A ruling of the Danish Supreme Court in 2003 acquitted a woman of slander against populist leader Pia Kjærsgaard, after she said on the radio that she would be unwilling to be identified with Kjærsgaard's "racist views." That ruling followed a new, broader definition of "racial discrimination," which was now "discrimination and oppression of, or merely dissociation from groups of individuals who may be of the same race as oneself."[26] On that count, vegetarians could be branded racist for dissociating themselves from meat eaters (or vice versa). Socialists were racists if they dissociated themselves from conservatives, and there was almost no limit on what kind of critical speech could be deemed "racist."

At least the woman was acquitted. The court thus ruled that calling a politician racist was not punishable by law. However, the new, wide definition of racism continued to be employed in calling for constraints on freedom of speech in other contexts. In 2010, a complaint was lodged against the head of Copenhagen's police homicide squad for racism following a comment he made when a Romanian man randomly murdered a Norwegian flight attendant in a Copenhagen hotel. "The Romanians are without scruples. They'll kill for a couple of hundred kroner. It's a whole different culture," the officer said.[27] The context made it very clear that it was a comment made with specific reference to the case in question, and that no generalization was intended. The officer swiftly retracted his comment and publicly expressed regret if what he had said had been taken to apply to all Romanians. The case sparked lively discussion in the Danish media, demonstrating that free and open debate was by far the best way of regulating the bounds of freedom of speech in a democracy. Yet the officer in question was reported to the police for racism. What such tendencies will lead to may be rather difficult to predict. Perhaps, it won't be long before we see media taken to court for racism on account of (authentic) headlines, such as "Mexicans Smuggle Cocaine in Sharks," "Swedish Men Impotent," or "Danes Enjoy Cocaine."

In today's grievance culture, with its identity politics and cultivation of the victim, the grievance lobby has succeeded in shifting the fulcrum of the human rights debate from freedom of speech to the necessity of countering hate speech; from the individual pursuing individual liberties to the individual aggrieved by the liberties taken by others. That shift becomes counterintuitive, the logic increasingly absurd. Those aggrieved by free speech are defended, while those whose speech is perceived as offensive to such a degree that they are exposed to death threats, physical assault, and sometimes even murder are deemed to have been asking for it: "What did they expect, offending people like that?"

When we focus on nondiscrimination and equality, and aim to empower the aggrieved, tolerance is no longer about the ability to tolerate things that we don't like; it becomes the ability to keep quiet and refrain from saying things that others may dislike. That is the basic, and very flawed, premise underlying the much-touted phrase "Freedom of speech is not the same as freedom to offend."

Following the collapse of the Berlin Wall and the march of freedom through Central and Eastern Europe, a number of European countries have adopted new insult codes. In Norway and the Netherlands, measures have been taken to replace outdated blasphemy codes with new legislation to safeguard groups and ideas central to personal and group identity. So far, legislators in the two countries have not succeeded, but the idea is being pushed.

British sociology professor Steven Lukes mapped out the grievance fundamentalists' ideal society in his novel *The Curious Enlightenment of Professor Caritat*, in the author's words "a comedy of ideas."[28] The novel is about Nicholas Caritat, a professor of the Enlightenment, who, after being rescued from prison in the military state of Militaria, is assigned the task of journeying to find the best of all worlds. On his travels, he passes through Utilitaria, Libertaria, and Proletaria, but ends up in Communitaria, a society based on the notion of multiculturalism and equality of all its 34 ethnic groups and 17 religions.

Communitaria was once an ethnically and religiously homogeneous society. Then came the great wave of immigration. Individual rights no longer exist. The only right acknowledged is the right of the various communities to be respected.

People are forced to remain within the religious and ethnic communities to which they belong, and marriage across community borders is frowned on. Individuals attempting to establish new communities are ostracized and branded as rootless cosmopolitans. Communitaria is founded on the so-called Principle of No Offense, manifest throughout its legislation. Freedom of speech does not exist. Indeed, it is a punishable offense on the grounds that speaking freely involves the risk of offending others.

The citizens of Communitaria are constantly on their guard to defend freedom, that is, the freedom of others from insult. For that reason, humor and satire have been abolished. In fact, no one knows what they are, so when a reviewer deems a rock opera to be a satire dealing with the fanaticism of faith and the intolerance of ethnicity, a need arises to investigate the concept. Thus, the rock star composer discovers to his horror that satire seeks to expose human folly and malice through ridicule.

The religious and ethnic communities of Communitaria demand that the composer dissociate himself from his work and apologize in public. Subsequently, he is forced into hiding when it transpires that his satire is deemed sacrilegious, the worst of all crimes in Communitaria, and the only one commanding the death penalty on account of its violating the absolute right of communities to be respected.

That prompts Professor Caritat to investigate the extent to which Communitaria is familiar with tolerance, a concept that he considers would make it easier to find a solution to the problem. Tolerance, though, is not practiced, not least because it entails the acceptance of offensive speech on the part of others, and why should one accept that? Why, indeed, should it be necessary at all to offend anyone else?

Citizens of Communitaria's religious and ethnic communities are quite simply unable to tolerate a lack of respect for what they hold to be sacred. "Why?" Professor Caritat inquires again in a last-ditch attempt to plead the case of tolerance, a concept in which he has conducted considerable scholarly research.

"The problem lies in the giving of offense. What you call tolerance, so far as we understand it, is to accept being subjected to an offense without objecting; respect is refraining from causing it. Our whole society is committed to the second, not the first," explains the chairman of one of Communitaria's parliamentary groups.

Does that sound familiar?

In the spring of 2006, I visited liberal law professor Ronald Dworkin, an ardent advocate of free speech, in New York. He had recently published a noteworthy commentary on the Muhammad cartoons in the *New York Review of Books* titled "The Right to Ridicule." "In a democracy no one, however powerful or impotent, can have a right not to be insulted or offended. That principle is of particular importance in a country that strives for racial or ethnic fairness," Dworkin wrote.[29]

Sitting in his office on Washington Square, I asked him to expound on the idea. "The democratic process is founded on the idea of freedom of speech," Dworkin told me.

> In a democracy we discuss things and then vote, and we expect those who lose the discussion and the vote to accept the decision of the majority and uphold the laws it has adopted. That's quite an extraordinary thing to ask of people. My conviction is that the only way we can ask that is if everyone in the democratic process has had the chance to put forward their arguments in exactly the way they wish. If we suppose one group has the special right not to be ridiculed, what that automatically entails is that others are deprived of their right to voice their opinions about that group.[30]

"Why can't we just ask people to word their criticism politely and respectfully, avoiding scorn, mockery, and ridicule?" I asked him.

"We can't do that, because scorn, mockery, and ridicule are specific modes of expression, which present their content in such a way that it cannot be duplicated less offensively without that content being changed," he said. "We cannot force some other taste on people, or some different standard as to how they should voice their opinions in the public debate, at the same time as we ask them to accept the decisions of the majority."

In contrast to Europe, the United States has not legislated against hate speech. Throughout the 20th century, the limits on what individuals in America can say without running the risk of prosecution have gradually been pushed back. The U.S. Supreme

Court's interpretation of the First Amendment to the Constitution, which safeguards freedom of speech and religion and separates church and state, has become increasingly broad.[31] The American tradition avoids regulating speech, no matter how injurious or insulting it may be. Government does not interfere with what its citizens say. Moreover, the courts focus on the consequences of speech when addressing whether it should be protected under the law. In the United States, even threats or incitements to violence are punishable only where there is a risk that they will be followed by immediate action. Things are very different in Europe.

Although freedom of speech enjoys a hallowed status in the United States, in Europe it is but one among a number of related rights. Others, such as the right not to suffer affront or indignity, are in some instances considered more important than the right of free expression. That is particularly so in Germany, where the right of dignity is held higher than free speech, a fact that has spawned a series of restrictions on the latter, leading to convictions against artists and media for publishing satirical drawings depicting politicians as animals.[32] Moreover, Germany has been able to push through framework agreements in the EU obliging member states to introduce new legislation against hate speech.[33]

Several recent incidents in Europe serve to illustrate the difference further.[34] In July 2007, four British Muslims were sentenced to long prison terms for inciting racism and murder in connection with protests against the Muhammad cartoons outside the Danish embassy in London in February 2006. One of the men convicted had put on a belt similar to those worn by suicide bombers, while placards urging the killing of those who had offended Islam were clearly visible in press photos of the event.[35] It is hardly likely that the four men would have been convicted in the United States, since none of the individuals being threatened (I was among them) was within reach at the time. There was no clear and present danger.

In October 2008, the European Court of Human Rights dismissed as being without merit a complaint by French cartoonist

Denis Leroy, who six years previously had been convicted of glorifying terrorism because of a cartoon he published on September 13, 2001.[36] It depicted the Twin Towers in New York with the caption "We have all dreamt of it . . . Hamas did it." From an American point of view, that utterance was horrifically offensive, yet in the United States, it would hardly have been brought to court at all. Instead, the cartoon would have been condemned by civil society in the media.

A third example again involves the European Court of Human Rights. In 2004, the court dismissed an appeal by Mark Norwood, a member of the British National Party who had been convicted of insulting Muslims after putting up a BNP poster in his window showing the Twin Towers in flames, with the words "Islam out of Britain—Protect the British People." The Muslim symbols of a crescent and star were also shown, inside a prohibition sign.[37] In the United States, the Constitution would most likely have protected Norwood's freedom of expression, whereas in Europe his words were regarded as hate speech and made him liable to prosecution.

Even racist hate speech is permitted in the United States, though like Europe's, the country's history is a painful one, encompassing slavery, civil war, lynching, and widespread discrimination against black Americans. Nazis have the right to demonstrate in neighborhoods housing Holocaust survivors; the Ku Klux Klan is free to set its crosses ablaze in black neighborhoods; and critics can burn the American flag, or indeed that of any other country, pretty much as they please.[38]

The history of free speech in the United States undermines those who in Europe insist on a causal link between legalization of hate speech on the one hand and racist violence and killings on the other.[39] Throughout the 20th century, the United States saw a gradual relaxation of restrictions on free speech; nonetheless, at the beginning of the 21st century, racism is far less of a problem than it was a hundred years ago.

Yet in the view of a number of observers well versed in the history of free speech, the European trend will be consolidated in coming years, whereas the United States, with its liberal interpretation of the concept, will become more isolated.[40] Paradoxically, the European stance is that a more religiously, ethnically, and culturally diverse society demands less diversity of speech, whereas in the United States, diversity of speech is viewed as a natural requirement of a diverse society.

Some may counter that the differences I have noted between the United States and Europe do not accord with the reality of the Cartoon Crisis. The drawings were published by a number of European newspapers, while the U.S. media generally steered clear. Does that mean that in a crisis, Europeans are more willing to defend freedom of speech? I don't believe so. The original idea that led me to commission the cartoons as input for the debate on self-censorship was more relevant to Europe than to the United States. Fear of Islam in the United States did not at that time entail theaters censoring plays or pulling them from their programs; it did not prompt museums to remove works from exhibition; comedians felt no imperative to hold back; and filmmakers saw no reason to cut scenes from their films. True, there were booksellers in 2006 who refused to carry a magazine that included the Muhammad cartoons, and the same year, a scene was cut from an episode of *South Park* dealing with the Muhammad cartoons, but the issue was not a challenge to American culture in the same way as in Europe.

Moreover, most Americans considered the discussion of Islam to be primarily an issue of foreign politics. The perpetrators of 9/11 were Muslims from without, not from within; the murder of Theo van Gogh and the London and Madrid terror bombings were attributable to Muslims from within. American Muslims are traditionally a lot better integrated into the society than their European counterparts. They are better educated than most; they earn more money; and they speak the language. They are not a burden on public funding, so in contrast to Europe, American satire and comedy had nowhere near the same focus on the integration of Muslims, or on Muslim attempts to enforce their own norms on the society.

Another difference probably lay in the much deeper religious sentiments held by many Americans. Though ridicule of religious sensibilities is protected speech, civil society has worked out unwritten rules that make that kind of speech rare. And finally, the issues of immigration, integration, and values now under debate in Europe are questions that have already been dealt with in the United States. Dutch sociologist Paul Scheffer outlines three phases of immigration.[41] In the first, immigrants and indigenous citizens of the receiving society avoid each other. At some point, maintaining separate worlds becomes less tenable, and a second phase involves confrontation of values, lifestyles, constraints, and what it means to be a citizen of that society. In Scheffer's view, the Cartoon Crisis was a highly significant episode in the debate on what freedom of speech and the right of religious free exercise entail in modern Europe. Eventually, the third phase occurs in which the society negotiates a common understanding of how its basic values are to be understood. The United States has already been through those three phases, and thus the Muhammad cartoons seemed of little interest to most American media. It was a European thing, a story that may well have echoed through the Islamic world, but one that had no domestic political dimension in the United States.

That was before all hell broke loose. In January and February 2006, the Cartoon Crisis was a global news story. As such, one can only marvel at the reluctance of the American media to show the drawings and to permit their readers and viewers to make up their own minds. That reluctance gave the impression that the drawings were a lot more offensive than was actually the case. I spoke to a couple of American editors during the Crisis, and what they told me led me to conclude that there were two further reasons for their refusal to reprint the cartoons.

The first was to protect their own correspondents in the Islamic world. Less than four years had passed since Daniel Pearl of the *Wall Street Journal* had been kidnapped and executed by Islamic terrorists in Pakistan. In Iraq and Afghanistan, violence was on the upsurge, animosity toward the United States was fierce, and the media were having problems ensuring the continued safety of their staff in the field. The second reason had to do with political correctness and an erroneous notion that religion and race could be put on equal footing. In the view of a number of American editors, Muslims in Europe had the same status as the black community in the United States. For that reason, the Muhammad cartoons could be deemed racist.

In the United States, it is held that a multireligious, multicultural society has need of a greater diversity of speech than a homogenous society. That belief entails religious groups enjoying the freedom to proselytize and to attack others, while being prepared to tolerate the same kind of treatment when it goes the other way. In 1940, the U.S. Supreme Court ruled in defense of the right of a member of Jehovah's Witnesses to proselytize on the streets of a Catholic neighborhood using a portable phonograph and to openly declare in that context that the Catholic Church was the instrument of Satan.[42] Conversely, in Europe, the feeling was to hold back and show respect, justifying constraints on free speech in the name of peaceful coexistence.

In a celebrated essay in 1988 on the history of censorship, Michael Scammell, founder of the journal *Index on Censorship*, a significant forum of international debate on free speech since the 1970s, pointed out that the establishment of a distinction between words and actions had been epochal in the Western European history of the right of free expression. Until the 17th century, actions and words were treated identically throughout Europe. Verbal expression of deviant or unorthodox notions in religious matters was taken to be a physical attack on the Church, its members, and God. Speaking out in favor of political change or against the existing order was perceived as incitement to rebellion and treason. Exactly the same was true of totalitarian societies of the 20th century.[43]

Criminalization of speech is the closest a society can get to controlling the thoughts of its people.[44] Thoughts cannot be made the object of government surveillance, but speech is positioned somewhere between thought and action; whereas authorities cannot interfere in the former, all, regardless of political inclination, believe the latter in some cases may or ought to be regulated. It is not forbidden to think that black people belong to an inferior race. If, on the basis of that notion, blacks are separated from the rest of society, that is unlawful discrimination. But if one merely states that black people do not deserve the same rights as other citizens, without actually discriminating in practice, the legal consequences are far from clear-cut. Some people feel that speech has more in common with thought than with action. Others feel speech begets action. Or more radically, that utterances are actions, and that racist speech should be prohibited because it is in itself discriminatory, or is likely sooner or later to lead to discrimination.

Many believe that freedom of speech is essentially rooted in the right to speak out against the powers that be. It therefore ought not to be used to attack the weak in society. *Jyllands-Posten* thus misused its right to free speech to step on a group generally held in low esteem and often kicked around by the media. As such, the whole affair was a perversion of free speech.

That argument is built on a series of false premises. If freedom of speech is a universal right, it includes the right to voice sentiments or opinions that may be considered objectionable, obscene, or derogatory. One of the most important tasks of the media is indeed to monitor those in power. It isn't, however, the only responsibility of a free and open press.

British philosopher John Stuart Mill, author of the classic work *On Liberty*, pointed out in the 19th century that the task of the press was not merely to safeguard citizens against the authorities.[45] The tyranny of predominant opinion presented an equally large threat to the liberties of the individual. Mill possessed a keen eye for prejudice in society, for taboos and repression, and he warned forcefully against the despotism of custom, its often aggressive intolerance of opinion, and oppressive moralism with respect to deviant viewpoints and behavior. Mill believed it was the task of the press to put accepted truths to debate and to challenge the dogmas that form the framework of a society's self-image, whether they involve attitudes on immigration, taxation, the monarchy, the relation between church and state, the wars in Afghanistan and Iraq, or self-censorship.

Mill's most controversial idea concerned what is referred to as the "harm principle": government is entitled to restrict the freedom of its citizens only if an action is harmful to others. Mill did not consider the offending of religious sentiments to be an action that fulfilled the harm principle; he called for state intervention only if there was a risk of imminent violence.

During the debate concerning the Muhammad cartoons, some resorted to a broad interpretation of the harm principle. It ran like this: your freedom stops where practicing free speech hurts my religious sentiments. Others added that offending religious conviction was a breach of the victim's right of free exercise of religion. That was an argument I heard put forward by leading Syrian filmmaker Najdat Anzour when he visited Denmark in 2010. In 2007, Anzour had made a 30-episode television series, *Roof of the World*, based on the Cartoon Crisis. In it, I was portrayed as a Ukrainian Jew with close ties to neoconservative circles in the United States, as well as to the Israeli intelligence service Mossad. Anzour apparently saw me as a Dr. Evil–type, heading up a conspiracy whose purpose was to create confrontation between the West and the Islamic world into whose clutches the hapless Danes had fallen. When I suggested to him that the whole thing was lies from beginning to end, he defended himself by saying that his assistants had researched the matter fully on the Internet. Their error appeared to issue from the first biographical article about me on *Wikipedia*, in which it could be read that I was Jewish and hailed from Ukraine. That erroneous information was swiftly exploited by various obsessives. Some Muslims were so caught up in their hatred of Israel that it amounted to a form of paranoia. One could almost see the light bulb appearing above their heads: aha, so he's a Jew, now we get it!

Initially, I'd decided not to engage in debate with Najdat Anzour when he was scheduled to appear at the Danish Film School in Copenhagen to discuss his work with students. But when he reiterated his twisted version of the harm principle with respect to the boundaries of free speech, I found myself unable to hold back. I pointed out that publication of the Muhammad cartoons did not in any way prevent Muslims from taking part in prayer five times a day, from attending mosque, fasting during Ramadan, abstaining from the consumption of alcohol and pork, or practicing their faith. To claim that the cartoons were a violation of the right of Muslims to free religious exercise was, to put it mildly, nonsense.

But many others believed that *Jyllands-Posten* should have been taken to court on charges of blasphemy or racism. Former Danish foreign minister Uffe Elleman-Jensen quoted Article 4 of the 1789 Declaration of the Rights of Man. Freedom, he said, consists only in the right to do anything that does not harm others; since many Muslims believed their religious sentiments were damaged by the cartoons, *Jyllands-Posten* was in breach of a founding principle of democracy.[46]

Sadly, our former minister had omitted to read on. The text of Article 4 in its entirety reads:

> Liberty consists in being able to do anything that does not harm others: thus, the exercise of the natural rights of every man has no bounds other than those that ensure to the other members of society the enjoyment of these same rights. These bounds may be determined only by Law.[47]

The cartoons never stopped anyone from practicing their religion nor prevented them from speaking freely. But Elleman-Jensen was by no means the only one to twist essential concepts so as to justify crackdowns on offensive speech.

In 2009, British Foreign Secretary David Miliband defended the British government's decision to ban Dutch parliamentarian Geert Wilders from entering the United Kingdom where he was to show his anti-Islamic film *Fitna* to colleagues in the British Parliament. Miliband's grounds for defending the decision and putting Wilders on the next plane back to Amsterdam were as follows: "We have profound commitment to freedom of speech, but there is no freedom to cry 'fire' in a crowded theatre and there is no freedom to stir up hate, religious and racial hatred, according to the laws of the land."[48]

Miliband's analogy of crying "fire" in a crowded theater was taken from a ruling of the U.S. Supreme Court in 1919, which has since entered into the language as an aphorism, often being used as a yardstick for determining whether speech should be afforded the protection of law. I had been confronted with the analogy on several occasions by American and British journalists who suggested that publishing the Muhammad cartoons might be considered akin to crying "fire" in a crowded theater.

But if we look at the original quote, by Oliver Wendell Holmes Jr., one of the Supreme Court's most legendary judges, it reads, "The most stringent protection of free speech would not protect a man falsely shouting fire in a theater and causing a panic."[49]

Miliband overlooked the fact that cries of "fire" have to be made falsely in order to fall outside the protection of the law. If someone's house is on fire, or even merely smoldering, the good citizen has a duty to cry fire, inform those inside, or to call the fire department.

Holmes coined the phrase when the Supreme Court upheld a ruling against one Charles Schenck, a Socialist who had passed out flyers on the street referring to the government draft for World

War I as slavery that should be combated using legal means. The authorities did not look lightly upon criticism of U.S. involvement in the war, and Congress had passed a bill outlawing disloyalty and opposition to the draft.

It would be unthinkable today that governments could take people to court for protesting against the participation of Western nations in the wars in Iraq and Afghanistan. Moreover, as Harvard professor Alan Dershowitz has pointed out, the analogy seems ill placed even in the situation in which it was put forward by Holmes.[50] Schenck's flyers contained a political message urging the reader to think for himself and to decide on the basis of sound common sense. Shouting "fire" in a crowded theater is not a call to reason; it is an urgent and unambiguous appeal for swift action, rather than thoughtful reflection. A more suitable analogy to the Schenck case would have involved a man standing outside a theater passing out flyers suggesting that the theater was unsafe, and therefore urging the public to stay away.

To return to Miliband's endeavors to justify his ban on Geert Wilders's entering the United Kingdom, Wilders had not threatened anyone. Nor had he said or done anything that could have been construed as incitement to violence. He had uttered some opinions on Islam and Muslims in Europe that were found by some to be morally reprehensible; his film included a number of elements that seemed to be unreasonable generalizations; but so do the documentaries by filmmaker Michael Moore. So what was the problem? A British imam had threatened riots in the streets if Wilders was allowed to screen his film in the United Kingdom. The British government's grounds for banning Wilders's entry at Heathrow had nothing to do with anything he had said or done; they were motivated solely by what others were intending to do to him.

That decision was unworthy of an open society. Incidentally, a year later, Wilders was finally allowed into the United Kingdom, where he presented his film and held a press conference. A few people protested, but no riots occurred.

In the spring of 2009, I was in Israel to discuss freedom of speech. When I said that I believed that the EU ban on Holocaust denial should be lifted, there were protests from people whose families had perished in the Holocaust. I explained that banning all speech that is demonstrably false and offensive would result in a lot of things that couldn't be said, and a lot of people who would have to be prosecuted. Quite aside from how morally reprehensible, wounding, and offensive such utterances were, the only thing in my opinion that could justify a ban was if it were clear that Holocaust denial led to an immediate risk of racist attacks and genocide. As far as I could judge, no such risk existed in modern-day Europe.

The risk we ran, I said, was that an increasing number of groups in society would exploit the ban on Holocaust denial to call for protection of their own taboos. In a society of increasing diversity and an attendant grievance culture, acknowledging such calls, and criminalizing speech that some ethnic and religious groups might feel undermines their dignity and identity, would put us on the road to a tyranny of silence.

Criminalization of Holocaust denial itself constitutes a problem in the context of the growing European Muslim population. Schools have been pressured by Muslim parents and pupils to stop teaching about the Holocaust.[51] Teachers have been abused for relating historical events in Europe during World War II. In some Muslim circles, it is held that the Holocaust is a myth constructed by the Jews in order to secure a homeland in Palestine. In such a context, what is needed is a free and open debate to shed light on Muslim standpoints on the Holocaust, to challenge, to enlighten, to discuss, and to force proponents of such views to account for them and to defend them objectively and with documentation.

Many Muslims see criminalization of Holocaust denial as an expression of European double standards. Publishing satirical cartoons of the Muslim prophet is OK, whereas questioning a Jewish myth is not. Clearly, the perception that society finds no place for Muslim opinion seriously undermines the confidence of Muslims in the democracy. Moreover, it expresses a profound lack of confidence in the values of the free and open society.

From time to time, I receive messages of support for my position from Muslims. One Danish Muslim wrote that my struggle was identical to his own for civil rights in the Muslim community, and for that reason it was important that I not back down. Another was sent to me in May 2009, when I was attending a UNESCO conference in Doha; some Arab newspapers had condemned me as the "Danish Satan." The email's author was a Jordanian woman living in another Arab country.

She wrote:

> I have seen and heard a lot of things about the Cartoon Crisis, but only through my work today did I discover the details of what occurred and I feel the need to thank you. I am sure that thanks have been few from my part of the world, but I would like to be among those to express gratitude, for I find your viewpoint highly respectful and forthright. I wish our own media would present the events in all their detail in order that people might get the full picture before condemning.

Such expressions of support helped convince me that my taking part in debates and discussions around the globe had not at all been in vain.

8. From Russia with Love

Silence is a way of talking, of writing. Above all, it is a way of thinking that obfuscates and covers up for the cruelty that should today be a central preoccupation of those who make talking, writing, and thinking their business.

—Kanan Makiya

It was October 30, 1972, and a 38-year-old Russian astrophysicist and biologist stood accused of anti-Soviet agitation and propaganda. The trial was taking place in the small town of Noginsk, and the man's name was Kronid Lyubarsky. Until then, Lyubarsky had been pretty much unknown to the state security agency KGB (Komitet gosudarstvennoy bezopasnosti), despite being a key figure in the underground dissident press, or *samizdat*. He held a position in a research facility just outside Moscow that worked on the Soviet space exploration program for the planet Mars. He had been arrested 10 months earlier in the wake of KGB raids targeting people who edited, stored, and distributed the *Chronicle of Current Events*, the most important publication of the Soviet human rights movement.

The trial was taking place away from Moscow to discourage Western media and activists from following the case. But when Lyubarsky was eventually allowed to speak, eyewitnesses said the tension in the courtroom was electric.[1] He laid out arguments against Soviet censorship: the tyranny of silence that forbade Soviet citizens to discuss or even to mention a long list of issues. He pointed to the double standards of the Soviet regime and the variability of prohibitions over time.

Lyubarsky did not take part in public demonstrations against the regime. His "anti-Soviet agitation and propaganda" limited itself to editing and distributing the *Chronicle*, possession of several hundred *samizdat* publications that he lent to friends and acquaintances, and political opinions that he aired in private company, in particular criticism of the gradual rehabilitation of Stalin and the Soviet invasion of Czechoslovakia.

"Information is the staple diet of the scientist," Lyubarsky stated in his concluding defense speech. "A farmer works with corn, a worker works with metal; in the same way, an intellectual works with information. One can only form an independent opinion to the extent that one possesses information."[2]

Kronid Lyubarsky was sentenced to five years in a labor camp. He was released in January 1977, though he was prevented from returning home by laws denying former convicts the right to live within a 100-kilometer radius of Moscow. Lyubarsky resumed his work collecting information on violations of human rights and headed Aleksandr Solzhenitsyn's fund for the aid of political prisoners. Within months, the authorities were threatening him with renewed internment of 10 years or emigration. As a result, he and his wife Galya left the Soviet Union in October of the same year, with the firm conviction that they would never see their homeland again.

"I felt like I was in a crematorium, saying goodbye to friends and family at the airport," he would recall years later.[3]

The majority of Soviet dissidents, including Lyubarsky himself, were sentenced under Article 70 of the Soviet Penal Code. That article prohibited anti-Soviet agitation and propaganda whose effect was to undermine or weaken Soviet power, along with the propagation of slanderous fabrications targeting the Soviet political and social system, and the production, dissemination, and storage of anti-Soviet literature. The Kremlin exploited such insult codes to muzzle human-rights activists. To my mind, legislation in Islamic countries and calls by Muslim groups elsewhere to ban speech critical of religion on the grounds of causing offense to Islam echo the Soviet Union's use of such laws to persecute free-thinkers. Indeed, there are many similarities between dissidents in communist and Islamic regimes.

Kronid Lyubarsky was an extraordinary individual. I got to know him after Mikhail Gorbachev came to power in 1985, though I had followed him for some years through my contacts in dissident circles in the West. For 10 years, I enjoyed the privilege of working with him. I contributed to his bulletin and carried messages back and forth between him and his contacts in Moscow. When he returned home in the wake of the Soviet collapse, I was a frequent guest at his office on Pushkin Square, where I related impressions from my travels around the great country, and he told me what was happening in the corridors of power. He was a fantastic conversationalist, never concerned with his own vanity or endeavors to display the depth and breadth of his knowledge, always focused on content and substance, effervescent with insatiable curiosity and dedication.

My 10 years of dialogue with Kronid came to an end when he drowned in May 1996 while on holiday. The news of his death was a shock; even today, some 15 years later, I still think of him. Our discussions shaped my understanding of the upheavals that took place in Russia in the late 1980s and early 1990s. His moral clarity gave me insight into the essence of totalitarianism and the significance of the dissident movement for Russia's development during those years. All of that information considerably informed my view of the Cartoon Crisis.

Two groups of events in particular proved significant for the Soviet human rights movement.[4] The first was the imprisonment in the autumn of 1965 of writers Andrei Sinyavsky and Yuli Daniel, both of whom had published satirical work in the West under pseudonyms. Stalin was dead; the reins of power appeared to be growing slack; but again, writers of fiction were imprisoned because of the content of their books. To the great surprise of the authorities, the charges brought against Sinyavsky and Daniel triggered a wave of protest that marked the birth of the Soviet human rights movement, including the first public demonstration since 1917 in support of human rights.

Then in August 1968, the Warsaw Pact invaded Czechoslovakia, crushing the dream of socialism with a human face. That prompted eight demonstrators to protest against the invasion in front of the Kremlin on Red Square. "Long live a free and independent Czechoslovakia!" proclaimed one of their banners in the Czech language. Others carried the words "Shame on the occupiers!" and "Hands off Czechoslovakia!" The eight were arrested after 20 minutes, several of them subsequently receiving prison sentences or being sent into exile.

Next came Andrei Sakharov's 1968 manifesto, "Reflections on Progress, Peaceful Coexistence, and Intellectual Freedom,"[5] the document that most clearly voiced the intellectual basis for the human rights movement in the Soviet Union. Some 18 million copies were published around the globe, unheard of for an essay on social issues and international politics. Sakharov highlighted the correlation between the way a state treats its own citizens and its ability to exist in peace with its surroundings, that is, the link between democracy and security. The world, Sakharov said, cannot be dependent on leaders who are not dependent on their own peoples. Any state that respects the rights of its citizens to free speech, free religious exercise, free assembly, and free movement will also likely respect the rights of citizens in other countries, including their right to decide for themselves the kind of society in which they want to live. In such a society, elected representatives of the people will have a stake in solving conflicts between government and society by peaceful means, whereas states that oppress their citizens will be more likely to solve conflicts with violence, be it at home or abroad.

The second significant milestone in the history of the Soviet human rights movement was the founding of the Moscow

Helsinki Group in 1976. Formed to monitor Soviet implementation of the Helsinki Accords of 1975, which called for the recognition of universal human rights, the Moscow Helsinki Group was a shining example of how a small group of people with no power or standing in society—among them Yuri Orlov, a 52-year-old physicist, and Lyudmila Alekseyeva, a 49-year-old historian—could, with acumen, courage, and good fortune, succeed in setting an international agenda by consistently defending the ideals of freedom.

Thanks largely to their monitoring of the groundbreaking 1975 Helsinki Accords between the Soviet Bloc and the West, Soviet violations of human rights increasingly became a focus in the Western media, and the Soviet image became ever more tarnished, not least in the eyes of leftist intellectuals.[6]

Although the KGB kept their group under constant surveillance, from time to time issuing warnings and harassing its members, no arrests were made until January 1977. In the meantime, they produced thousands of typewritten pages documenting evidence of everything from conditions endured by political prisoners to how the authorities were cutting off the private telephone connections of difficult citizens. They detailed the harsh sentence imposed on the leader of a movement for the right of Tatars to return to their Crimean homeland, from which they had been deported during World War II; they registered the unlawful exclusion of six Catholic boys from a school in Lithuania, violating the right of Christians to exercise their religion freely; and the authorities' refusal to allow Soviet Jews to emigrate to Israel. As word of the group's efforts spread, individuals, groups, and organizations all over the Soviet Union turned to Yuri Orlov seeking help in their struggle for rights: Catholics, Baptists, Seventh-Day Adventists, and followers of the Pentecostal movement; Jewish activists wishing to emigrate; Crimean Tatars; Russian nationalists, Lithuanians, Estonians, and Ukrainians, all striving for severance from the Soviet Union.

Helsinki watch groups were established in the same year in Ukraine and Lithuania; later, others were set up in Georgia and Armenia. The same thing was happening in Poland and in Czechoslovakia with its Charta 77. As 1976 progressed, reports of the Helsinki Group's work found their way increasingly onto the front pages of newspapers in the West. In 1978, the Helsinki Watch Committee was formed in New York following Orlov's example. Later, it evolved into Human Rights Watch, one of the largest human rights organizations in the world, with offices in cities throughout Europe, Asia, and North America. Inspired by Orlov's work, the International Helsinki Federation for Human Rights was established as an umbrella organization with locations in 41 countries, from the Netherlands to Uzbekistan. Following the Soviet collapse, the Helsinki Group established offices throughout Russia, manned by scores of full-time staff members and hundreds of volunteers.

The key to the group's success lay in its use of foreign media—not only those that broadcast to the West, but also Western radio stations broadcasting in Russian to the Soviet Union—to spread information about Soviet violations of human rights to millions of people all over the world, thereby exerting pressure on the Soviet government. The huge scope of media coverage turned the issue of human rights behind the Iron Curtain into a legitimate concern for politicians in the West. By focusing so clearly on an international agreement between East and West, and by his high-lighting of the ties between peace, security, and human rights, Orlov smoothed the way for Western politicians to understand and identify with the Helsinki Group and its efforts. Several of its members were accorded celebrity status in Western media.

Orlov and the Helsinki Group even gained rare success in the Soviet dissident community, which so often had difficulty collaborating because the aims, methods, and standpoints of the various groups and factions were so disparate, and internal suspicion and skepticism were widespread. Nevertheless, the Helsinki Group managed to unite dissidents across national, political, religious, and cultural boundaries. It was a first.

In early 1977, the leading figures in the group were arrested or forced into exile. Yuri Orlov was sentenced to 7 years in a labor camp, and Aleksandr Ginzburg was sentenced to 8, both on the grounds of anti-Soviet agitation and propaganda; whereas Natan Sharansky was found guilty of espionage and sentenced to 14 years' internment. Lyudmila Alekseyeva immigrated to the United States, returning to Russia following the Soviet collapse to resume her work in the human rights movement and stepping in as leader of the reestablished Helsinki Group after its previous leader, Kronid Lyubarsky, died in 1996. It was in Russia that I interviewed her in 2001 on the occasion of the group's 25th anniversary, celebrated with pomp and circumstance at the Hotel Kosmos, one of the hotels built for the Olympic Games in 1980 at a time when several of the group's members were incarcerated in the camps. Now, a weighty three-volume work had been published documenting the group's history and containing essays on its work.

Alekseyeva was by no means resting on her laurels, being heavily involved in the struggle to establish a true constitutional state in Russia. On New Year's Eve in 2009, dressed as Snow White, the 83-year-old Alekseyeva was detained by police in Moscow for taking part in an unlawful protest against the authorities' repeated violations of the right of free assembly, otherwise guaranteed by the Russian Constitution. Orlov, Ginzburg, and Sharansky all left the Soviet Union after having served their sentences. Orlov settled in the United States; Ginzburg became a journalist on the Russian emigrants' bulletin *Russkaya Mysl* in Paris; and Sharansky went to Israel.

While Sharansky awaited arrest in January 1977—everyone knew it was but a question of time—he confided in Alekseyeva.

"Do you know something?" he said. "The last eight months have been the happiest time of my life."

"Indeed," Alekseyeva replied. "I've been living that way for ten years. Allowing yourself to think freely and to live accordingly is wonderful. The only drawback is they put you in prison for it."[7]

Following imprisonment of the group's leading members in 1977, the KGB further tightened its grip on Soviet society, and in 1982, a decision was made to cease the group's activities when one of the three members yet to be imprisoned was detained for slander against socialism. The *Chronicle of Current Events*, published since 1968, also folded, since no one was available to continue the work. The human rights movement in the Soviet Union was largely wiped out. Its most prominent figure, Andrei Sakharov, had been deported to the closed city of Gorky, and most others were either interned in the labor camps or had been sent into exile in the West, from where, however, human rights monitoring continued. Kronid Lyubarsky devoted most of his time to it after emigrating.

The apparent stability and the absence of a visible opposition prompted American historian Arthur Schlesinger Jr. to speak optimistically of the perseverance of the Soviet regime following a visit to Moscow in 1982: "Those in the United States who think the Soviet Union is on the verge of economic and social collapse are wishful thinkers who are only kidding themselves." Yet although in 1982, it seemed like the human rights movement had lost its confrontation with the regime, it soon turned out that the processes that had been set in motion were unstoppable, regardless of the numbers imprisoned. The movement found resurgence with the rise to power of Mikhail Gorbachev. In 1990, when I asked an acquaintance belonging to the new generation of activists to sum up the history of the Soviet human rights movement, he said this: "If you think of the last 30 years of the Soviet Union as a struggle between dissidents and the Soviet authorities, you would have to say that the dissidents won in the sense that their ideas were absorbed by Gorbachev. They have become the common property of the society."

In the spring of 1988, the Louisiana Museum of Modern Art, located north of Copenhagen, was the scene of a historic event that demonstrated that the Soviet human rights movement, after decades in the cold, was on its way to being rehabilitated in Moscow. The occasion was a conference on literature and perestroika, in which Soviet intellectuals met with exiled Russians for the first time.[8] Soviet participation had been approved by the highest powers—according to one of those taking part by Communist Party second-in-command Yegor Ligachev. The Soviets were represented by leading figures of the liberal reform movement, while the emigrant Russians sent writers and intellectuals who acknowledged that change was under way in the Soviet Union. Among them were three former political prisoners: author Andrei Sinyavsky, who had emigrated to France after having served seven years' exile and imprisonment in the camps; Boris Weil, who, with the aid of Amnesty International, had been granted asylum in Denmark in 1977; and Kronid Lyubarsky, who had left the Soviet Union with Weil, but had settled in Munich, where he occupied the same tiny apartment during his 15 years in exile before returning to Russia and entering the struggle for an open and democratic society.

I was the go-between for Kronid and the organizers of the conference. As an active campaigner for human rights and political prisoners in the Soviet Union, he was its most controversial delegate. He was the driving force behind three publications that, in their own ways, influenced decisionmakers in the West and Russian opinion. One was a twice-monthly bulletin on Soviet violations of human rights, a source of information favored by the foreign ministries of governments in the West. The second was the yearbook *Political Prisoners in the Soviet Union*, published annually in Russian and English, and the third was the journal *My Country and the World*, which published essays on and analyses of developments in the Soviet Union, as well as translations of Western philosophers, authors, and historians, such as Isaiah

Berlin, Francis Fukuyama, Karl Popper, Arthur Koestler, and Richard Pipes.

My Country and the World also published an excerpt from the most controversial chapter of Salman Rushdie's novel *The Satanic Verses*, complete with an introduction penned by Kronid himself, in which he defended publishing material that allegedly was offensive to Muslims. "We do so not to provoke, but because we believe that no restrictions can be placed upon free speech other than the ban on incitement to violence," he wrote in his preface.[9]

Kronid's talk was the bombshell of the conference. As he spoke, those present followed intensely the reactions of the Soviet representatives. Would they walk out? What could be read into their body language, their facial expressions? Were they smiling? Were they incensed? Were they talking among themselves, discussing how they should react? What were they thinking? How far could free speech be taken under Gorbachev?

Only two years before, Gorbachev had claimed that there were no political prisoners in the Soviet Union and had rejected the charge that Soviet courts were sending people to labor camps because of their convictions.

That emotional spring day in Denmark, Kronid touched an issue that despite glasnost and perestroika remained a taboo in the official Soviet press. He spoke of the role of the human rights movement in the reform process. He spoke of the individuals who 20 and 25 years before had pointed to the very same weaknesses that the Kremlin, Soviet economists, and social scientists were now acknowledging, but who then in the 1960s, 1970s, and even the 1980s had paid for their critical analyses with internment in the camps, exile, and destroyed livelihoods.

In Kronid's view, it was the dissident community that had opened Gorbachev's eyes, whether the Soviet leader realized it or not. He had taken their insights and their slogans as his own, and the very problems the dissidents had illuminated in their work were now firmly setting the agenda. Calls for glasnost had come from the dissident community, just as demands for transparency in relevant matters of society had been central to dissident thought and action. Nonetheless, in the spring of 1988, many of them were still behind barbed wire in Soviet prison camps.

Kronid's talk made an indelible impression on those present. In 2000, Kronid was one of 50 journalists and editors who, on the 50th anniversary of the International Press Institute, were named World Press Freedom Heroes for their efforts to ensure press freedom in the face of particularly adverse conditions. Although the West allowed itself to be carried away by Gorbachev's fluffy talk of a common European house in which the Soviet Union was a part, Kronid continued to keep a watchful and objective eye on his homeland.

A year and a half later, Kronid moved back to Moscow, becoming the editor of the liberal weekly *Novoye Vremya* (*New Times*) for whom he penned a flow of dazzlingly insightful articles on such varied topics as the transition of a totalitarian regime into democracy, the adoption of constitutions in Germany and Italy following World War II, Portugal and Spain in the 1970s, President Boris Yeltsin's dissolution of the Supreme Soviet and the deployment of troops to Moscow in October 1993, ballot rigging, and the unconstitutional decision to wage war on Chechnya in December 1994. He was involved in wording new legislation restoring citizenship to all exiled Russians. It was typical of him. He would never be satisfied with a decree that encompassed only a few select groups; he called for legislation institutionalizing changes to benefit all citizens. He took part in hammering out the constitution that was adopted in December 1993, and he stood for parliament and lost.

Kronid resumed his work for human rights in Russia that had occupied him so fully during his exile. In 1989, he was among those who initiated a revival of the Helsinki Group, whose chairman he was from 1994 until his death.

When I began studying Russian at the University of Copenhagen, my life changed. I was drawn, for some reason, to the language and culture of Russia; somehow, I sensed that immersing myself in this strange and distant world would help me gain an understanding of myself and of the deeper layers of existence. I was so eager to learn that in my first year of study, I went all out, reading day and night so as not to fall behind. It was as though a whole new world was opening up: a republic of scholarship. Almost from one day to the next, I gave up soccer. Most of my time was spent immersed in Russian grammar and phonetics, painstakingly spelling my way through incomprehensible rows of words aided by dictionaries as heavy as bricks. Occasionally, I would have time to read a proper book. Two in particular made an impression on me, though their influence at first was rather modest. Yet they were to become important sources for my understanding of Soviet society.

The first of those books was Nadezhda Mandelstam's *Hope against Hope*,[10] a memoir of her 19 years with the poet Osip Mandelstam, from the first years following the 1917 Russian Revolution until he perished in a transit camp near Vladivostok in late 1938. Mandelstam was briefly imprisoned in 1934 after having written a poem critical of Joseph Stalin, but he escaped lightly at first, being sentenced to three years of exile in the Russian provinces. Her memoir was written in the certain belief that no one elsewhere had the slightest idea of what was actually occurring under Stalin, that sheer barbarity had caused a silence to descend on the great country, allowing only lies and propaganda to slip out. Besides her wish to secure her late husband's work for posterity, she saw her book as a message to future generations, the endeavor of a single voice to penetrate the lies and the repression. As she so graphically described it, on each day that passed, it became more and more difficult to speak with a tongue torn from the mouth.

What struck me in reading Nadezhda Mandelstam's memoirs was the significance attached to literature in the Soviet Union. Osip Mandelstam, presumably not without irony, even considered the regime's persecution of dissidents, himself among them, to be a kind of homage. To think, he said to his wife, in our country people get killed on account of a poem. That's how we honor and respect literature. We are afraid of literature because it is power.

The second book to make an impression on me was *The Oak and the Calf*,[11] Aleksandr Solzhenitsyn's memoir of the period extending from his sensational 1962 debut *One Day in the Life of Ivan Denisovich* to his enforced exile 12 years later following publication in the West of *The Gulag Archipelago*. Solzhenitsyn was the calf, the regime the oak, but now and then the reader found himself believing it was the other way round. David inflicted on Goliath a succession of calculated, painful blows, and deportation of Solzhenitsyn to the West was in reality the Kremlin's capitulation to a writer whose words were feared more than the long-range missiles of the North Atlantic Treaty Organization.

Once again, I was amazed by how seriously the Soviet government and its people took literature and the written word. That was brought home to me by Solzhenitsyn's harrowing depiction of the publication of *One Day in the Life of Ivan Denisovich* in the journal *Novy Mir*, which broke open one of the greatest of all Soviet taboos: discussion of the labor camps. Every word in it was weighed. Party leader Nikita Khrushchev had an adviser read the manuscript aloud to him while vacationing on the Black Sea coast before approving it personally. Subsequently, the novella was discussed in detail at a plenary meeting of the Central Committee.

Solzhenitsyn's life as a writer—first in a labor camp after the war, then in exile in central Asia, and eventually as a teacher in the Russian province in the latter part of the 1950s—revealed an astonishing confidence in the power and capability of the written word to survive and exert influence through centuries. He viewed the word in an eternal perspective, convinced he would never have so much as a single line of prose published as long as he lived. He was writing for future generations.

Like Nadezhda Mandelstam, Solzhenitsyn learned lengthy stretches of prose and thousands of lines of poetry by heart, but he found himself spending an increasing amount of time remembering what he had written. Whenever he completed a new version of a work or edited it, he would burn the draft. It was a practice he was forced to give up in 1953 when he was struck by what was deemed to be an incurable cancer. He found himself in a dilemma: how was he to ensure that his work survived if it was to vanish along with his memory? He set about writing everything down in the evenings and at night, hiding it in small tubes pushed into champagne bottles and buried in the garden, before leaving for Tashkent, certain that he now was to spend his final days in a hospital.

But he survived. Not only that, he shook the world when in 1973, his Russian-language publishers in Paris released *The Gulag Archipelago*, a harrowing depiction of the development of the Soviet Union from Lenin's decree to establish labor camps, shortly after the revolution, to Khrushchev's so-called Secret Speech in 1956 denouncing Stalin's purges.[12] To Solzhenitsyn, Stalin's regime was a logical progression of the political project Lenin had initiated; labor camps and an economy based on slavery were integral to the Soviet project. His account detailed massacres and riots in the camps, and waves of purges. That lent a documentary style to the narrative and shocked the West profoundly.

The Soviet authorities considered *The Gulag Archipelago* to be a ticking bomb. Simply possessing a copy of it could cost you seven years in the camps. It would not be published in Solzhenitsyn's homeland until 1989. Six months before, Gorbachev's chief ideologist, Vadim Medvedev, had declared that the work would never be published in the Soviet Union. But at that time, things were moving so quickly that the Kremlin was far from fully aware of what was actually going on and how close the people were to regaining control of the printed word.[13]

Solzhenitsyn had originally wanted his compatriots to be able to read *The Gulag Archipelago* before it became available elsewhere. However, when the KGB got hold of a copy in the summer of 1973, he realized that he would be unable to hold off any longer on publishing. His loyal aid, Elizaveta Voronyanskaya, had been coerced by the KGB into revealing the whereabouts of one of just three complete copies. Following her detainment and interrogation, Voronyanskaya was released and committed suicide.

As the drama of *The Gulag Archipelago* was played out, Solzhenitsyn had installed himself in a rented house northwest of Moscow where he completed an appeal to the Russian people, an essay titled "Live Not by Lies."[14] That essay was a call to challenge fear, to no longer take part in the official lie that served as the basis of the regime, a lie that concealed violence, intimidation, and coercion. It read: "The simplest and most accessible key to our self-neglected liberation lies right here: Personal non-participation in lies. Though lies conceal everything, though lies embrace everything, but not with any help from me."

Andrei Amalrik, author of the prophetic essay "Will the Soviet Union Survive Until 1984?" would later word his view on self-censorship as follows:

> I prefer the police to silence me rather than to do so myself. The need to change the outside world through one's own creativity is greater than the need to adapt to it. If a person refuses the opportunity to judge the world around him and to express that judgment, he begins to destroy himself before the police can destroy him.[15]

One insight came in 1994 in Moscow, when classified documents were made public containing minutes of Politburo discussions on Solzhenitsyn in the period 1963 to 1979.[16] The arguments put forward by the communist high priests were riddled with religious metaphor, and rank-and-file communist fury at Solzhenitsyn's scorn, mockery, and ridicule of their faith was born along by a sense of grievance that brings to mind that of many Muslims during the Cartoon Crisis. In fact, I find it genuinely difficult to distinguish between causing affront to Muhammad, Moses, Vladimir

Lenin, Karl Marx, Adam Smith, Maharishi Mahesh Yogi, or any other prophet we may care to mention, or indeed their ideas, whether they be inscribed in the Koran, the Bible, *The Communist Manifesto*, or a treatise hailing the blessings of the free market.

For the Politburo, Solzhenitsyn's *The Gulag Archipelago* had the same effect as a satirical cartoon depicting Lenin with a bomb in his turban and excerpts from *The Communist Manifesto* printed on his headband, the only difference being that Solzhenitsyn did not stop at pointing to Stalin's or other communists' abuse of a fundamentally beautiful idea aiming to eradicate social injustice. Solzhenitsyn was boiling with rage, his gall dripping from the pages: the Marxist-Leninist ideology was the very embodiment of evil and the root of all misfortune that had befallen 20th-century Russia and those countries that had fallen under the communist yoke.

The documents that were published made it clear that even people who had spent 10 or 15 years in the Soviet camps for anti-Soviet activity fiercely defended Lenin and the regime against Solzhenitsyn's criticism. One factory worker in Moscow wrote as follows to a Soviet newspaper in late 1973 when news of *The Gulag Archipelago* first emerged: "Solzhenitsyn smears our socialist system and its advances. All we have achieved thanks to the work of the Soviet people, all that is sacred and dear to each and every Soviet citizen, is rejected by this apostate."[17]

Solzhenitsyn had violated what was held to be "sacred" and was therefore branded an apostate. In the view of the Politburo, Solzhenitsyn had to be punished: he had committed sacrilege and had defamed what was held to be sacred. He had, as the Politburo put it, "slandered the Soviet system, the Soviet Union, the Communist Party and their domestic and foreign policies, and smeared the memory of V. I. Lenin and other prominent persons of the Communist Party and the Soviet state, victims of the Great Patriotic War and the Fascist-German occupation."[18]

At a meeting of the Politburo in January 1974, at which the guardian council in the Kremlin discussed whether the heretic

Solzhenitsyn should be sent into exile or incarcerated, Party Leader Leonid Brezhnev resorted to religious imagery in arguing the need for firm action: "We have every reason to imprison Solzhenitsyn, for he has attacked the most sacred of all—Lenin, our Soviet system, the Soviet power, and everything we hold dear."[19]

If you believe in maintaining—or even, as in a number of European countries, extending—present laws that criminalize verbal offense, and if you believe that insulting people by words or images is to be consistently avoided at all costs, then no fundamental distinction exists between offending the feelings of communists or Muslims, whether it be in Denmark (where both groups are minorities); or in Islamic countries, such as Iran and Saudi Arabia (where Muslims make up the majority and religious and political minorities are persecuted); or in communist countries, such as Cuba and North Korea. Of course, there may be slight differences here and there, but none are substantial, unless you believe that some feelings deserve to be protected more than others.

Would the world have been a better, more peaceful place if Soviet dissidents had followed the examples of West European museums and galleries, newspapers, visual artists, and filmmakers—if they had submitted themselves to self-censorship rather than offend communist sentiments? Would radical leftists and terrorists in Western Europe, from communist parties to the Red Army Faction and the Red Brigades, have moderated themselves if criticism of their methods and ideology had been withheld?

The answer, of course, is no. But that is precisely the kind of warped logic that gave rise to double standards in the debate on freedom of speech in the new millennium. There was a strong desire to protect groups that the political left saw as being particularly vulnerable, while groups and sentiments that did not enjoy the same kind of attention, or whose opinions one disagreed with, were not protected in the same way.

One baking hot day in the summer of 2007, many years after Solzhenitsyn had penned his poignant appeal not to go on living with lies, I found myself seated in Natan Sharansky's tiny office on a quiet residential street in Jerusalem. It was the third time I had met him. The second had been during his term as Israel's interior minister, when he had been leader of the Russian Jewish party Yisrael Beiteinu (Israel Our Home). The first time, he had greeted me on a breezy terrace in Jerusalem wearing shorts, flip-flops, and his characteristic cap. At the time, he was leader of the Zionist Forum, a forerunner of the parliamentary party that looked after the interests of a million immigrant Jews from the former Soviet Union. Sharansky, who spoke quickly, often snapping off words and half sentences in midspeech, grinned as he divulged his recipe for making a career in politics:

"I got here first, then a million voters followed me."[20]

More than 21 years had passed since Sharansky was released from Perm-35 in the northern Urals, where he had been imprisoned for 9 years, falsely convicted on trumped-up charges of high treason and spying for the United States. Exchanged for a Soviet spy, he was immediately flown to Israel.

"I involved myself in two movements at once," Sharansky recalled. "I got into the movement for the rights of Jews to emigrate and the human rights movement that was informally led by Andrei Sakharov. For me, the two movements were a natural extension of each other," he explained. "On the one hand, I'd been deprived of my right to go back to my Jewish roots, to find my place in history, and on the other, they'd taken away my freedom and rights as a citizen of the Soviet Union."

Solzhenitsyn's call to stop living with lies was still clearly of key significance as Sharansky endeavored to put into words what in particular had marked the dissident movement:

> The notion of no longer upholding the lie, of no longer pretending, playing the game of the regime, submitting to its intimidation—that had the most tremendous liberating effect on us. As dissidents, we found it gave us enormous

strength to free ourselves from the second-guessing that so permeated Soviet society. The regime understood that perfectly, so it spent considerable amounts of energy trying to shut dissidents up, even though at first sight we were a small and insignificant group. But in the end, the Soviet Union did collapse. And what made the difference was the desire not to go on living a life of lies.

In Sharansky's view, the dissident community made doing business very uncomfortable for Western politicians such as Henry Kissinger, who emphasized a "realistic," pragmatic approach to the Soviet Union. And here he saw parallels with the West's relationship with oil-producing dictatorships in the Middle East today:

> The West's fear of the Soviet Union and its policies of appeasement is something I still see now. Supporting dissidents and listening to their insights were embarrassing and awkward because it involved confrontation with the regime. So what happened was they tried to reduce it down to a minor humanitarian problem of no real importance for what was happening elsewhere in the Soviet Union or for its relationship to the outside world. Kissinger and those who were in agreement with him said they wanted to help Sakharov, but that the Soviet Union was a dictatorship that was going to be around for a very long time, and for that reason it was essential to remain on good terms with Moscow, and in so doing, they would in Kissinger's view be able to do more for Sakharov and other dissidents. Sakharov tried to explain to them that it wasn't about helping dissidents, but about how the West could help itself, defend the free world, and not become a victim of its own illusions.

The world can be divided into two kinds of society, Sharansky suggested: free societies and fear societies.[21] In free societies, conflicting opinions coexist, even ones that are opposed by the majority in power. In a fear society, that is prohibited. Societies that do not allow divergence of opinion and disagreement will inevitably be founded on fear and will never protect the rights of their citizens. Importantly, in the struggle for a free society, the existence of diversity of opinion is more significant than the specific nature of individual opinions:

> Although an enormous diversity of opinion was behind bars in the Gulag, dissidents shared one belief in common: we all wanted to live in a free society. And despite our sometimes contradictory visions of the future, the dissident experience enabled all of us to agree on what freedom meant. A society is free if people have a right to express their views without fear of arrest, imprisonment, or physical harm.[22]

Sharansky, a founding member of the Helsinki Group, one of history's most successful human rights groups, a man who had endured nine years in a labor camp for his part in it, believed that the struggle for human rights had since been discredited. In his view, it had become removed from the vision of a free society. Now, the most brutal regimes spout about human rights even as they murder their own people or violate their rights across the board. As such, Sharansky wrote in his book, the link between democracy and liberty on the one hand, and peace and security on the other, had been undermined.

The idea of human rights today has become synonymous with showing sympathy for the poor, the weak, and the infirm. The fundamental distinction between a free society and a fear society is thereby being dissolved. Sharansky perceived this in the United Nations Commission on Human Rights, which regards Israel as the world's primary violator of human rights, although it is a free and democratic society surrounded by vicious dictatorships. The same pattern, Sharansky suggested, can be found in the annual reports of Amnesty International and other human rights organizations, all of which devote more space to violations of human rights in Israel than they do to the entire Islamic world. The reason for that is that Israel is an open society in which information is freely available, whereas gathering exact and reliable information about what is happening in Saudi Arabia and Iran is impossible.

Sharansky approached Amnesty International and suggested that it operate with categories of totalitarian, authoritarian, and democratic societies in the manner employed by Freedom House in its reports. Doing so would, in his view, allow information to be read within a context; it would allow the public to distinguish between countries in which human rights were violated daily by the very nature of the regime and countries in which violations occurred occasionally because of error and abuse of power. His suggestion, however, was declined on the grounds that the organization wished to remain nonpolitical, registering violations of human rights rather than focusing on the political systems of individual countries.

The same logic—the wish to distinguish between the struggle for freedom and democracy and the struggle for human rights—is also the reason why Denmark, in the view of the International Convention on the Elimination of all Forms of Racial Discrimination, figures as one of the most racist countries in the world, Danish nongovernmental organizations having filed more complaints with the convention than any other country. In 2010, the figure was 20 out of a total of 45 cases.[23] Yet Denmark consistently occupies a top-10 position in global surveys of freedom, tolerance, and equality.

Sharansky suggests that in fear societies, that is, those prohibiting dissent, three categories of citizens emerge. One group comprises those loyal to the existing order insofar as their support is heartfelt. These are the true believers, a relatively small group growing smaller as citizens increasingly reject living in a society founded on fear and because freedom takes on universal appeal. Lack of freedom will moreover significantly weaken the competitive position of any society and in time will cause its decay and decline. An even smaller group of citizens comprises those who are prepared to confront the existing order, who refuse to live the lie regardless of the punishment they may endure. Those people are dissidents, freethinkers. They are a virus lethal to the fear society, a foreign body to be eradicated. Between those two minorities lies society's largest category. Its members are not undyingly loyal, but they are prepared to live the lie. They are afraid to voice their opinion. Sharansky calls them double-thinkers. They live in a state of permanent tension between thought and action, between what they think for themselves and voice in close company and what they say at work and in public. Double-thinkers continually submit themselves to self-censorship. They are driven by the fear of what will happen if they speak freely.

Sharansky explained:

> Even if you think freedom is for everyone, including those in the Islamic world, it doesn't automatically imply that they prefer a Western model of democracy. But it does mean they want to live in a world without fear. When a person is forced to lie and to say something other than what he thinks and feels because he's afraid of what's going to happen if he tells the truth, his fear is controlling him. That's not going to make anyone a loyal citizen. On the contrary, they're going to become less and less loyal as time goes on. This is true of all dictatorships—the Soviet Union, Iran, Saudi Arabia, whatever. Just as the free world tried to keep on lying to itself about the Soviet Union, the West is lying to itself about the dictatorships in the Middle East. It's convenient for them: confrontation is avoided, and no responsibility is assumed.

I asked him if he thought the experiences of Soviet dissidents could be relevant to the Islamic world today.

He replied:

> Indeed, and not only for the Islamic world. In my opinion, the lessons we learned then are of crucial importance for the whole world. Sadly, though, the free world doesn't seem to want to know and learn from what we went through. When I met with the Egyptian dissident Saad Eddin Ibrahim, he criticized the United States for supporting Mubarak on the grounds that the Muslim Brotherhood is worse. Even though we're politically opposed on many issues, his defense of human rights and freedom as a way of challenging the dictatorship reminds me of my own experience. We understand each other; I can acknowledge what he's going through, his understanding of the strength and appeal of liberty. Unfortunately, though, his situation is a lot more difficult than ours, because we at least were in the public eye of the world whenever we were arrested. In the Islamic world, that's not the way it is.

Can dissidents of the Islamic world gain the same kind of significance as those in the Soviet Union, I asked, if they receive the support of the West?

> To begin with, the West could at least stop supporting dictatorships so openly. As soon as President George W. Bush put pressure on Mubarak in the wake of 9/11, civil society suddenly woke up. Suddenly, there were protests going on in the streets in Egypt, but as soon as the United States stopped being critical again, the regime threw Saad Eddin Ibrahim in jail and silenced a lot of other voices. It's a difficult task, but to say beforehand that the Arab world can never become democratic is immoral and wrong. Nobody has done as much as the West to

ensure that democracy enjoys such miserable conditions in the Arab world. After World War I, when nation-states were established in the region, the West went all out to support local dictators. They'd find a family in one country, another in a second, and then hand them the power. That's how Jordan, Iraq, and Saudi Arabia came into being. So when the West says, "What are we to do? That's just the way they are," my answer is: give them a chance at least, starting, for example, by cutting off support to the dictators. Or at least make demands, ask for something in return. Instead, they reduce the whole issue to a choice between religious fanatics and secular dictators.

When I wrote the brief introduction that accompanied *Jyllands-Posten*'s publication of the Muhammad cartoons, explaining our desire to use that project to investigate self- censorship, my point of departure was my encounter with the fear society that was the Soviet Union.[24] Of course, as my piece suggested, I would never claim that free societies in the West were seriously threatened by the specter of Soviet-style fear. But the examples of recent self-censorship about Islam among museums and galleries, transla-tors, artists, theaters, television stations, and comedians made me think of the kind of fear society Sharansky so precisely had described.

In the Soviet Union, I had seen how, as those mechanisms spread through society, they eat away the soul and cause people to lose dignity and self-respect. Censorship, intimidation, and threats led to almost total self-censorship in the Soviet Union, so the authorities rarely needed to step in. People toed the line, adapting themselves and their behavior to the boundaries set for them by the regime. As Solzhenitsyn and others pointed out in their calls to challenge self-censorship and refuse to live the lie, the citizen was eventually held down, not only by the regime but also by himself.

That is what I had in mind when I wrote the short article that accompanied the Muhammad cartoons, "It is no coincidence that people living in totalitarian societies often end up in jail for telling jokes. . . . It has not come to that here in Denmark, but we are on a slippery slope where no one can predict where self-censorship will end."[25]

9. Questioning the Harassers

When the Cartoon Crisis was at its peak in January and February 2006, I recognized among critical Muslims and ex-Muslims in the West a pattern similar to the one I had seen among Soviet dissidents. I found it striking that so many Muslim dissidents, regardless of where they positioned themselves in the political spectrum, supported the cartoons' publication. They viewed the drawings as input to the struggle for free speech and free religious exercise against totalitarian regimes and movements. Like the Soviet dissidents, they were speaking out against the fear society and warning of the consequences of bowing down to intimidation.

That view was evident in a manifesto published in several European newspapers (including *Jyllands-Posten*) in February 2006, titled "Together Facing the New Totalitarianism."[1] That manifesto was a reaction against the violence and threats that had issued from publication of the cartoons. It was signed by prominent former Muslims and secular Muslims, all of whom had grown up in Muslim societies and were now critical of Islam as a political instrument of persecution wielded against freethinkers. All had personally received threats because of their opinions, though they assumed widely different political standpoints—from Iranian-born communist Maryam Namazie and left-wing activist Chahla Chafiq to the liberal Ayaan Hirsi Ali from Somalia; from practicing Muslim Irshad Manji to atheists Ibn Warraq and Salman Rushdie; from professors Antoine Sfeir and Mehdi Mozaffari to author Taslima Nasreen. In addition, the statement was signed by three French intellectuals: Bernard-Henri Lévy,

Caroline Fourest, and Philippe Val. The latter two were from the satirical publication *Charlie Hebdo*, a magazine that was sued in 2007 for reprinting the cartoons, only to be acquitted.

The statement read:

> After having overcome fascism, Nazism, and Stalinism, the world now faces a new global totalitarian threat: Islamism. We writers, journalists, intellectuals, call for resistance to religious totalitarianism and for the promotion of freedom, equal opportunity and secular values for all. Recent events, prompted by the publication of drawings of Muhammad in European newspapers, have revealed the necessity of the struggle for these universal values. This struggle will not be won by arms, but in the ideological field.
>
> Islamism is a reactionary ideology that kills equality, freedom, and secularism wherever it is present. Its victory can only lead to a world of injustice and domination: men over women, fundamentalists over others. On the contrary, we must ensure access to universal rights for the oppressed or those discriminated against.

The statement concluded:

> We refuse to renounce our critical spirit out of fear of being accused of "Islamophobia," a wretched concept that confuses criticism of Islam as a religion and stigmatization of those who believe in it. We defend the universality of the freedom of expression, so that a critical spirit can exist in every continent, towards each and every maltreatment and dogma. We appeal to democrats and free spirits in every country that our century may be one of light and not dark.

As a reaction to the debate on the Muhammad cartoons, so-called Councils of Ex-Muslims were established in a number of European countries under the unifying banner "We have renounced religion!" The significance of this movement for people of Muslim background and their rights as individuals to convert, give up, or practice their religion can hardly be exaggerated, but it was also of considerable importance for Europe as a community upholding the freedom and rights of the individual. The Councils of Ex-Muslims began speaking out against the culture of fear in Muslim societies, challenging intimidation of the individual by Islamic movements and governments. Rejecting fear, they openly stepped forward and appeared, with their photographs, on websites and brochures for branches set up in Belgium, Denmark, Germany, Great Britain, Sweden, Switzerland, and other countries. It was a direct challenge to the totalitarian society, which can only exist as long as its people submit to the intimidation that forms the basis of social control.[2]

It reminded me of Charta 77, the Helsinki Groups, and other Eastern European human rights movements in the days when East and West subscribed to vastly differing views of the rights of the individual. In the capitalist West, importance was attached to civic rights, the right to free speech and free religious exercise, freedom of assembly, freedom of movement and economic freedom; the socialist countries highlighted social and economic rights, the right to work, the right to housing and to education. As such, two standards of human rights emerged, and in the clash between East and West many insisted on a balance between them. West attached importance to freedom, East insisted on equality, so the ideal was probably somewhere in between.

It was a view rejected by the human rights movement behind the Iron Curtain. It did not accept differing conceptions of human rights, one socialist, one capitalist, another Asian, another Islamic. It held that only one set of human rights existed, that they issued from civic rights, and that as such they were natural. As citizens of socialist countries, members of the Helsinki Groups and of Charta 77 were claiming exactly the same rights as enjoyed by those in the West. This is what ex-Muslims are doing today when they step forward publicly to insist on their right to renounce their religion. They reject the notion of specifically Islamic human rights, as well as the idea that universal rights are a Western invention with no bearing on and without validity in other cultures.

A number of Islamic countries punish apostates by death or imprisonment. Even in the West, where legislation is secular and Islamic law has no validity, many former Muslims, or Muslims whose opinions are taken to be deviant, feel intimidated and afraid to speak their minds. That fear was the reason Ibn Warraq in 1995 published his bestseller *Why I Am Not a Muslim* under a pseudonym. Politicians, activists, writers, scholars, and artists of Muslim background have all received death threats for publicly criticizing their religion, for leaving it, or for practicing it idiosyncratically. Women especially are subjugated.[3]

Subjugation of women was exactly what the short film *Submission*, by Dutch filmmaker Theo van Gogh and feminist former Muslim Ayaan Hirsi Ali, was about.[4] It contains monologues of Muslim women addressing Allah on the subject of abuse and oppression. The characters say that if religious submission causes them such pain and suffering without intervention from Allah, then they may decide to submit themselves no longer. One is lashed for fornicating, a second is married off to a man she despises, a third is beaten by her husband, and a fourth is cast out by her father when he discovers that she has been raped by her brother. The perpetrators of that violence justify their misdeeds by referencing verses of the Koran painted on the women's bodies.

The film cost van Gogh his life, when he was murdered by a Muslim who believed the film had insulted Islam. His assassin declared in a letter addressed to Hirsi Ali and left at the scene that she would be next. She did not, however, submit. She published a number of books about her own story and her experiences in Muslim societies, and described how, following 9/11, she experienced a personal crisis when she realized that the terrorists had been driven by their faith in Islam and the Prophet Muhammad—a faith she, at least nominally, shared. She pored through the Koran and found that a number of passages could clearly be used to justify the attack. She then broke with Islam, a decision that involved a painful conflict with her parents and close family. Reading a book while on holiday in Greece, she understood that she no longer needed to believe in any God.

"One night in that Greek hotel I looked in the mirror and said out loud, 'I don't believe in God.' I said it slowly, enunciating it carefully, in Somali. And I felt relief." she wrote.[5]

Her books became international bestsellers. *Infidel*, published in English in 2007, and *Nomad: from Islam to America*, in 2010, made Ayaan Hirsi Ali an influential voice, perhaps the world's most prominent ex-Muslim.

In November 2007, I interviewed Ayaan Hirsi Ali, about her views on the Muhammad cartoons. I was in New York to discuss my own book project with a number of American publishers. I found a great deal of reluctance; I kept hoping that was not a fear of stirring up trouble with Islam. But the thought gained strength a few months later, when Random House canceled its planned publication of a historical novel about the Prophet Muhammad's child bride, Aisha, though it had already paid a $100,000 advance to the author, Sherry Jones. Then, in 2009, Yale University Press, which was publishing Professor Jytte Klausen's book *The Cartoons That Shook the World*, decided to remove from the book all images of the Prophet—including the original page of cartoons in *Jyllands-Posten* and historical images from Muslim and non-Muslim sources.

To return to my encounter with Hirsi Ali: she had to cancel our first meeting, being heavily involved in negotiations about setting up a fund to finance her security in the United States. She was being driven around in bulletproof vehicles and was shadowed by bodyguards wherever she went. The next day, though, we met over tea and biscuits in the bar of one of Manhattan's most fashionable hotels. She was in good spirits, bubbling with self-deprecating humor. Every so often, despite the bodyguards, she cast a swift eye around the room to see who was coming and going.

Hirsi Ali told me that the cartoons, and the first reactions to them in autumn 2005, had reminded her of something that happened in the Netherlands in 2003. In an interview in the Amsterdam daily *Trouw*, she had made some critical comments about Muhammad. By modern, Western standards, she said, Muhammad was a pervert: he had married a very young child and had sex with her. He was also a tyrant who oppressed freethinkers and ruled by fiat. He was therefore an inappropriate role model for Muslims in a secular democracy.

Her comments prompted a Dutch Muslim group to file a complaint with the police on the grounds of discrimination. The public prosecutor, however, dismissed the case, stating that Hirsi Ali's comments had not exposed the Muslim community to scorn.

"I said that people like bin Laden, Khomeini, and Saddam Hussein saw him as an idol," she told me. "And that kicked off a crisis in the Netherlands. Four Muslim ambassadors approached my party leader, urging him to punish me and throw me out of parliament, demanding an apology. When I saw the cartoons, I showed them to him and said, 'Take a look at what's going in Denmark.'"

In Hirsi Ali's view, we needed more depictions of Muhammad, not fewer. She said she longed for an Islamic version of Monty Python's Jesus comedy, *The Life of Brian*. She wanted stories, comedies, illustrations, historical research, and philosophy to delve into the teachings of Muhammad, employing popular as well as more serious genres:

> One and a half billion Muslims see Muhammad as a role
> model. If you call yourself a Muslim, you have to follow

his example, not just praying five times a day but living according to his moral values. So it's hugely important to investigate the more exact nature of those values, in order to liberate oneself from the chains of ignorance, as Kant said. It's crucial, not just for Muslims, but for all who value freedom.

Hirsi Ali compared the teachings of Muhammad with those of Karl Marx. The more people who understood why and where Marx was wrong, the greater the chances that society would be able to avoid the pitfalls of Marxism:

> Marx took up important issues, the divide between rich and poor, but every time it was tried out in practice the recipe he suggested for solving the problems of poverty led only to bloodshed, prisons, need, and more poverty. In practice, it all turned out so different from the ideal he envisaged in his books and articles. The same is true of Muhammad.

Hirsi Ali felt the cartoons had a beneficial effect on opinion in the West, particularly on leftist social democrats. It sparked a debate that Europe badly needed:

> The cartoons raised a series of issues. Can Western Europe keep pretending to live on a desert island far from the true tragedies of the world? Can Europe open its borders to millions of people from parts of the world that do not enjoy the freedoms of the West—people from countries ruled by authoritarian regimes, ravaged by civil war and anarchy—and pretend it doesn't bother us? Those images of angry crowds in the Middle East attacking embassies, boycotting Danish goods, and protesting were a vivid picture of how small the world has become, how much the free world is in the minority and can be swept aside, and how much we need to safeguard and look after it.

That was one important debate kicked off by the cartoons. Another was about freedom of speech and Islam:

> All of a sudden the issue was no longer about how the political right and left considered free speech and its boundaries in the West. Now, the very institution that allows us in the first place to debate each other without violence was under attack. Some wanted Islamic moral values and rejected free speech. They believed only Allah and his Prophet could decide what could be said. Everything else was taboo, and they were willing to force their view of the world and their norms upon others. Many thought they had seen the back of that kind of thing once and for all in Europe with the collapse of totalitarian ideologies like Nazism and communism, that it had all come to an end in 1989. But the Cartoon Crisis brought home a new reality and made Europeans realize that major parts of the world think in a different way altogether.

Hirsi Ali believed the cartoons demonstrated the extent to which the people of Europe had taken freedom of speech for granted, and the Crisis revealed that many intellectuals were not prepared to analyze and confront a new totalitarian movement based on Islam:

> The cartoons made that clear. Therefore, it was only natural that so many intellectuals didn't care for them. The whole thing showed how a small group of intolerant people could force a large group into silence when that group lacked the will to confront tyranny even when it gets up and punches you in the face.

The Islamist threats reminded Hirsi Ali of her years as a student in Leiden in the Netherlands, where she was confronted with historical accounts of World War II. There was the political history of the war, and the history of the major powers, but there were also attempts to unravel how anti-Semitism could ever have progressed as far as it did:

> They looked on as their neighbors were branded and driven from their homes. All these people just standing by and watching and doing nothing. I studied with young people of the second and third generations after the war. For them it was history, but I remember in class—whether it was the lecturers or the students—there was always this common assumption that if they had been alive in the 1920s and 1930s, they would have protested; they would have been on the side of good. The Muhammad cartoons revealed another, more prosaic reality. It transpired that the number of people willing to challenge tyranny is actually quite small, and that many were driven by the same motives as in the 1920s and 1930s in Europe and other places where atrocities take place. People want to keep their jobs, and they want their children to stay at the same schools and kindergartens. They want to keep in the same social circles, go to the same parties, and have what they write published in the same newspapers. How could they go on doing all that if they put themselves at risk of threat, if their surroundings were made unsafe, and neighbors turned on them for being a danger to their children? So the Cartoon Crisis showed there was a great gap between talking about the importance of not submitting to tyranny and actually doing something about it when the situation arises.

I said to Hirsi Ali that some people felt, in connection with the Cartoon Crisis, that freedom of speech was not an imperative to speak out, but that it also entailed the right to remain silent, and that the whole thing was not actually about freedom of speech at all. "I don't agree with that," she replied.

> I think they confuse social etiquette and good manners with freedom of speech as a civic right. Imagine we were

sitting in a restaurant. Think of how we're seated, how we behave, how we eat, all of it social etiquette. We are aware that we have the freedom not to adhere to it, but we do so anyway. With freedom of speech it's different. Let's say I see children in school being segregated, boys and girls separated, the girls brought up to submit to men all their lives; a school in which children belonging to minorities learn to live apart from society, where they are taught to hate other children, taught to hate Jews and Christians and to consider themselves more worthy than others. If I hear that children are being made more vulnerable in that way, that people are making it more difficult for them to get an education and find work; if in that situation politeness and social etiquette and sensitivity cause us to say that freedom of speech is not an imperative but entails the right to remain silent, then I would say that we have become slow-witted, hard-hearted, and cruel, oblivious of what freedom of speech even is.

It's the same thing with the cartoons. We heard there was an author who couldn't find an illustrator for his book because people were afraid, and then we discovered that a lot of people were submitting to self-censorship for fear of how some Muslims would react. To keep silent about that would be morally wrong. What would a journalist do if it were rumored that the mafia in Denmark were controlling people and that you weren't allowed to write about them? Wouldn't it be your duty as a journalist to investigate that? Or if you found out that Danish politicians were receiving bribes, would you say then that freedom of speech is not an imperative? Should we show sensitivity, respect the families who risk being affected, and for that reason remain silent? Of course not—not even if you knew that innocent people were going to feel injured. If a journalist learns that people are declining to illustrate a book about Islam because they are afraid of what will happen to them, and in misguided deference, the journalist decides not to pursue the matter further, then he or she is not a worthy member of the profession.

But, I said, critics of the cartoons claimed that basically a large and influential newspaper used the drawings to bully and deride a weak minority; it was really about the right to mock a marginalized group of society.

"In my view," Hirsi Ali said, "the real bullying would be to let the minority steep in its own seclusion and fail to integrate its members into Danish society." She explained:

> If Muslims are to be a part of Danish society and find jobs as teachers, politicians, doctors, journalists, nurses, shop assistants, bus drivers, or whatever, then employers are going to have to start treating them on an equal footing with everyone else. That means that every time someone arrives in Denmark, the Netherlands, the U.K., or France and is given a residence permit, he or she also receives a parcel of rights. In return, the recipient society must make it clear that with rights come duties. That has nothing to do with discrimination. Among those duties is the duty not to demand special treatment or special rights; and the duty to respect freedom of speech and the right of free religious exercise, which entail the right to be critical, to question and challenge.

> Those who talk of bullying a minority are guilty of the racism of low expectations. When you approach a blond, blue-eyed, white Dane, you expect a high degree of tolerance and reason. But faced with someone like me, you say OK, let it go. That is the racism of low expectations, and that's what you are guilty of when you reduce the Cartoon Crisis to a story about a powerful newspaper bullying a minority. It's a distortion of the essence of the matter. To harbor lower expectations of my ability to be tolerant and reasonable compared to the majority is to discriminate against me.

Fortunately, there were Muslims in Denmark and other countries too who did not wish to take on the role of victim. They said that as practicing Muslims, they considered the Prophet Muhammad to be infallible, but that freedom of speech had to be defended, and that newspaper artists had to maintain the freedom to draw what they wanted. I don't like it, but I can live with it, they said. That is a mature standpoint, and it shows that those who believe that we can expect uncontrolled rage across the board are wrong.

I pointed out that many people appear to think that it is immoral to satirize another religion: satire should instead be turned inward against one's own beliefs. Similarly, criticism should be leveled upward to those in power rather than targeted downward against a weak minority.

"Well," Hirsi Ali said, "the amazing thing about that argument is that what all those who speak of being tolerant and of including Muslims really are saying is this: let's exclude Muslims." She explained:

> To become a part of the community of Danes, one has to be integrated in the Danish culture, which includes the culture of satire. Being a community means that *Jyllands-Posten* in principle is just as much their newspaper as any other Dane's. Why should they be excluded from its satire? Integration means inclusion all the way round—in film, theater, literature, satire, and cartoons.

What about the other argument, I asked—that scorn, mockery, and ridicule should only be targeted upward?

"That's indicative of the Marxist approach to human existence: the division of the world into powerful and powerless," she said.

> I'm not a supporter of that idea, and that's what the United States is so good at. Everyone can come here, and opportunities are equal for everyone. Society's approach is

equality for individuals, not groups. Those born into low-income families with poor education can move up in the world, and the rich can fall. There's movement both ways. Education and being included by satire, being included in the culture, and critical thinking increase the opportunities of the minority individual with respect to moving up in the world.

If you accept the Marxist view of the world, things aren't that simple. Muslims who are lacking in resources, who live in ghettos in Europe, are being brainwashed with totalitarian doctrine, and those behind it all are exploiting those people's vulnerability. They indoctrinate and preach an ideology of totalitarianism that exceeds that of Marxism, and at the same time, they claim to be a weak minority whose ideology must be spared criticism. This is a doctrine issuing from a rich oil state, Saudi Arabia, and is therefore very powerful indeed when you start looking at it from a new angle. They are extremely authoritarian and oppressive; they have the money and the influence to export their ideology to our part of the world and indoctrinate Muslims with low incomes.

Satire is a wonderful instrument by which to combat that. The funny thing is that many of those who claim that this is all about strong versus weak are not against the use of hard, military power, but all of a sudden, they're against satire, the softest form of power imaginable.

People like to compare Christian and Jewish communities in the West with Muslim communities, but Christians and Jews have accepted the division of divine and secular power. Only few Muslims have done that. In the United States, a Christian can be just as fundamentalist, just as orthodox as he wants. He can read the Bible as literally as he sees fit, but he has accepted that outside his home and his church resides a different reality, an open, secular space in which the American Constitution is law. When Muslims say the American president rather than God is sovereign, they are committing a sin. Many Muslims live in secular societies without having accepted that model as the prerequisite of democracy and freedom of religion. Recognizing that principle means becoming an infidel.

Ayaan Hirsi Ali was one of the 12 signatories of the anti-totalitarian manifesto published during the Cartoon Crisis. A second was Maryam Namazie. Both are women, both were born and brought up in Muslim environments; they are roughly the same age; and they have both left Islam, are deeply involved in the women's rights movement, subscribe to the idea of universal human rights, and are prominent figures in the debate on Islam. And despite threats against their lives, neither intends to step back from the public eye and give up the struggle for what they believe in.

Yet the two women have positioned themselves at different ends of the political spectrum. Ayaan Hirsi Ali is a classical liberal in the sense of Friedrich von Hayek and Milton Friedman—a believer in the free-market economy. Maryam Namazie is a socialist, a member of the Central Committee of the Worker–Communist Party of Iran. She combines criticism of capitalism with a defense of human rights, and she believes political Islam and U.S. militarism to be the greatest threats to world peace and development.

Initially, Maryam Namazie declined to sign the manifesto, since it put communism on a par with Nazism and fascism as totalitarian ideologies of the 20th century. When "communism" was replaced by "Stalinism," however, she agreed. At the end of May 2008, I traveled to Cologne to attend a conference organized by the Central Council of Ex-Muslims in Germany, which saw itself as a counterweight to the Central Council of Muslims, and I spoke with Namazie. I met with her again in the autumn of that year when she organized a similar conference in London.

Namazie is a founding member of the Council of Ex-Muslims in the United Kingdom, set up in June 2007 as a response to the British Council of Muslims. She holds a number of prominent positions, is actively involved in the fight against Sharia law and stoning, and hosts her own program on New Channel TV, a 24-hour station broadcasting to the Middle East and run by the Worker–Communist Party of Iran.[6]

After forming the Council of Ex-Muslims, Namazie received an email from a Muslim believer pointing out that Islam could not be renounced. Namazie replied that she would demonstrate the falsity of that claim, for she had indeed renounced her religion, and that many others would follow her example. The aim of the groups of ex-Muslims that were being formed around Europe was to break down the taboo that said Muslims could not leave Islam, and that those claiming to have done so were apostates, guilty of a crime deserving of the harshest punishment. The law in many Islamic countries punishes apostates with death.

A number of Muslims in the United Kingdom apparently believed such punishment to be only fitting. One day, there was a message on Namazie's phone saying, "You are going to get your throat cut." She has received a number of others since, but Namazie refuses to be intimidated, though she admits the threats do affect her more since she became a mother.

In Namazie's view, the open proclamation by ex-Muslims of their renunciation of Islam has clear parallels with the situation of homosexuals some 30 years ago. Sexuality and religion are private matters, but when homosexuals were threatened or marginalized, it was important for them to publicly demonstrate that they would not be intimidated. She told me:

> We hope that our manifestation can reduce fear and the
> feeling of being stigmatized that ex-Muslims experience.
> We can tell from people's reactions that there are a great
> many ex-Muslims, but that many of them are afraid to

be counted even anonymously. It's rather like being an ex-Christian during the Inquisition, but we're doing it to make people here in the U.K. and in Europe aware that not everyone who comes from an Islamic country is Muslim, that there are various takes on the issue, and that imams do not speak on behalf of the majority.

Maryam Namazie was 12 years old in 1979, when the mullahs came to power in Iran. She remembers how a man with a long beard and strange clothing appeared one day at her school and said that boys and girls were to be kept apart. Later, the school was closed down so the building and teaching materials could be Islamized. Members of the Islamic Hezbollah movement shouted obscenities at her on the street whenever she appeared without a hijab, and graphic images of televised executions remain etched on her memory. In 1980, the family decided to move to India, from where they relocated to the United Kingdom. They finally gained asylum in the United States, where Namazie attended university.

Islam and her personal take on religion were not big issues for Namazie until she traveled to Sudan in 1988 to work for the United Nations with Ethiopian refugees. Six months later, Colonel Omar al-Bashir seized power in a military coup and introduced an Islamic government. It was the second time in 10 years that Namazie had witnessed religious fanatics taking power and introducing Sharia law. It made an indelible impression on her. She realized that she was no longer merely a nonpracticing Muslim: she was an atheist. She became involved in a Sudanese human rights group that so incensed the authorities that they began harassing her:

> They believed they had the right to violate my private life. They pressured me and asked questions of a very personal nature, things I didn't think were any concern of theirs. They didn't care for my answers and started threatening me. One guy from the security services warned that I could have an accident on my motorcycle if I kept up my work.

The UN acted, evacuating Namazie out of fear for her safety. She devoted herself to humanitarian work for Iranian refugees around the world and has since been fiercely opposed to movements and governments seeking to constrain civil rights in the name of religion. "They want to control every aspect of people's lives. They interfere in what you wear, what you eat and drink, what kind of music you listen to, who you have sex with in your own home, and what you draw. Everything has to be monitored, controlled, and regulated."

In Namazie's view, all media should have reprinted the Muhammad cartoons in 2006, and she refers to *Jyllands-Posten*'s apology for having offended Muslim sentiments as naive. She posted the cartoons herself on her own blog and spoke at a demonstration in March 2006 on London's Trafalgar Square in support of free speech, with the cartoons prominently displayed on placards, together with the slogans "Religion: Hands Off Women's Lives" and "Long Live Unconditional Freedom of Belief and Expression."

She rejected criticism of the cartoons as being racist or attacking Muslims:

> *Jerry Springer: The Opera* or *Monty Python's Life of Brian* are satirical takes on Christianity, and I don't think they can be seen as being racist towards Christians. Criticism and ridicule of religions and ideas, or even hatred of ideas, regardless of what the pope or Islamic governments say, is not racism. It just doesn't make sense. They try to tell people that ideas, religions, and cultures can lay claim to rights because someone says they're sacred, but only people are sacred and entitled to rights.

Those who saw the Cartoon Crisis as a conflict between a powerful newspaper and a weak minority were, Namazie said, narrow-minded and submissive. She believed they were ignoring the past 30 years of history, a time in which Islam had steadily gained ground as a political ideology, and she saw their view as overlooking those who had been persecuted and discriminated against in the name of Islam:

> I don't think women who are stoned to death would see those responsible for their deaths as representatives of a persecuted and oppressed minority. People are slaughtered in the name of religion by Islamic governments and movements. So claiming that publication of the cartoons was not about freedom of speech but more about a big newspaper stepping on a weak minority is a poor excuse to appease and justify one's own silence in respect of Islam.

> If you criticize Islam, you're attacked for being out to get Muslims, but freedom, civil rights, and respect are for people, not religions and faiths. Anyway, how long must those of us with Muslim backgrounds live in Europe before we're considered to be part of the majority and the population as a whole? Why should a certain reaction to the cartoons be identified as the view of the entire minority? That's a problem, because political movements ideologically based on Islam have an interest in claiming that we are all of us Muslims. It lends them credibility, so those who claim that the cartoons offended all Muslims or the greater majority of them are in that way giving credence to the Islamic movements and enhancing their opportunities to exert influence upon society.

Namazie snorted her disapproval when I laid out the widely held view that as a non-Muslim newspaper *Jyllands-Posten* ought not to have published the Muhammad cartoons and instead should have left it to Muslims to break the ban on depiction and to satirize Islam:

> How dare they? How dare they? By that logic, Danes, Dutchmen, Britons, and others who took part in the struggle against apartheid in South Africa should have left the

South Africans alone in their Bantustans, deprived of their civil rights, until they managed to crawl their way out themselves. They didn't have the same moral right to criticize the apartheid regime. I thought all of us were humans before we were Muslims, Christians, Hindus, blacks, whites, communists, or capitalists? I was actively involved in the struggle against apartheid, but I've never been to South Africa, so that would mean I ought to have kept well away.

I'm also actively involved in the gay rights movement speaking out against homophobia, though I'm not a lesbian myself. But the logic would say I would have to be, otherwise I would have no moral right to support the rights of homosexuals. Some say, too, that only theologians should discuss Islam, because ordinary people aren't knowledgeable enough. I could go on. People are always looking for excuses to restrict the right of others to criticize. But it won't work. The right to criticize Islam is like the right to criticize Zionism. I don't like either of them, and I criticize both. Unfortunately, far too many people think Islam should be treated as a human being equipped with rights, and they'll drag you into court for libel if you dare to attack Muhammad and his religion.

Maryam Namazie's compatriot and peer, Afshin Ellian, involved himself at a young age in the politics of his Iranian homeland. He was 13 when revolution broke out in 1979, but like many of the youth on the street, he had only vague ideas about what the demonstrations were for. "During the daily protests, we shouted about wanting freedom, but if anyone had asked me what that meant, I would have been unable to give them a satisfactory answer, and the same was true of those who were older than me," Ellian says.

It's a grimy day in January 2009, and we are sitting in Afshin Ellian's office at the University of Leiden. Leiden is a quaint Dutch town with canals, narrow alleys, and 115,000 inhabitants. Ellian, now 42, has worked on the university's law faculty since completing his doctoral dissertation in 2003 on the South African Truth and Reconciliation Commission that followed in the wake of apartheid. The waves of his hair are black as ebony, and every now and then, his narrow spectacles slide down his nose. At regular intervals, he asks politely if I mind his smoking and lights up another cigarette. He laughs easily, though he is also clearly a very serious person.

To get to Ellian's office, I must first pass through an electronically secured glass door and state my business to one of the two bodyguards who accompany Ellian to work each day. It's been like that since just after the assassination of Theo van Gogh, in November 2004, when Ellian called for intellectuals to make jokes about Islam and more generally to make Islam the object of the same kind of ridicule, artistic exploration, and philosophical investigation as Christianity.

"I hereby call upon all artists, writers and academics to stop discriminating against Islam," he wrote in *de Volkskrant* on November 6, 2004.[7]

> When on television and in hundreds of theatres jokes are made about Islam, and when academics begin to treat Islam more critically, then Muslims will learn tolerance. The terrorists can intimidate and eliminate a handful of critics of Islam, but they can never kill hundreds of critical minds. Come, my friends, and enter the brothels and torture chambers of Muhammad and Allah. You will find great inspiration there. Come, my fellow scholars, and put Islam upon the operating table of philosophy. Otherwise it will remain a question how many murders our society can deal with.

Death threats were not long in coming, and the desire of Dutch comedians, newspaper editors, and scholars to follow Ellian's call has been subdued, to say the least. Ellian completely understands that reaction. He himself felt a strong reluctance to confront Islam when the terrorist attacks on the United States in 2001 so devastated and shocked the West. He and his wife had arrived in the Netherlands as refugees in 1989, and he had devoted many years to learning Dutch, getting an education in law and philosophy, and trying to fathom where the Islamic revolution back home in Iran had gone wrong. He had laid it all behind him when New York and Washington were struck on that fateful day, September 11, 2001.

Afshin Ellian grew up in northern Iran in the 1970s, the youngest of six children. His father was a retired army officer who cared little for the mullahs. On Fridays, he took the children with him to his own "mosque," the local cinema, where the family was transported around the world with Hollywood as its guide. It provided a cosmopolitan background for which Ellian to this day is profoundly grateful.

Ellian's father was killed in a traffic accident a few months after the revolution of 1979. The years that followed were full of drama and pain. Ellian protested for freedom along with others on the political left, but no one had any real sense of where they were going. "We had a real and burning desire for freedom, but we didn't know what freedom entailed." Ellian recalls.

> That's the debate going on in Europe right now, because many Muslims are in the same situation as we were in Iran in the 1970s and 1980s. Many Muslims have yet to grasp that the price of freedom is that others are allowed to disagree with what you believe in and can criticize your ideology and cultural background.

Some six months after the revolution, the regime commenced persecuting freethinkers—first from the far left, then the Islamic Marxists, Mujahedin, and moderate leftists. Two of Ellian's relatives were executed for counterrevolutionary activities, one an uncle's son active in the same circles as Afshin himself:

> I was only 15 or 16 at the time and was forced into hiding. For a while, I hid out at my uncle's. My being there

reminded him constantly of his son. One day, he was in
tears and asked me why I was alive when his own son
was dead. It was painful, but I could understand his
question and told myself: OK, this is how life is now; you
risk being executed or tortured, but I have to try and understand how it got this far.

A few months later, Ellian fled the country, traveling by camel to
Pakistan, from where he went on to Afghanistan after six months.
He ended up in Kabul, began to study medicine at the university there, met his wife, and involved himself in the Iranian exile
community where he ran into communists who had supported
Khomeini during the revolution. It was a source of conflict, and
eventually he feared so much for his safety he sought refuge with
the UN mission in Kabul, where with the aid of a shrewd Swedish
diplomat, he was accorded status as an asylum seeker, allowing
him to leave the country as a political refugee.

Looking back now on his first encounter with the West, Ellian
recalls one vivid contrast with the world he had fled: The Dutch
openly and loudly discussed politics and social issues in public.
They spoke critically of the government without having to glance
over their shoulder.

That was completely new to me, and it surprised me. I
was used to keeping quiet and not uttering a superfluous
word outside the home. What freedom, I thought. They
say what they think, and no one comes after them. That
was the reason I decided to study law. I wanted to find
out how the Dutch could live together like that without
killing each other; how people could openly express disgruntlement without it leading to violence.

What did Ellian learn from his study of law?

I came to understand what freedom entails, and what
they should have done in Iran to ensure freedom after

the revolution. Back then, unfortunately, Khomeini was the only one who knew what he wanted and how to go about it. Studying law made me understand how a political idea becomes constitutional and translates into an order of democracy. I learned the imperative of accepting a diversity of opinions, even those that are wrong and abhorrent, and the importance of acknowledging a political opposition.

Studying Western philosophy, Afshin Ellian became aware of an undercurrent of self-hatred running through European culture. A lack of faith in the strengths of their own culture had caused many Europeans to give themselves up to totalitarian ideologies, such as fascism, communism, and Nazism:

> It surfaces in an uncritical, romantic cultivation of foreign cultures, even when there is nothing whatsoever romantic about those cultures up close. That self-hatred is only partly rooted in postcolonial guilt. It runs a lot deeper. European self-denial means that Europe is viewed as more racist and intolerant than most other parts of the world, even though the opposite is true.

In Ellian's view, that self-denial involves a diminished ability to distinguish between good and evil, between what is ethical and what is not. That inability to distinguish explains why people can even think to juxtapose Theo van Gogh's assassin, Mohammad Bouyeri, with Ayaan Hirsi Ali and to declare them both to be fundamentalists in their own way—he an Islamist fundamentalist, she an Enlightenment fundamentalist:

> Time and again, Europeans demonstrate an inability to distinguish between the criminal and the victim. The criminal becomes the victim and the victim the criminal. Beneath it all, one clearly senses the consequences of European nihilism. If Europeans are unable to separate

out their own fundamental values in that way then eventually, there will be no one left to defend Europe at all.

Ellian continues:

> You see it very clearly in the debate on freedom of speech.
> In that area, we are no longer Europeans. Maybe we've
> become Arabs, or maybe we've taken on the Islamic or
> the Soviet view of freedom of speech. Whatever, it's cer-
> tainly not the European conception of free speech we
> champion. To begin with, Europe's great strength was
> its defense of freedom. In the European view, tolerance
> entailed being willing to accept all the pain and affront
> that accompanied the right of the citizen to exercise his
> freedom of speech. Christians learned to withstand the
> pain that followed from the rejection of God and the
> scriptures, and in that sense, they became free. But it's
> not like that anymore.

I asked Ellian what, then, he understood by the term "European
civilization."

> The ability to establish a political order that takes free-
> dom and justice as its points of departure, and the abil-
> ity to question one's own culture and way of life. A
> philosophical approach to life. These are things that are
> essential to European culture. The Judeo-Christian cul-
> ture tried from day one to reconcile itself with the Greco-
> Roman tradition. That's a painful and complicated story,
> but a path was found from the Old Testament to the New
> Testament. Europe has reconciled all the various ele-
> ments of its past; they have been integrated and included
> and form a bridge into the present.

> In Islam, the opposite is the case. Everything that has to
> do with a pre-Islamic Arabia is discarded. Anyone not
> adhering to the Koran is misguided and wrong. They call
> it the Age of Ignorance. In the view of Islam, the past is

not to be reconciled, and its various elements are not to be integrated into the tradition in the manner in which that has occurred in Europe.

For Afshin Ellian, the Muhammad cartoons were an example of the kind of challenging approach to Islam that he had urged following the murder of Theo van Gogh in 2004. He welcomed the cartoons as input to Muslim understanding of the concept of tolerance. He believes it would be wrong to claim that the drawings were not so much about freedom of speech but more about the right of a big newspaper to bully a weak minority:

> That's a false argument. We're not dealing with a minority at all in the traditional sense. This is a minority that enjoys great power. Geert Wilders has been taken to court here in the Netherlands because the Muslim lobby demands it. The mayor of Rotterdam, a very large city by Dutch standards, is a Muslim. Two ministers of the Dutch government have Muslim backgrounds. The same kind of thing is seen in other European countries. That's not what they would call a weak minority in Iran. Muslims in Europe are a powerful minority with representatives in European parliaments and governments. Or take freedom of speech: a minority that can stop others writing about and discussing Islam freely is not weak.

Ellian rejected criticism of the cartoons that claimed that only Muslims have the moral right to make fun of Islam and that criticism from within a culture possessed more moral weight than that from without:

> All right, then, let's begin by telling the Islamic world it has no right to criticize the Jews. It's a ridiculous argument. First, Islam is a part of Europe. It's absurd to say to Europeans that they should keep silent because Islam is a foreign religion, and Muslims are a minority. Muslims have been in Europe since the eighth century. There

was an Islamic culture in Andalucía in Spain, in parts of France and Italy. Sicily was Islamic for 200 years. Islam was predominantly a military power in Europe, but then it became a part of Europe in cultural terms. So Islam is a part of Europe, and criticizing Islam is necessary, just as it is necessary to criticize Christianity and Judaism.

Second, criticism of other cultures and religions is not about a moral right, it's about arguments. If, as someone not from Zimbabwe, I say that Robert Mugabe is a lunatic, the question is not whether I have the moral right to call Mugabe a lunatic. The only thing that matters is the quality of my analysis and the arguments I put forward. To claim that non-Muslims are less entitled to express their opinions about Islam than Muslims is absurd. Essentially, it's a totalitarian demand. Muslims are fully entitled to criticize and make fun of Europe, Christianity, and Judaism, and the same is true of Europeans. Why should a Muslim enjoy a greater moral right to draw a cartoon of Muhammad than you? Where is the rational argument? Is Muhammad not a man of this world? It's nonsense. Everyone has the right to say what they want about Islam.

Ayaan Hirsi Ali, Maryam Namazie, and Afshin Ellian are all more or less the same age, born between 1966 and 1969, at a time when the dissident movement in Eastern Europe was taking shape. A line of continuity runs from Eastern Bloc dissidence through the triumph of freedom in the Soviet Union in 1989–1991 to the struggle for civil rights that is going on today.

Russian writers Andrei Sinyavsky and Yuli Daniel received long prison sentences in 1966 for publishing works of fiction in the West. Their trial set off a storm of protests in the Soviet Union that lay the groundwork for the human rights movement. During a dramatic court case brought against four critics of the Soviet system in Moscow in 1968, two prominent dissidents sent out a declaration to the world.[8] It was the first time dissidents had addressed the outside world over the head of the Soviet regime on an issue of human rights. It was a new departure, and it was to be a yardstick for the dissidents' insistence on making respect for human rights an issue in East–West dialogue.

Recall that also in 1968, Andrei Sakharov published his famous manifesto on "Progress, Coexistence and Intellectual Freedom," in which he so clearly worded the idea of the close link between respect for human rights and freedom on the one hand, and peace and security on the other. The idea was taken up in the latter part of the 1970s by the Helsinki Groups that were set up behind the Iron Curtain and were significant to Eastern Bloc collapse. The first issue of the Soviet human rights movement's legendary *Chronicle of Current Events* was published in the spring of 1968 with the aim of registering violations of citizens' rights and establishing a forum of news and debate.[9]

In many ways, the year 1968 proved epochal in the history of the Soviet human rights movement. It was also a crucial year in Central Europe. In August 1968, the Prague Spring had become such a threat to Kremlin rule that troops of the Warsaw Pact invaded Czechoslovakia and shattered the dream of the human face of socialism. On January 30, 1968, Warsaw's National Theatre played its final performance of *Forefathers' Eve*, a Romantic drama by Poland's national poet Adam Mickiewicz, following demands by the regime that it be canceled. The play was about the struggle of the Polish people to win freedom under foreign rule. Although set in the 19th century, it was interpreted by all as a comment on current events. Rumors of its censorship had abounded, and the final performance turned into a demonstration when students without tickets showed up in droves to express their support.

After the final curtain, an enraged audience tumbled out into the winter night and gathered at Mickiewicz's memorial. Here, banners were unfurled demanding an end to the regime's violations of the freedom of speech. A number of students were arrested; still others arrived to join the demonstration; and in the weeks that followed, protests were stepped up in support of Article 83 of the Polish Constitution guaranteeing freedom of speech and the right of assembly. Unrest culminated in March 1968 in clashes between demonstrators and security forces. Hundreds of students and professors were either jailed or forced into exile, and a malicious anti-Semitic campaign ensued.

Among those arrested was 22-year-old Adam Michnik, one of the leaders of the Polish youth rebellion. Later sentenced to three years in jail for rioting, he was released after a year though prohibited from continuing his university studies in history. Michnik carried on his involvement in the anti-communist underground until the final collapse, following which he was elected to the Polish parliament and became editor-in-chief of Poland's biggest newspaper, *Gazeta Wyborcza*.

"For my generation, the road to freedom began in 1968. While students in Paris and Berkeley were rejecting bourgeois democracy, we in Prague or Warsaw were fighting for a freedom that only the bourgeois order could guarantee," Michnik told the *UNESCO Courier* following the collapse of the Berlin Wall.[10]

> The main difference between us and revolutionary movements was that we, the anti-communist opposition, did not harbor any illusions about the 'utopia of a perfect society.' . . . Western intellectuals have made a specialty of placing their hopes in the Vietcong, Fidel Castro, Mao Zedong, the Soviet Union, the Sandinistas of Nicaragua, and I don't know what else. Our movement—that of Czechoslovakia's Vaclav Havel, Russia's Andrei Sakharov, Solidarity, did not strive for utopia. What we wanted was a return to "normality."

The political upheavals on either side of the Iron Curtain in 1968 were of vastly different character. Revolutionary students in the West demonstrated for a socialist utopia to be realized by abolishing the constitutional state, whereas dissidents struggled for its establishment in the East, even going to prison for their insistence on a civil order. Dissidents like Michnik, Havel, and Sakharov put their faith in a society that for all its imperfection was open, whereas rebels in the West insisted on the perfect society, attaching their hopes, as Michnik noted, to a string of totalitarian regimes, each of which left its own particular trail of blood.

During my time in the Danish Gymnasium (upper secondary school or senior high school) in the 1970s, many convinced themselves that the youth rebellion still taking place at European and American universities heralded a new age in which the socialist utopia lay waiting on the horizon, while Eastern Bloc intellectuals saw their own protests as the beginning of the end for organized socialism. Today, we know that the dissidents behind the Iron Curtain were right.

When I look back on 1968 and all it brought with it, the dissidents from the Baltic to the Black Sea are for me the great historical victors. Their struggle for freedom was a guiding star. They practiced what they preached; for them, there was no divide between words and actions, even though in many instances, it cost them dearly. They were the exact opposite of the Western generation of 1968, who spoke with passion but whose private actions often directly contradicted their speech. In the human rights movement of Eastern Europe, there were no easy rides. Everyone who got involved knew that they could wind up incarcerated for years behind barbed wire, careers spoiled, families split.

For Ayaan Hirsi Ali, Maryam Namazie, and Afshin Ellian, there is no moral free lunch either, even though they all live in the West. They pay a price for stepping forward and insisting on the right to say no to religion. When they demand the same critical approach to Islam as to Christianity and other belief systems, they know the price will come in the form of death threats and ruptured families and friendships.

When ex-Muslims insist on their right to say no to religion, when they stress that individual rights take precedence over group rights, they are saying exactly the same to Muslims around the world as the seven courageous people who, in August 1968, protested on Moscow's Red Square against the Warsaw Pact's invasion of Czechoslovakia. On a banner they managed to unfurl before being taken away by the KGB were the words, primarily addressing the Czech people but in principle addressing all those in the Eastern Bloc, "For Your Freedom and Ours."[11] It was a quote by Russian author Aleksandr Herzen, who had supported Polish rebels fighting for their independence from Russia in the 19th century. In January 1991, I noticed that those same words appeared again during demonstrations in Moscow in support of the Baltic countries' struggle for liberty in the wake of attacks by Soviet troops in Lithuania and Latvia. When ex-Muslims insist on the right to say no to their religion, and stress that individual rights have priority over group rights, they are saying exactly the same thing.

10. A Victimless Crime

It's not dark yet, but it's getting there.

—Bob Dylan

In the end, we will remember not the words of our enemies, but the silence of our friends.

—Martin Luther King Jr.

On August 12, 1553, a middle-aged man arrived in Geneva, one of the centers of the Protestant Reformation in Europe. He was on the run from the Catholic Inquisition in the French town of Vienne, where he had been charged with heresy and inciting rebellion. Evidence of the man's heresy had been sent by Jean Calvin, the head of the Reformed Church of Geneva, who had corresponded privately with the man. That act was highly unusual. To draw a Cold War parallel, it would be like Jesse Helms informing on a Soviet dissident to the Kremlin.

Michael Servetus was a 42-year-old theologian, physician, and book editor of Spanish descent.[1] He was aware that the most prominent theologian of the Protestant Church had given him away to the Inquisition. Why he decided to pass through Geneva after he escaped his arrest in France remains a mystery. Some believe he entertained plans of a coup to remove Calvin. According to Servetus himself, he intended to remain in the city for only a few days.

Some years before, Servetus and Calvin had engaged in an impassioned and polemical correspondence. Servetus had stated that he would be prepared to travel to Geneva to meet his old acquaintance and opponent face to face should Calvin so wish. Calvin mentioned that possibility in a letter to a friend, noting, "If he comes, I shall never let him go out alive."

And so it came to pass. The day after his arrival, Servetus attended a church service in the St. Pierre Cathedral where Calvin preached. Attendance was compulsory, and perhaps he feared drawing unnecessary attention to himself by remaining behind. Inside the church, however, he was recognized by Calvin, who ordered that he be detained.

There was a lengthy trial. Thirty-nine charges were brought against Servetus, encompassing his early writings, claims of the mortality of the soul, mockery of the Church in Geneva, pantheism, infant baptism, and the denial of the Trinity. All but the last two were dropped during the trial. Servetus denied the doctrine of the Trinity to which both Catholics and Protestants subscribed, that is, the unity of Father, Son, and Holy Spirit as three entities in one divine Being. He also did not believe in the need to baptize children since unlike Calvin, he did not consider children to be sinful beings in the same way as adults. That view outraged Calvin, who in a fit of anger declared, "Servetus deserves those sweet, innocent little chicks of his to dig out his eyes a hundred thousand times." A written dispute in Latin between Calvin and Servetus was the highpoint of the process. Servetus held that the idea of man as a sinful and depraved being from the moment of birth, and the claim that human destiny is predetermined, reduced him to little more than a dead creature with the free will of a stone. By contrast, Calvin felt Servetus elevated man to divinity, blaspheming.

On October 27, 1553, sentence was passed. Servetus would be burned alive at the stake.

It took an hour for the procession to reach the Plateau de Champel, the place of execution. Heading it were local officials in capes and the garb of authority, members of the city council, church dignitaries, clergy in their priestly robes, and the chief of police. Behind them came the guards, officers, and archers on horseback. The citizens of the city brought up the rear in order of civil rank and status. Along the way, prayers were said.

The clergy continued their efforts to talk Servetus into confession. Weak and tormented, he refused. When the procession arrived, the condemned man was brought to a high pile of firewood and green branches. A crown of straw and leaves covered with sulfur was placed on his head. Then, he was fixed to the pyre with chains, and a copy of his book *The Restoration of Christianity*—the work that had sparked the accusations of his heresy—was tied to his arm. A thick rope was wound around his neck four or five times; Servetus pleaded that it not be bound tighter. When the executioner stepped forward with a lighted torch, Servetus let out a howl so violent that many in the crowd were transfixed in terror for a moment. With Servetus still breathing, onlookers threw fresh branches onto the fire. It took half an hour or so for him to die.

Michael Servetus was the first man to be executed for heresy by the Reformation Protestants in Geneva. That deed sparked international protests and kicked off a major debate on religious tolerance. Thousands of people had already been executed on grounds of heresy, and there were many more to come. But here, for the first time, the Calvinists were resorting to the same macabre methods for which they had criticized the Catholics.

The Reformation challenged the Catholic Church's monopoly on correctness of faith. In Germany, Martin Luther spoke out in favor of complete freedom of faith. Faith—or indeed incorrectness of faith—was a free matter for the individual. To the extent the secular authorities violated that freedom, they overstepped in Luther's view the bounds of their powers and could be disobeyed. Luther's distinction between the secular and the spiritual was a significant step in a development that would later bring forth the rights of free speech and free religious exercise, and indeed secular democracy, although there is little to indicate that it was what Luther intended.

In the early 1520s, that German father of the Reformation found himself engaged in an intense confrontation with the Catholic Church and secular authorities. In 1521, the pope excommunicated him. His teachings were branded as heretic; orders were issued to seek out and burn his books; and printing, selling, and buying them were made punishable offenses.

Yet later, when Luther's Protestantism had been officially introduced in a number of German principalities, Luther lent support to the execution of people who believed in other schools of thought, and he distanced himself from the kind of tolerance he had previously championed. He condemned the Catholic Mass as an abomination and a crime of blasphemy that authorities should suppress. When a town or a principality converted to Lutheranism, Catholic dogma, the Mass, and the adoration of the Virgin Mary and various saints were forbidden. Altars, images, and ornaments used in Catholic rituals were destroyed, and monasteries were closed down.

"I can envisage no reason why tolerance should be justifiable to God," Luther wrote in a letter in 1541.[2] With the execution of Servetus, the Protestants in Geneva demonstrated their religious intolerance. Europe was to be infested by religious wars for the next 150 years.

The Reformation forced Catholics to address a question with which they had no particular reason to concern themselves for a thousand years: who are we? Even though there had been clashes with the Muslim world—and although Europe was also home to a number of Jews—the established Church had seldom before been challenged so fundamentally with regard to its identity. In many ways, it was a situation similar to that in which Europe finds itself now at the beginning of the 21st century. Who are we? What does it mean to be a European in the 21st century? What does it mean to be a citizen of a liberal democracy? What is freedom of speech and of religion in a multicultural society? What rights does the citizen possess, and what are his responsibilities? How can people of different cultures and religious backgrounds live together in peace and democracy?

The religious divisions of the 16th and 17th centuries sparked a theological mobilization of all Christians. Previously, individual religious practice had broadly concerned ritual rather than substance. Prayers were recited in Latin (a language few understood), and religious festivals were observed, yet most people had only a vague understanding of what their faith actually implied in a dogmatic sense. That had not mattered much in a world in which everyone shared the same Christian faith. But that changed with the Reformation. Competing dogmas emerged. Suddenly, faith required discovery of the fundamentals of religion, what it entailed, and where it differed from other faiths. The Christian Churches began to conduct religious identity politics focusing not on points of similarity with other Christian doctrines, but on what separated them. Lines were drawn.[3]

In a way, the lines drawn then were similar to those drawn between groups in the present-day multicultural society of modern Europe, where a tribal mentality and cultivation of religious and cultural separation are often seen as a basis of democratic society, to the detriment of common, universal values that safeguard all citizens' equality before the law. They are similar, too, to the lines drawn during the Cold War, when the world was split in two, each side considering the other to be the embodiment of evil: truth against lies, black against white, capitalism against communism.

In the 16th- and 17th-century confessional state, dissidents were viewed as a threat and did not enjoy the same rights as those who subscribed to the dominant Church. Cultivation of other beliefs was an offense to God and the state. Freethinkers were considered to be potential traitors, regardless of how loyal they might be to the authorities. In Britain, France, and Poland, that view of religious dissidents was widespread until the mid-18th century or later. In Denmark, the Lutheran Evangelical Church enjoyed a monopoly of faith until 1849, when the country adopted a constitution that ensured freedom of religious expression.

But the execution of Michael Servetus sparked the first major European debate on religious tolerance. Was there an alternative to enforced orthodoxy? Could any multireligious society exist, and how could it then be organized? Some 200 years later, the debate culminated in the American Bill of Rights and the French Declaration of the Rights of Man and Citizen, in 1791 and 1789, respectively, both of which embodied the principles of free speech and free religious exercise. But long before either, a dialogue began between the two most brilliant scholars of the French Reformation, John Calvin and Sebastian Castellio.[4]

Castellio was a theologian who had known Calvin personally—had even stayed with him in Strasbourg in 1540, after witnessing the first Protestant heretics being burned at the stake in Lyon, an experience so horrific that for the rest of his life he would champion humanism as the essential core of Protestant thought and practice. Later, at Calvin's suggestion, Castellio moved to Geneva as rector of the Collège de Genève, but following a disagreement with Calvin, he moved on to Basel in 1545, where he was appointed professor and lived until his death in 1563. Basel was where an anonymous account titled *Historia Mortis Serveti* (*Account of the Death of Servetus*) was published in 1553; although its author was never identified, scholars believe—and Calvin clearly felt—it was written by Castellio.

The *Account* highlights Calvin's hypocrisy. If he truly believed in predestination—the idea that God has already determined which of us should be saved and which doomed—then believers had no reason to fear Servetus's heresy. It also condemns Calvin for conspiring with the Inquisition against Servetus. Rome and

Calvin were not one iota better than Pilate and Herod, rivals who had conspired to have Jesus crucified for heresy. The issue was not for the civil authorities to decide.

Calvin was furious and made repeated attempts to convince the authorities in Basel to arrest Castellio. In his *Defense of Orthodox Faith against the Prodigious Errors of the Spaniard Michael Servetus,* published in 1554, Calvin stated that Servetus had not acted alone but had conspired with fanatics who opposed the death penalty for heretics. Those who defended heretics were themselves guilty of heresy. Later he said that Castellio's defense of the individual's right of doubt would ultimately destroy the Church altogether.

But Castellio was already immersed in preparing a more expansive work titled *Concerning Heretics: Whether They Are to Be Persecuted* that came out in the spring of 1554 under the pseudonym Martinus Bellius. It comprised a collection of texts by scholars, ancient and modern, including Luther, Erasmus, and Calvin himself. In his preface, Castellio again suggested that Calvin and his supporters should tread carefully when branding others as heretics, since that was the crime for which Christ had been crucified. Moreover, Christ had declared that he would be tolerant of his enemies; how then could men be given the right to judge who were the true believers?

Castellio's defense of religious tolerance was a thoroughly modern work, though his ideas would long be ignored; it would be several centuries before they entered the common wisdom. He held that Christians should concentrate on what could be agreed to be essential and leave the rest up to individual conscience and the revelation of the Savior.

The agreed essentials were the Ten Commandments, that God was the source of all good, that mankind was lost because of Adam and Eve's disobedience, and that mankind was saved by Jesus Christ. Studying the Holy Scriptures uncovered no justification for definitive statements about predestiny, the Trinity, or notions of heaven and hell, and in Castellio's view it was impossible to condemn people to death for their stance on dogmas so disputed:

> He makes himself (by what right I do not know) the judge and sovereign arbiter. He claims that he has on his side the sure evidence of the Word of God. Then why does he write so many books to prove what is evident? In view of all this uncertainty we must define the heretic simply as one with whom we disagree. And if then we are going to kill heretics, the logical outcome will be a war of extermination, for each is sure of himself. Calvin would have to invade France and other nations, wipe out cities, put all the men to the sword, sparing neither sex nor age, not even the babes and the beasts. All who bear the Christian name would have to be burned except the Calvinists. There would be left on earth only Calvinists, Turks, and Jews, whom he accepts.[5]

Castellio's conclusion has come to stand as a fundamental critique of religious and political fanaticism: "By persecution and violence one can no more build the Church than one can construct a wall with cannon blasts. To kill a man is not to defend a doctrine. It is to kill a man."[6] It was Castellio who laid the first stone of the house in which tolerance and the right of free religious exercise eventually found a home.

It's a bitterly cold day in December 2009, and I'm walking around Geneva in the footsteps of Servetus and Calvin. The Old Town mirrors some of the asceticism, the lack of pomp found in the Protestant church service. I stroll from the railway station, passing the Place du Molard where Servetus took lodgings, then head through a cobbled alley to the square in front of the St. Pierre Cathedral where he was recognized and arrested. He sat imprisoned in the bishop's cellar next to the cathedral for two and a half months. The building no longer exists. The city's Hôtel de Ville, however, where the trial took place, has survived in all its splendor. I nose around in the courtyard from where the sentence was pronounced on the morning of October 27, 1553, most likely from a balcony on one of the upper floors.

I'm in Geneva trying to fathom what led to the Cartoon Crisis. I've met with diplomats and nongovernmental organizations active in the UN Human Rights Council. Over the past four years, I've increasingly felt a need to understand the Cartoon Crisis within a broader historical and global context. I've immersed myself in issues of which I previously had only rudimentary knowledge, at best: constitutional law, the history of free speech and religious tolerance, Holocaust denial. The things I have learned have convinced me all the more that publishing and defending the Muhammad cartoons was the right thing to do, and that a number of crucial issues are still at stake.

I jump onto a bus that will take me out to the Plateau de Champel where Servetus was killed, triggering one of the most important debates a society can conduct with itself: how to guarantee religious freedom and maintain social harmony. It is a struggle that each new generation must work through, and its outcome is never certain. In Servetus's day, religious tolerance was seen at best as a necessary evil to appease the regrettable, but unavoidable, reality of multiple viewpoints. Today, tolerance is no longer exclusively about religion, but extends through notions of intellectual, political, and cultural freedom. It has become an ideal, and because being tolerant has become modern and fashionable, takes on what it involves are many. Who may claim tolerance and who may not? Where should its boundaries lie? In the debate on the Muhammad cartoons, many—Muslim and non-Muslim alike—believed *Jyllands-Posten* and its 12 cartoonists to be intolerant. Others—Muslim and non-Muslim alike—found intolerance in those who reacted with violence, demanding that the cartoons be banned.

I sit down at a café and think about the challenges of intolerance in my own life. When I married Natasha in 1981, the Soviet Union was Denmark's enemy. Her nation was a threat to my own. When we married, neither of us had any particular interest in politics. Natasha had never been an active critic of the system, though many things about the Soviet Union appalled her. She did not see her country as a threat to the West and was surprised by people's reactions in Denmark when she told them where she was from. People balked at her accent, avoided interacting with her. She was turned down when applying for jobs. She remained aware that no one in Denmark—besides me—had asked her to go there, and for that reason, she never blamed society for it or complained about discrimination. But she felt Denmark was rejecting her. Even now, some 30 years later, with her firm command of the language, two Danish children, friends and family, and a Danish passport to boot, Natasha does not feel herself to be Danish.

I think that feeling has to do with the way we are in Denmark. Being Danish is about the way you look, what you eat, how you dress, the way you talk, how you interact with other people. It's how we recognize each other. All those things will gradually change, I'm sure, and I feel they are changing already. Danish people are not more xenophobic or more skeptical of outsiders than anyone else. But they will need time to get used to the idea that you can be Danish even if your skin is a different color, you speak with an accent, and you wear unusual clothes.

Neither Natasha nor I ever thought much about the ideological war that separated our countries. That became visible, however, whenever we visited her parents. Her father, Vasily Ivanovich Salnikov, was devoutly Stalinist. Passions often ran high when we discussed the news on TV or as we drove through the stunning beauty of the Caucasus or jogged around the track at the local athletic club. But he was also a warm, sensitive, and intelligent man who wrote love poems to my mother-in-law, taught children at an orphanage, and selflessly engaged in volunteer work for veterans of World War II.

Our relationship was a test of tolerance, and it taught me that pigeonholing people according to one identity—communist, Muslim, atheist, whatever—is simplistic. We all possess many identities. I was extremely fond of my father-in-law. We spent many enjoyable times together. I like to think he felt the same way, even though it must have been extremely difficult for him, having grown up in Stalin's Soviet Union, exposed to daily doses of propaganda about the enemy in the West, to accept a son-in-law from a capitalist country. I did not care for his religion, Stalinism, and he did not believe that Russia was mature enough for democracy, though in his later days, he found some benefit to the market economy. In the end, our mutual disapproval of each other's ideas no longer prevented us from seeing the individual behind them.

Things go wrong when people have identities forced on them. That is true whether we're talking about the Soviet Union and its imperative of communist ideology, or of Muslim societies that hold that no person born a Muslim can ever be allowed to leave Islam. Things go wrong too when immigrants or descendants of immigrants from the Islamic world are pigeonholed as Muslims, even though some may be agnostic or atheist, and many clearly wish to highlight other aspects of their identity.

The story of John Calvin's confrontation with Michael Servetus points to some of our current threats to free speech and freedom of religion. That is hardly surprising. To legitimize one's wish to censor speech one doesn't like, or that one considers being a threat to society, it is convenient to claim justification from an ideology, a religion, a nation, or other higher idea. If your enemies can be said to have violated something sacred, then your chances of winning support among the population are greatly enhanced.

In modern-day Europe, a number of conceptions of tolerance compete. One model takes as its point of departure the individual and his inalienable rights at birth, among them free speech and freedom of religion. Other citizens and the state itself are obliged to tolerate the individual's exercise of those rights, even if they disapprove of them. You can believe or not; you can leave your faith, convert, and proselytize to others. You can shop from faith to faith, and if none is satisfactory, you can start your own. People are free to criticize and to believe what they want about their own religions and those of others. Faith is voluntary.

In liberal democracies, rights are possessed by the individual. But citizens may belong to religious, ethnic, or cultural minorities also tolerated by the society as groups, even when such groups subscribe to ideas at odds with the values of the liberal democracy. Communist parties and other revolutionary groups of the left were tolerated in Western Europe during the Cold War, even though they fought to undermine the rule of law and abolish democracy. Today, liberal democracy is tolerant of Islamists who work for the introduction of a strict Islamic state; and Denmark has no law against Nazi parties. As long as anti-democratic movements merely argue their case in words, the state will not interfere to stop them.

In liberal democracies, groups have no right to exercise power over their members, other than the right to expel them. If a member of a religious minority wishes to leave the group or fails to obey its rules, the group may not impose other punishments; if it seeks to do so, the nation-state is obliged to step in to ensure respect for the individual's rights. Michael Walzer maps it out in his 1997 book *On Toleration*.[7] Although the state may be less tolerant of groups than of individuals, it may force groups to be more tolerant of individuals. That is because in the nation-state, the group is a voluntary association. Sects that constrain the liberties of their members will attract few members in an open society, and the more radical they become, the fewer they will be able to recruit. In the liberal nation-state, Walzer says, the majority tolerates cultural and religious differences in the same way that government tolerates political opposition, that is, by establishing a system that by independent courts may effectively ensure the civil rights of the individual.

A second model of tolerance has most notably been practiced by multinational empires in which different ethnic and religious groups coexisted, though it has now also found its way into European multicultural society of the 21st century. Groups exercise a certain degree of self-determination and self-justice, from time to time gaining the consent of the authorities to employ parallel systems of justice. The object of tolerance is the group rather than the individual. That was the state of affairs in the Ottoman Empire, in India under British rule, in ancient Persia and Egypt, and elements of it exist today in modern Britain, where the state in some cases has an approach to minorities that is similar to the British Empire's attitude in India.

For instance, until 1829, the British did not prohibit traditional self-immolation of Hindu widows on the funeral pyres of their husbands, and they did so then only with reluctance, wishing to interfere as little as possible in local custom. In Britain today, minorities are often treated as collectives rather than individuals. Self-proclaimed spokespeople without democratic mandate may approach the authorities, make demands, negotiate, and enter into agreement with them on the group's behalf. Individuals whose opinions are considered deviant by the group may find themselves squeezed out of the equation. According to a Swedish government report, a number of women from the Middle East now living in Malmö have stated that they enjoy fewer freedoms in their Swedish public housing blocks than in their homelands, because Muslim "thought police" demand they cover in public and consistently strive to constrain their liberties.[8] In some areas of Great Britain, Sharia courts have been established to deprive women of rights guaranteed by British law.[9] Thus, some individuals are unable to enjoy the tolerance accorded by the liberal democracy to its citizens, since the group prevents them from doing so. That model may increasingly prevail elsewhere in Europe, in neighborhoods where the state fails to exercise its sovereignty.

Those two approaches generate very different societies. The first, liberal model furthers a religious melting pot in which loyalties and identities are changeable. People of different faiths mix with and influence another. Individuals are not bound by their affiliation to any group but are free to determine the role faith plays in their lives. Citizenship transcends religious, cultural, and ethnic boundaries. Any group into which the individual is born may be left at any time. The second model furthers a society in which groups are walled off from one another, allowing no movement between them. Each group establishes its own parallel society of schools, nursing homes, laws, customs, associations, and authorities.

The future of Europe depends to a certain extent on the way in which we practice tolerance. Are we to be tolerant of the individual or of the group? Whose rights are to be held highest? Under pressure from increasing diversity, the institutions of the nation-state face a dilemma.

One path consists of deferring to the group's self-esteem, accepting that only the group has the right to speak critically of itself, while others who do so are called intolerant. In that case, freedom of speech is not a duty to speak; it involves refraining from saying anything critical of, or offensive to, another group. That form of "tolerance" closes its eyes to intolerance of individuals within the minority group, because to draw attention to that intolerance would be "racist." Individuals are walled in to their groups, which exist apart from others. That, to me, is anathema. It is the kind of society I would hope my children will never have to live in, not least because they are the product of Natasha and my meeting and joining together despite belonging to very different groups.

A second path for adapting to the multicultural reality of Europe today is to build on the American model of tolerance. Walzer calls it the model of the immigrant society.[10] Tolerance is of the individual rather than the group, and it is more radical than what is practiced in the nation state. In the immigrant society, the state is not committed to one group over any other; it is neutral. All speech, even racist speech, is protected, so long as it does not imminently incite violence. Government is not an arbiter of taste, and citizens of the society must learn to tolerate one another as individuals, even within the group. Tolerance is of the individual's personalized version of religion, culture, or ethnic affiliation rather than the religion, culture, or ethnic group itself. Thus, individual group members are obliged to be tolerant of other members' idiosyncratic versions of their shared religion. That tolerance entails a kind of individual freedom that I personally find appealing, though I acknowledge that groups and communities less tolerant toward the individual may be crucial for society's continued cohesion.

More than 450 years have passed since Michael Servetus was burned at the stake in Geneva. Since then, the West has seen wars of religion, world wars, and bloody revolutions, but also progress in science and the establishment of democratic institutions. It has engendered unique prosperity and ensured individual rights and freedoms that make its open societies attractive to immigrants striving for a better life. A culmination came with the triumph of freedom in 1989, when socialist dictatorships collapsed in the East. A new and free Europe began to emerge.

In 1989, many in the West, myself included, were under the illusion that the ideas and values that had eventually developed from the dispute over religious tolerance had won a conclusive victory. The world may perhaps not have been approaching "the end of history" as Francis Fukuyama put it, but it was hard to see what kinds of ideas and values could challenge the West and the values that had won the Cold War.[11] In 1990, U.S. President George H. W. Bush succeeded in mobilizing the world community into supporting some of those principles when Iraq invaded Kuwait. Giddy in the moment, Bush and Western media spoke of a new world order based on the UN Charter and the Universal Declaration of Human Rights.

But things went differently. Although the old enemies, the United States and the Soviet Union, joined in condemning Saddam Hussein and imagining a new and better world, the Organization of the Islamic Conference (OIC), numbering 57 Islamic countries across four continents, met in August 1990 in Cairo to adopt the Declaration on Human Rights in Islam.[12] That event passed unnoticed. The eyes of the world were focused on Saddam Hussein's army and its occupation of diminutive Kuwait, and few paid much attention to the OIC anyway.

Since its inception in 1969, the OIC had seldom been able to reach agreement on anything. True, when foreign ministers of the OIC met in Riyadh in March 1989, they were able to put out a joint declaration condemning Salman Rushdie's novel *The Satanic Verses*. Iran's Ayatollah Khomeini had issued a fatwa against Rushdie and put a million-dollar price on the writer's head. The novel had not appeared in Iran, but in the United Kingdom; thus, Khomeini's death sentence and the OIC's statement were in effect a demand that Islamic law be extended into the West. Thus, even in 1989, that magical year when freedom celebrated triumph upon triumph in Europe, the OIC claimed the right of censorship over what could be published in the West. It was to become a habit.[13]

The Declaration on Human Rights in Islam was hammered out at a meeting of the OIC in Tehran in December 1989 and signed by 45 foreign ministers in Cairo in August of the following year. The collapse of socialist regimes behind the Iron Curtain suggested that the formerly communist world and the West were now in agreement on a new, joint value system grounded in universal human rights. A new era was heralded for the United Nations. The dictators of the Islamic world reacted by stressing that human rights were a Western invention. Using them as a yardstick of global norms amounted to imperialism. They were supported on that by many non-Muslim countries in Asia.

The Islamic human rights declaration contained no protection of free speech or freedom of religion. There was no safeguarding of the rights of religious minorities, women's rights, or the principle of equality before the law. As a political instrument, it was engineered to deflect criticism of human rights violations, such as using the death sentence against apostates; it was also a way of justifying the punishment of dissidents and religious minorities on the grounds of their offense against Islam. Sharia became the only legitimate source of citizens' rights, and any previous agreements to human rights covenants were made conditional on their lack of conflict with Sharia.

The Declaration was meant as both a sword and a shield. It would defend the Islamic world against criticism from without and would strike out at freethinkers from within. Although the UN's Universal Declaration of Human Rights was meant to ensure the spread of civil rights throughout the world, the aim of the OIC's Declaration on Human Rights in Islam was to make sure they were undermined.

It wasn't easy for the OIC in the early 1990s to get across the idea that there was a set of specifically Islamic human rights, but that changed with time. Russia and China began once again to see themselves as counterweights to the West; power gradually shifted away from the United States and Europe toward Asia. Support in the UN General Assembly for the European Union's stance on human rights dropped from more than 70 percent in the 1990s to under 50 percent in 2008.

In 2010, the Freedom House think tank, which compiled and published annual reports documenting the state of freedom in the world, noted that on the global level, freedom of the press had suffered for the eighth year in succession, mostly in the former Soviet Union, so that only one citizen in six in the world could claim to live in a country that enjoyed a free press.[14] That same year, the human rights organization Article 19 noted that human rights were under pressure even in Western Europe. Several countries had seen violence and threats against journalists. Anti-terrorist legislation had constrained freedom of speech and made it more difficult for the press to protect its sources. Governments blocked Internet access to certain kinds of information. A number of countries maintained violation codes making it an offense to insult the honor of the armed forces, the nation, the president, members of the royal family, public institutions, courts of law, and even deceased persons. In Germany, a total of 193,617 criminal cases were brought in 2008 alone involving one or another form of defamation, and with British laws particularly amenable to cases of libel, the United Kingdom became a locus of so-called libel tourists: wealthy individuals of doubtful repute seeking to silence critical media, journalists, and scholars.[15]

Meanwhile, in Geneva, the OIC continued to work to globalize censorship. First in the UN Commission on Human Rights and later in the Human Rights Council and General Assembly, the OIC pushed through resolutions condemning defamation of religion and urging UN members to adopt legislation to outlaw it.

There was something symbolic about the OIC doing that in the city in which Calvin and his tyrants of piety imposed the death sentence on Servetus for offending God and challenging the existing order. Only a few kilometers separate the Plateau de Champel where Servetus was burned in 1553 and the Palais des Nations, where the OIC hectors the UN Council of Human Rights and garners support for laws criminalizing speech considered offensive to God, punishing it, in several instances, by death.

In 2010, Ann Elizabeth Mayer, a human rights lawyer and author of a standard work on human rights and Islam, looked back on the resolutions that had been initiated by the OIC and adopted by the UN Commission on Human Rights and the Human Rights Council from 1999 to 2009.[16] Her findings are not encouraging. The OIC has shifted from defending an Islamic version of human rights to attacking the West for supposed rights violations. When the EU states decline to punish people who allegedly offend religion—as in the Cartoon Crisis—the OIC sees that as violating the rights of Muslims. Some European opinion makers concur, seeing Muslims as "the new Jews" of Europe: a persecuted minority deserving of special protection from scorn, mockery, and ridicule. At the same time, they close their eyes to the OIC's refusal of that logic when it persecutes minorities and freethinkers in its homelands.

The OIC has learned to adapt its demands to modern human rights jargon. It no longer demands the protection of Islam as such. Instead, it pleads protection of Muslims, individually and collectively, and refers to Article 20, paragraph 2, of the UN Covenant on Civil and Political Rights, which defines situations in which countries should constrain freedom of speech.

Thus, in an interview given to *Jyllands-Posten* in 2008, OIC Secretary General Ekmeleddin Ihsanoglu categorically rejected the notion that the OIC had anything against criticism of religion.

"We have no problem with that. But when freedom of speech is abused in order to demonize and ridicule, with the intention of sowing seeds of hatred against a group of people or citizens, that is when the problems begin," Ihsanoglu said. "What we are saying is that incitement to hatred should not be permitted as long as this specific action comprises a crime . . . under Article 20 of the Covenant on Civil and Political Rights of 1966, which obliges governments at the national level to take measures against incitement of religious hatred."[17]

In Ihsanoglu's view, European countries violated universal human rights when they refused to criminalize the Muhammad cartoons. It was, he maintained, in contravention of international human rights legislation.

The precise wording of Article 20, paragraph 2, is hardly as broad as Ihsanoglu claims, though the phrasing is vague and subject to interpretation. In Europe, Ihsanoglu's vision of it is shared by many lawyers, politicians, and activists who support a far wider definition of racism. The paragraph reads as follows: "Any advocacy of national, racial or religious hatred that constitutes incitement to discrimination, hostility or violence shall be prohibited by law."[18]

The wording raises several questions, though there is little consensus about their answers. How are we to define hate speech, and how do we decide when hate speech begins to incite discrimination and hostility? What is meant by hostility anyway? In 2009, the European Council commissioned a human rights lawyer to prepare a handbook of hate speech.[19] The work ascertains that there is not a single approved definition, although the notion is widespread in the jurisprudence of the European countries. In a number of rulings, the European Court of Human Rights has referred to hate speech as "all forms of expression which spread, incite, promote, or justify hatred based on intolerance (including religious intolerance)."[20] As such, it might on the face of it seem easy to agree with the OIC's view that Kurt Westergaard's depiction of Muhammad with a bomb in his turban constitutes incitement to religious hatred and promotes discrimination against Muslims.

The basic problem in all definitions is that recipients of the speech are granted wide powers to decide whether it constitutes an expression of intolerance. That power turns the concept of tolerance on its head. Initially, tolerance was the ability to accept speech that one disliked. It meant that people of different faiths and nonbelievers could live in peace together, accepting that one's neighbor preached a faith that saw itself as superior to one's own. The imperative of tolerance applied to the person who heard the speech rather than to the speaker.

Today, we make demands of the speaker. The territory in which we combat discrimination and inequality has become so broad that almost any speech may be branded intolerant or racist. That is how *Jyllands-Posten*'s publishing of the Muhammad cartoons was condemned as intolerant, while threats, violence, and calls for them to be banned were interpreted as the perhaps regrettable, though in principle wholly understandable, reactions of a persecuted minority. Rarely was such intolerance called by its proper name.

Article 20, paragraph 2, was adopted in 1953 as part of the process of negotiating the International Covenant on Civil and Political Rights. The majority of the Western democracies voted against it, citing its vagueness and the accompanying risk of abuse. Several predicted that governments would be able to use it to silence critical voices, and Eleanor Roosevelt, who had presided over work on the Universal Declaration of Human Rights, warned against the wording's lack of distinction between words and actions.[21] Today, Article 20, paragraph 2, has become a trump card in the hands of the OIC, Russia, China, and other countries wishing to safeguard themselves against criticism on human rights.

Besides reference to Article 20, paragraph 2, the OIC also invested much effort into linking offense against religious belief with racism. Secretary General Ihsanoglu put it this way in his interview with *Jyllands-Posten*:

> We believe that incitement to religious hatred is a new form of racism. Western institutions concerning themselves with Islamophobia agree that Islamophobia is worse than racial discrimination. In practice they may be difficult to distinguish, but when Muslim immigrants on

a daily basis are subject to physical and moral attacks in Western countries it is the negative result of a campaign of hatred that undermines the human rights of those Muslim victims.[22]

The OIC wanted relevant conventions to be rewritten to ensure that no one would be able to invoke freedom of speech when defaming a religion; moreover, it wanted the obligation of conventions banning racism also to encompass insults to religion.

Equating racism and defamation of religion would oblige EU member states to introduce laws that would make the Muhammad cartoons a punishable offense. Moreover, would it be defamatory of Islam for a Muslim individual to leave the faith? Could demands on Muslims to obey secular laws in the West be perceived as defamation of the Muslim faith? All that may seem far-fetched, and most of us would undoubtedly be hard-pressed to imagine any of it happening in Europe. Yet as Kenan Malik observed, if Khomeini's fatwa on Rushdie had within two decades become so internalized by Europeans that consensus now deemed that under no circumstances should Islam be defamed, then perhaps there were no limits to what fundamentalists could achieve.[23]

In 2009, the OIC tabled a proposal in a committee of the UN to make defamation of religion part of international human rights legislation. It was a proposal that repeated word for word the content of legislation recently passed by the Irish government, which made it a crime to be "grossly abusive or insulting in relation to matters held sacred by any religion, thereby causing outrage among a substantial number of the adherents of that religion."[24] In a decade, the OIC had turned criticism of Islamic human rights into a movement that took its point of departure from international agreements and the language of Western human rights movements. Instead of distancing itself from universal human rights as an expression of Western cultural imperialism, the

OIC now ostensibly subscribed to the idea of such rights and had turned them on the West.[25] It was a skillful maneuver. The only thing Europe can hope for, as one British diplomat in Geneva put it in the autumn of 2009, is to maintain the status quo. Any hope of progress in the struggle for human rights around the world is, in the view of many observers, little more than a pipe dream.

How seriously should we take those OIC attempts? Are the many resolutions more than declarations of intent? Are they merely words on paper with no binding effect? Although they may be regrettable and detrimental to the image of the United Nations, many hold that they cannot seriously endanger freedom of speech and of religion in countries whose citizens enjoy full civic rights.

Ann Mayer is of the opinion that the OIC offensive in the UN should be taken seriously, and people working for nongovernmental organizations in Geneva with whom I spoke in the period following the Cartoon Crisis share her view. They point out that the UN system has now assimilated the concept of defamation of religion. Resolutions are not merely words on paper but documents that are acted on. Reports are compiled in which concepts and wordings are repeated and reiterated. Conferences are organized, recommendations are made, and plans of action are prepared.

According to Ann Mayer, from 1999 to 2009, the OIC succeeded in creating the impression that the world is under an obligation to combat defamation of religion. The concept is well on its way to becoming an accepted principle of international human rights law.[26] So when Denmark and other liberal democracies in the not-too-distant future speak out in the UN and reject defamation of religion as a principle at odds with the right of free speech, the UN will, with reference to a new convention, dismiss that criticism as defending a specifically Western version of human rights having little bearing on universal principles.

After World War II, a coalition of countries led by the Soviet Union exploited the Nazis' genocide of the Jews to gain UN support for including severe constraints on freedom of speech in both the Covenant on Civil and Political Rights and the Convention on the Elimination of All Forms of Racial Discrimination. It meant that the distinction between racist and discriminatory speech and actions was blurred. The oppressive regimes that voted for those constraints were subsequently able to employ them to justify laws used to incarcerate champions of national independence in the former Soviet Union. The OIC exploited the Muhammad cartoons in much the same way, to demand that the UN sanction further restrictions on free speech. Insisting on assigning rights to cultures and religions at the expense of the individual, those efforts overturned all previous understanding of the notions of human rights.

Diplomats skilled in the language of international rights and the rhetoric of grievance demanded that the world crack down on Islamophobia—an ambiguous concept that had wormed its way into UN documents, covering a hodgepodge of legitimate criticism of religion and illegitimate discrimination against Muslims.[27] They called for imposing sanctions on those who offended religious sentiments, while in their own countries, courts punished rape victims for extramarital sex; persecuted Bahá'is (Iran), Ahmadi Muslims and Christians (Pakistan), Shia Muslims (Saudi Arabia), and Copts (Egypt); and sentenced apostate Muslims to death and imposed long prison terms for blasphemy.[28]

But to see all that, you had to actually go to the countries in question. If you did, it soon became apparent that governments and religious movements in the Islamic world viewed criticism by Westerners of the Muhammad cartoons as indirect support for their continued violations against freethinkers, dissidents, minorities, and other deviants—because they all defamed religion.

By attacking the Muhammad cartoons and the media in which they were reprinted, those Western leaders were trying to keep the peace. But it revealed a simplified view of the Islamic world. Muslim countries are by no means homogenous entities; all include religious minorities. And even in the Islamic world, there were different views on the Muhammad cartoons. I myself received numerous messages from Muslims in Iran who were supportive of the cartoons' publication.

Westerners often forget that Muslim communities in the West are diverse. When the media asked imams to speak out on behalf of the Muslim community, regardless of whether or not they spoke for a majority, important voices were being ignored. That approach polarized issues to the benefit of the radicals; it was provincial and narrow-minded, and the consequences were serious. There wasn't a thought for what freedom of speech meant to those whose views were never heard.

I would like to relate five stories from various countries. All of them demonstrate how claims of wounded religious feelings are used to persecute critics, dissidents, and other freethinkers. Critics of the Muhammad cartoons owe us an explanation of how they intend to maintain a distinction between their condemnation of the cartoons and the speech, images, and actions those five people discuss. Personally, I find it difficult.

The universal rule of law is not right around the corner. But in a world where barriers are falling and increasing numbers of individuals of different religions, cultures, and ethnic backgrounds live alongside one another under the same laws, the question of whether the OIC's "human rights" declaration will prevail is by no means irrelevant.

The events in the five examples—each its own Cartoon Crisis—took place in Egypt, Russia, India, Afghanistan, and Pakistan. There is no doubt that today, religious pressure on free speech comes especially from the Islamic countries and from Muslims in the West, though not exclusively so. I have included two cases, from India and Russia, illustrating attacks by militant Hindus and

Christians on the right of free speech; the exact same arguments and demands are put forward as in cases involving Islam.

Abdul Kareem Nabeel Suleiman

In 2003, in Egypt's second-largest city, Alexandria, a play titled *Once I Was Blind, Now I See* was performed in a Christian Coptic church. It revisited a Bible story about Jesus healing a blind man and involved a young Christian who decides to convert to Islam. After much anguish, he discovers that his new religion doesn't work for him, whereupon he returns like the prodigal son to his original Christian faith; but when Islamists learn of the man's decision to renounce their religion, they become enraged and try to kill him on grounds of apostasy.

Initially, the play caused not a ripple of reaction among Muslims of the city. But two years later, when it was released on DVD, Islamists of the Muslim Brotherhood in Alexandria took such offense that they resorted to immediate action. Coptic spokesmen emphasized that the play was in no way meant as an attack on Islam as such, but was more a comment targeting religious extremism as it begets intolerance and violence. Nonetheless, angry protesters of the Muslim Brotherhood attacked the church in which the play had originally been performed. They set cars alight in the Christian Maharram Beh neighborhood and plundered Christian shops. Riots went on for several days, and news reports suggested 3 were killed and more than 100 injured, among them an elderly nun who was stabbed in front of her church.

Those events were witnessed by a 21-year-old Muslim by the name of Abdul Kareem Nabeel Suleiman, later to be known by his pen name, Kareem Amer. Kareem was a law student at the world's leading Islamic university, Al-Azhar, whose main campus was in Cairo. From a strongly religious family, he had also attended Al-Azhar's preparatory school. His main interest was in natural science, and his preferred subject had been biology.

Gradually, Kareem had become more critical of the worldview he encountered at the university. To Kareem's mind, the distinction made by religion between believers and infidels was a source of division and unrest leading to unnecessary tensions and hostility toward non-Muslims. The day after the riots had subsided, October 22, 2005, a shocked and distressed Kareem wrote as follows on his blog:

> The Muslims have taken off their masks and shown their true hateful face, and they have demonstrated to the world that they are at the top of their brutality, inhumanity, and pillage. They have clearly revealed their very worst features and have shown that in dealing with others they are ungoverned by any moral codes.[29]

He continued:

> Some may think that the actions of the Muslims do not represent Islam and bear no relation to the teachings of Islam that were brought to us fourteen centuries ago by Muhammad, but the truth is that their actions cannot be separated from the original teachings of Islam whereby believers were urged to deny others, to hate them, and to kill them and take their property.

He concluded:

> Before you put on trial the people who are responsible for the crimes that occurred on this Black Friday in Maharram Beh, you should first put on trial the foul teachings that prompted them to go on a rampage of stealing and plundering and looting. Put Islam on trial and sentence it and its symbols and execute them figuratively so as to make sure that what happened yesterday will never be repeated again. For as long as Islam exists on this planet, all your efforts to end wars and disputes and upheavals will fail, because Islam's filthy hand will be found behind every catastrophic event to befall humanity.

251

It was a powerful and impassioned broadside. If anyone in Europe had expressed his opinions in the same way as Kareem, he would have been branded an Islamophobe—someone with a pathological fear of Islam. He might have been reported to the police for hate speech: speaking ill of a minority on account of religious faith. Others would have defended Kareem's right to express himself in a democratic society, though by no means would they necessarily have been in agreement with his opinions. Still others would have declared themselves in complete agreement and characterized his description as a precise and sober analysis of reality.

How was Kurt Westergaard's drawing—coming as it did in the wake of 9/11 and the terrorist attacks that took place in London in July 2005—any different from Kareem's shocked and scathing comments on the Alexandria riots in October that same year? One very major difference was that Westergaard's cartoon was a form of speech protected by law in Denmark, whereas Kareem ended up in jail. Three days after posting the comment on his blog, police pulled in Kareem for interrogation and detained him for 12 days. Following his release, he continued to speak out against Islam, against Al-Azhar (from which he was expelled in the spring of 2006), and against Egyptian President Hosni Mubarak. Al-Azhar, he claimed, was a breeding ground for terrorists, where, as part of the curriculum, students were taught to hate freethinkers.

Kareem also criticized the fact that the university would not admit Christians, though it was funded by all Egyptian taxpayers, and voiced dissatisfaction with its segregation of men and women, which meant female students were excluded from certain subjects.[30] In November 2006, Kareem was arrested again, and in February 2007, he was sentenced to four years in prison for the things he had written on his blog: three years for having defamed Islam and one year for slander against President Mubarak. Kareem's father, a retired teacher of mathematics, disowned his son two days before the ruling and urged the court to judge him in accordance with Islamic law. The court gave Kareem three days to repent his contempt of Islam; his father voiced the view that if he declined, Kareem should be executed. "They turned disapproval into libel and slander, and they took criticism of a terrorist ideology to be defamation of religion," Kareem later said.[31]

Was there anyone in Egypt besides the Copts prepared to defend Kareem? Fortunately, yes there was; support came from unexpected quarters. Two Muslim women set up a website at freekareem.org. Although making it clear that they disagreed with his views on Islam, they nevertheless insisted on defending his right to say what he believed. Here, then, were Muslims who fully lived up to that Enlightenment belief many in Europe seemingly had forgotten: I disapprove of what you say, but I will defend to the death your right to say it.

It was people like Kareem whom Egypt and the other OIC members had in mind when they sought UN support for punishing those who defame Islam.

Yuri Samodurov

From the mouth of the Nile, we now turn north to Moscow, where Yuri Samodurov, director of the city's Sakharov Museum, found himself involved in two cases concerning defamation of religion.

Following a visit by a group of men to the Sakharov Museum in January 2003, the word "blasphemy" was found scrawled on one of the gallery walls. It was clearly aimed at an exhibition titled *Caution, Religion!* Among the works on display was Alexander Kosolapov's depiction of Christ with a Coca-Cola logo and the words, "This is my blood." Another was a sculptural installation by Alina Gurevich representing a church composed entirely of empty vodka bottles. Disgruntled visitors to the exhibition had already sprayed paint on several works and vandalized others with knives and an axe. A quick-thinking custodian managed to close off the exit before the perpetrators had time to get away, and they were quickly arrested by police. The exhibition had been running for only three days; only 20 people had seen it.

"As the owner of the work, I am upset," said Alexander Kosolapov who had emigrated from the Soviet Union in 1975 to settle in New York, where he had made a name for himself as a leading representative of so-called Sots Art, mixing sacred Soviet motifs with icons of Western pop culture. Following the demise of the Soviet Union, he began to employ religious and national rather than Soviet symbols, which were no longer as provocative as they used to be. "Still, as an artist I am proud. I think the action adds value to my art, since it still is able to provoke such strong reactions," he added in a comment to a Russian art publication.[32]

An investigation was launched. Four of the six activists, who all belonged to Moscow's Russian Orthodox Church, were released without further charges, despite having been caught red-handed inside the gallery. A charge of vandalism was brought against the remaining two, only to be dropped on the grounds that the men could not be held responsible for their actions. They had been provoked by blasphemous and offensive artwork and had in fact probably prevented a crime rather than committing one. The judge justified the decision as follows: "These Russian Orthodox faithful were shocked, and that is neither exaggeration nor metaphor. . . . The theory of frustration and aggression explains the subsequent aggressive behavior of these religious people following their visit to the exhibition; they reacted with frustration to the exhibited works' destructive sociocultural effect."[33]

Thus, perpetrators were transformed into victims, victims into perpetrators. The distinction between critical words and violent actions, between a picture and a violent reaction, between tolerance and intolerance, civilization and barbarity, dissolved. That is what happens if you fail to grasp the distinction between words and actions.

The reasoning of the Russian judge brings to mind the Pakistani diplomat who, following the terrorist attack on the Royal Danish Embassy in Islamabad in 2008, accused *Jyllands-Posten* of being responsible for the attack; because the Muhammad cartoons had been so offensive, any violent reaction was the newspaper's fault.

The case against the Russian Orthodox vandals took place in an atmosphere of intimidation and coercion on the part of religiously and nationalistically inclined writers, filmmakers, and artists, such as Vasiliy Belov, Valentin Rasputin, Nikita Mikhalkov, and Ilya Glazunov, all of them well-known artists outside Russia. Angry protesters demonstrated outside the courthouse, demanding all charges be dropped. A petition was started in support of the iconoclasts. The case took a new turn when three victims of the attack—gallery director Yuri Samodurov, a curator, and an artist—found themselves under investigation, while the vandals, now released, were accorded the role of victims. The Russian Orthodox Church urged parliament to step in to ensure that the faithful in the future would not risk being confronted by such offensive and blasphemous exhibitions. And in March 2005, the Russian parliament raised the penalty for inciting religious hatred from three to five years in prison.

The debate between supporters and critics of the exhibition raised a number of fundamental questions. What kind of speech is entitled to protection, and who draws the line? Are religious sentiments special, or can religion be treated in the same way as other ideologies? What does it mean to defame a religion? Who in this particular case personified tolerance and who intolerance, and how far does tolerance go?

The result: in the spring of 2005, Samodurov and the exhibition curator were found guilty of "inciting religious hatred." The court ruled the exhibition to be "openly insulting and blasphemous."[34] The third person accused, a female artist, was acquitted. (She later committed suicide in Germany.) Samodurov and his curator were each fined 100,000 rubles (around $3,600). The intervention of a highly placed friend managed to ease them out of prison sentences.

The case prompted Elena Bonner, widow of human rights champion Andrei Sakharov, to comment that the whole affair had discredited the Russian Orthodox Church in much the same way as the fatwa against Salman Rushdie had discredited Islam. It demonstrated that the Church sought to take on the role of moral arbiter and censor in matters of ideology that had formerly been occupied by the Soviet Communist Party. And it showed, too, how Christians in the space of only some 20 years had gone from being a persecuted minority in Russia to becoming a powerful institution ready to oppress and persecute others.[35]

Samodurov and the museum's curator, Lyudmila Vasilevska-ya, appealed their sentences to the European Court of Human Rights, which in the spring of 2010 decided to adjourn examination pending further information.[36] It was a decision that gave rise to considerable concern. Particularly interesting was the reference made to the court's support of the British film censor's ban on a 19-minute short, *Vision of Ecstasy*, in 1989. That film contained no dialogue. It explored Saint Teresa of Avila's sexual fascination for the crucified Christ, culminating in images of the sexually aroused nun's caressing of his body and lips.

The film and the ban slapped on it triggered heated debate in the United Kingdom at the time, with prominent figures Fay Weldon and Salman Rushdie lending public support to director Nigel Wingrove.[37] But in 1996, the European Court of Human Rights upheld the ban, declaring that although freedom of speech was fundamental to a democratic society, it was a freedom accompanied by duties and responsibilities, among them "a duty to avoid as far as possible an expression that is, in regard to objects of veneration, gratuitously offensive to others and profane."[38] In other words, Wingrove's right of free speech extended only to the point where the Christian faithful considered their sentiments to be offended. No wonder Muslims were surprised that the Muhammad cartoons could not be outlawed.

The trial of Samodurov and his curator made it easy to grasp why Russia consistently voted for OIC proposals in the UN condemning defamation of religion. The judgment ran to some 40 pages and contained analyses of selected works from the vandalized exhibition, among them Alexander Kosolapov's Coca-Cola ad featuring Christ and the words "This is my blood":

> The work is clearly offensive and defamatory. . . . Mockery of Christian ritual, and in particular of the Russian Orthodox Church and the Gospel, is manifest. The work has a deliberately shocking, provocative nature, since it consciously compares what is sacred and revered with that which is ordinary and vulgar. Thus, its originator deliberately provokes in the viewer a hostile reaction, an aggressive action on religious foundation, and incites religious hatred.[39]

It was the same logic used by Danish comedian Anders Matthesen and filmmaker Erik Clausen in claiming that Muslims were unable to react to the Muhammad cartoons in any way other than with violence; therefore *Jyllands-Posten* itself was to blame when targeted by terrorists.

In the spring of 2003, Yuri Samodurov publicly defended *Caution, Religion!* in an article.[40] It was an impassioned expression of his concern for what would happen if society bowed down to the kind of grievance fundamentalism that had been used to justify vandalism of the exhibited artwork. He warned against restrictions on the right of individuals to address religious symbols in science, film, journalism, visual art, theater, and other fields:

> This would entail an attack on all institutions of society and culture: museums, galleries, publishing houses,

newspapers, universities, political parties, and so on. If we were to welcome such constraints, would Russian museums then be able to put on exhibitions dedicated to the Gulag and documenting the crimes of the Soviet Union? Would Russian publishers be allowed, in Moscow and Kazan, to publish books and organize conferences on the norms of Sharia law as seen from the viewpoint of modern Western legal systems? Would exhibitions of works of art dealing with the Russian Orthodox Church and its clergy be permitted? Would schoolchildren be permitted to study Lermontov's *The Demon* and Goethe's *Faust*? Would a film such as 'Andrei Rublev' even be conceivable?

Samodurov was describing a society in which grievance fundamentalism is consistently practiced—where nothing meaningful can be uttered, since any speech of any sort may potentially be characterized as offensive to some person or group. His queries reminded me of a similar list of 60 questions that philosophy professor Frederik Stjernfeldt asked the public in the Danish weekly *Weekendavisen* in 2006 in an attempt to gain an overview of the code of behavior that had emerged following the Cartoon Crisis: "May Jesus be caricatured? May Disney's 'Aladdin' still be distributed? May Human Rights Watch continue to publish its reports on violations of human rights in Muslim countries?" Stjernfeldt emphasized that his questions were by no means intended to be read as ironic.[41]

While Samodurov awaited the European Court of Human Rights' decision, he found himself embroiled in a new and similar case. In 2006, he was contacted by art historian Andrei Yerofeyev of the Tretyakov Gallery, who specialized in modern and contemporary Russian art. Yerofeyev had created a collection of some 3,000 works. Although many had been exhibited at home and abroad, a considerable number had still not been shown in any Russian gallery.

Censorship and self-censorship had not disappeared with the collapse of the Soviet Union. When religion regained a dominant social position in the wake of communism, many galleries were reticent to display works that used religious symbols in contexts other than those prescribed by the Church. The public was still suspicious of and confused by modern art, and many works were categorized as unsuitable for exhibition in public museums. So Yerofeyev proposed that the Sakharov Museum put on an exhibition highlighting "forbidden art." Samodurov was enthusiastic, believing it could kick off a debate on censorship and self-censorship in the Russian museum and gallery world.

Thus, March 2007 saw the opening of *Forbidden Art—2006*. Fourteen artists—13 individuals and 1 group—were represented by 23 works, among them an installation by Ilya Kabakov, paintings by Mikhail Roshal-Fedorov and Alexander Kosolapov, and caricatures by Vyacheslav Sysoev, whose drawings had cost him two years in a labor camp in the mid-1980s. The exhibition spanned the period from 1966 to 2005 and according to Yerofeyev deliberately excluded works that could be construed as directly offensive. One painting showed a Russian icon with black caviar where the sacred image should be and a caption asking, "Have you eaten caviar lately?" Another depicted Jesus on the cross, his countenance obliterated by the face of Vladimir Lenin and the hammer and sickle; a third showed a Russian general raping a rank-and-file soldier and the words "Long Live Russia." Viewers saw the works only through small peepholes.

"This is not an exhibition about art, it is an exhibition about exhibitions. It speaks neither about sex nor religion. In fact, it's not about anything, except for a new and highly dangerous trend of fear and anxiety," Yerofeyev explained.[42]

Forbidden Art—2006 escaped vandalism but became instead the object of fierce criticism in the media. Demonstrations outside the museum called for a crackdown. Elena Bonner, who had defended Samodurov and the *Caution, Religion!* exhibition when it was attacked in 2003, distanced herself from *Forbidden Art—2006*, urging the museum's governing board to close it down and opining that it ran counter to Sakharov's legacy. She went so far as to call it an attack on the humanism and human dignity that her late husband had championed in his confrontations with the Soviet regime.[43]

The chairman of the Board of Governors—Sergei Kovalev, the grand old man of the Soviet human rights movement—dismissed Bonner's charge. He noted that Russia's national poet Aleksandr Pushkin had written poems so openly blasphemous that modern champions of a ban on sacrilege would have to ban his work and suggested organizing a conference on the boundaries of artistic freedom and the right of blasphemy. Copies of the exhibition's most controversial works could be employed as arguments for and against.[44]

The board decided to continue the exhibition as planned, though Samodurov would later be forced to leave his position as director. In August 2008, a case was brought against him and curator Andrei Yerofeyev, who in the intervening period had been sacked by the Tretyakov Gallery for his part in the controversial exhibition. In July 2010, the two men were found guilty of inciting religious hatred and abusing their positions of authority to damage the dignity of the religious faithful. The prosecution had called for three years of imprisonment, but Samodurov and Yerofeyev "got away with" fines of 200,000 rubles and 150,000 rubles, respectively (roughly $7,000 and $5,500).

It is worth noting that Russian human rights groups had for years been citing Article 282 of the Russian Penal Code concerning incitement to religious, racial, or ethnic hatred; but they had done so in the context of frequent racist and anti-Semitic outbursts by politicians and other public figures in the Russian media. Here, the law was instead exploited to protect thugs who justified vandalism by reference to wounded religious sentiments. Again, legislation outlawing defamatory speech ended up being used counter to its intention.

Maqbool Fida Husain

In the spring of 2010, India's greatest living painter, Maqbool Fida Husain, accepted an offer of citizenship from the tiny Gulf state of Qatar. It was a decision that once and for all put an end to his dream of returning to his homeland; the culmination of 15 years of harassment, vandalism, persecution, court cases, and death threats issuing from grievance fundamentalists who had forced the then 91-year-old artist into exile in another Gulf state, Dubai, one of the seven emirates making up the United Arab Emirates.

Husain, a Muslim, had at various stages of his career created a number of works depicting naked deities of the Hindu mythology. A visit to any Hindu temple provides ample evidence of how often sex is depicted in the Hindu tradition. Hinduism encompasses a wealth of deities and many different scriptures to guide the individual's way, and the relationship between God and the believer is a matter for the individual. Acceptance of diversity and tolerance are widespread.

According to Indian-born journalist and writer Salil Tripathi,[45] all that changed when the Indian authorities began to shift the principles of the secular foundation of the state. The initial aim was to accommodate minorities, but the steps they took opened an avenue to the militant Hindus of India's majority population. In 1986, following a court ruling in favor of a Muslim woman that angered many Muslim men, the Indian government passed legislation depriving Muslim women of the right to alimony following divorce. In the view of the Supreme Court, that act was against the secular basis of the Indian Constitution, but the government ignored its opinion.

Two years later, India became the first country to ban Salman Rushdie's novel *The Satanic Verses*. As Tripathi sees it, the government was trying to appease extremists. It went on to censor newspapers, films, books, plays, visual art, and all manner of expression, and matters only snowballed. Calls for censorship were issued not only by religious and ethnic groups but also by professional groups like the police and lawyers, who protested a film in which a journalist told his attorney wife that all lawyers were liars. (The police also complained about their portrayal in a movie.) In 1989, a businessman demanded a ban on a film he felt would ignite tensions between Hindus and Muslims. Christians called on the authorities to cancel a play based on Nikos Kazantzakis's novel *The Last Temptation of Christ*. Grievance fundamentalism was allowed to run amok at the expense of secular principles and freedom of speech.

Militant Hindus were quick to exploit the situation. Every time the government appeased another minority, the militant Hindus claimed their identity was being damaged. In the first 40 years after Indian independence, Hindu nationalists and militants had been isolated and occupied a marginal position on the political spectrum, but from the mid-1980s, their profile rose hugely. The nationalist Bharatiya Janata Party became the country's biggest political party and in 1998, it came to power for the first time as part of a coalition government.

Militant Hindu attacks on Maqbool Fida Husain began in 1996, when the magazine *Vichar Mimansa* ran an article about him and his work, accompanied by one of his sketches of a naked Hindu goddess. Court cases were brought against him in eight different cities for causing affront to Hindu sentiments; at one point, he faced 1,200 lawsuits. A gallery planning a major retrospective of his work was plundered, and police decided to arrest him for disturbing the peace.

In September 2008, India's Supreme Court dismissed five cases that had been brought against Husain on account of a painting showing India as a naked woman, *Bharat Mata* (*Mother India*). However, his lawyers told him there was little chance he could return to India without being arrested.

Husain's story was remarkable. Not only was he acknowledged as one of India's greatest living artists; his dilemma demonstrated clearly that "speech" that would have raised hardly an eyebrow only a decade before was now met with outrage. The attacks on Husain, and the authorities' handling of the situation, constituted, in Salil Tripathi's view, an admission of India's failure as a secular democracy.

In India, as in Europe, laws restrict free speech in order to protect sentiments, identity, dignity, the public order, and so on. Article 295 of the Penal Code prohibited offending religious sentiments; Article 153 made it illegal to disturb social harmony and engender animosity between groups on grounds of religion, race, birthplace, residence, and language. The two provisions meant that a tidal wave of charges could be brought against writers, visual artists, filmmakers, historians, and journalists. The Indian state often opted to step in preventively and ban works it believed could be offensive to one or another group of society.

Such restrictions created a climate in which intolerance was increasingly cultivated. Militant Hindus got away with attacking galleries, destroying mosques, raping and killing Muslims, withdrawing books from sale, and demanding censorship of historical portrayals that did not accord with their ideals. In 2008, they called for a ban on the Academy Award–winning film *Slumdog Millionaire*, which they claimed showed Hindus in a negative light. Two points of grievance were highlighted: a scene in which a boy dressed as the Hindu deity Rama sends a nasty look in the direction of some Muslim children running away from a Hindu–Muslim conflict; and the fact that a Hindu girl falls in love with a Muslim boy.

Only Hindus had the right to relate Hindu history. Only Hindus had the right to paint pictures of a Hindu deity. Husain was a Muslim; therefore, the militant Hindus insisted, if he wanted to paint naked people, let him paint the Muslim prophet Muhammad with his child bride Aisha.

SAYED PERVEZ KAMBAKSH

Although the West spends billions on trying to wipe out a religious dictatorship in Afghanistan and to ensure a new and more democratic order, Afghans may still, even under their new constitution, be sentenced to death for offending Allah.

In the autumn of 2007, Sayed Pervez Kambaksh read an article criticizing Islam's view of women. It was written in Persian by an Iranian blogger living in Germany and bore the title "Verses of the Koran Discriminating against Women." Kambaksh, a 22-year-old university student, highlighted the following statement:

> Muhammad often sinned. Muhammad oppressed women. The Koran portrays women as though they were not of a right mind. Islam is a religion that is against women. The Koran justifies Muhammad's sins. When Muhammad wished for something, he would begin to sing a verse, claiming it came directly from Allah. He forbade everything that did not suit him, and he allowed the things he liked. It's a joke. This is the true face of Islam, Allah, and Muhammad.[46]

Kambaksh, who studied journalism at Balkh University in Mazar-i-Sharif, the principal city of the Uzbek part of northern Afghanistan, was known by friends and teachers alike as a rather rebellious type who enjoyed challenging accepted truths. He photocopied a few selected passages from the article, perhaps adding a couple of comments of his own, then printed out a few copies, which he handed out to fellow students with the aim of starting a discussion—just as he had done on other occasions with works by European philosophers and revolutionaries.[47]

A number of students and teachers expressed distaste for the text Kambaksh had distributed on Muhammad and his view of women. A copy fell into the hands of the security police. Kambaksh was questioned, then released, but someone at the university had photocopied and distributed hundreds of copies of the text with Kambaksh's name on it. Soon campus protests flared. Most believed that Kambaksh himself was the author. The clergy of Mazar-i-Sharif's mosque demanded that the blasphemer be taken to task. Fearing for his safety, Kambaksh stayed away from lectures and sought refuge with friends and acquaintances. In late October 2007, Kambaksh's elder brother, himself a journalist, was contacted by the security police. They wanted Kambaksh to turn himself in, to avoid falling foul of the mob. He did so the following day. After a week of questioning, Kambaksh signed a statement saying that he had copied the article from the Internet, added a couple of lines himself, and handed it out at the university. It was taken to be a confession.

The court case against Sayed Pervez Kambaksh took place in Mazar-i-Sharif on January 22, 2008, in the presence of a prosecutor and three judges. According to Kambaksh, no others were present, and no lawyer or anyone else represented the accused. In his defense, Kambaksh spoke of freedom of speech under the Afghan Constitution, a document that furthermore also incorporates the Universal Declaration of Human Rights. The prosecutor instead invoked the constitution's reference to Islamic law; directly descending from Allah, it was by definition infallible and took precedence over secular, human codes. Article 1 of the Afghan Constitution defines Afghanistan as an Islamic republic; Article 3 states that no law may be counter to Islam.

In the view of the court, Kambaksh's interpretation of freedom of speech was counter to Islam. He was guilty of blasphemy for his spurious interpretation of the Koran, and defamation of the Prophet Muhammad and Islam. He was sentenced to death.

Afghan Minister of Justice Sarwar Danish defended the sentence, commenting in the German weekly *Der Spiegel*:

> He published things attacking our religion. The Koran is held in honor and respected by Muslims. Therefore one cannot expect Muslims to accept unjustified, hostile attacks. Such attacks must be considered to be blasphemy and punished as such. Blasphemy is forbidden all over the world, certainly also in Germany.[48]

Der Spiegel confronted the judge who had imposed the sentence with Article 34 of the Afghan Constitution, which states that freedom of speech is inviolable. He responded: "Freedom of speech is a very valuable thing, but it does not mean that one has the right to offend religious sentiments. To defame a religion, any religion, has nothing to do with freedom of speech. It is a crime."

An adviser to the Afghan minister of culture told the British daily the *Independent* that he supported the verdict, contending that Europe restricted Holocaust denial in much the same way: "Every country has its own limits on freedom. European people have the right to protect their opinions about ideas which are supposed to be dangerous for their civilization."[49]

There was no consensus. The Afghan Journalists Association and the Committee for the Protection of Afghan Journalists were both critical of the verdict. But attempts to invoke international law to support Kambaksh's freedom of speech were complicated by support within the United Nations system for the criminalization of defamatory speech targeting religion.

"The concept of religious defamation serves to legitimize the violation of Kambaksh's freedom of expression, guaranteed under the International Bill of Rights," said Austin Dacey and Colin Koproske in a 2008 report titled *Islam and Human Rights: Defending Universality at the United Nations*. "Islam does not need protection from Pervez Kambaksh. Pervez Kambaksh needs protection from those who speak in its name."[50]

Sayed Pervez Kambaksh was pardoned in secrecy and released in September 2009. The risk of encountering Muslims intent on carrying out his death sentence themselves meant that he was compelled to leave Afghanistan. He now lives somewhere in the West.

YOUNUS SHAIKH

It was October 1, 2000. Pakistani human rights activist Younus Shaikh was taking part in a symposium in the country's capital Islamabad. The subject was tensions between Pakistan and India and the danger of nuclear war. Younus Shaikh was not an invited speaker, but at one point during the proceedings, he asked for the floor and spoke in favor of recognizing the existing demarcation line in the contested region of Kashmir as the border of the two countries. He leveled criticism at the Pakistani government's support of terrorists on the Indian side of the line and warned that if India followed suit, the two countries might end up with a disaster on their hands equivalent in scale to the civil war of 1971 that had led to the secession of East Pakistan and the establishment of Bangladesh as an independent state.

Shaikh's speech enraged an officer of the Pakistani security police. According to Shaikh, threats were made. Two days later, Shaikh, a physician, was fired from his teaching job at the Capital Homeopathic Medical College and was shortly afterward arrested on charges of having offended the Prophet Muhammad and thereby having committed blasphemy, a crime punishable by death.[51]

The charges were not formally motivated by Shaikh's comments during the symposium. A complaint filed by an Islamic movement referred to comments Shaikh allegedly had made during a lecture he had given a few days before, according to a letter signed by 11 students. He was said to have claimed that the Prophet had not been a Muslim before reaching the age of 40, when he received his first revelation from Allah; that the Prophet's parents had not been Muslims, since they died before the birth of Islam; that the Prophet's first marriage at the age of 25 had not had an Islamic marriage contract; and that the Prophet was not circumcised and did not follow the Muslim practice of shaving the hair under his arms or around his genitals, since the tribe to which he belonged never had those customs.[52]

"I had heard from the sermons in the mosques that those who blaspheme deserve to be killed immediately," one student told the *New York Times*.[53] "It was a weakness of faith that we did not do it," he added. Another noted, "Only out of respect, because he was our teacher, did we not beat him to death on the spot."

Shaikh explained that his students had asked about shaving underarm and pubic hair, and that he had answered in accordance with the historical truth that Arabs had not practiced the custom before the arrival of Islam. While he sat detained behind bars, concerned relatives approached the Islamic movement that had filed the complaint, the Movement for the Finality of the Prophet, to plead his repentance. The response of the movement's secretary general, Abdul Wahid Qasmi, was, according to the *New York Times*: "Even if someone is only half-conscious when speaking against the Prophet, he must die. . . . To be sorry now is not enough. Even if a man is sorry, he must die."[54]

Despite procedural errors and several discredited witnesses, the trial continued and in August 2001, Shaikh was sentenced to death. He spent the next two years in solitary confinement in a death cell at Rawalpindi, deprived of books and newspapers and medicine for his diabetes. Following a lengthy appeal process, a Supreme Court judge ruled that the case be retried on grounds of procedural error. However, fears of reprisal at the hands of Islamists meant that no attorney was willing to take on Shaikh's defense. In the end, he had to act as his own lawyer. Friends managed to smuggle law books into the prison so that he could prepare his case.

Eventually, Shaikh was acquitted. He was quietly released in late 2003.[55] Like Pervez Kambaksh, fears that Islamists would take the law into their own hands forced him into hiding, and eventually he fled to Europe, where he was granted asylum in Switzerland. In Pakistan, taking the law into one's hands to mete out "justice" against blasphemers is common. Some are murdered while in prison; others after they are released, or before police officially charge the suspect. Lawyers who defend blasphemers receive death threats, and in the mid-1990s, one retired judge who had acquitted a man of blasphemy charges was gunned down on a public street in Lahore.

People killing alleged blasphemers are rarely convicted in Pakistan. On the contrary, if they are ever reported by witnesses or relatives of the victims, the killers are received as heroes in police stations around the country. In January 2011, Salman Taseer, the governor of Punjab, was killed by one of his security guards. Taseer had publicly called for a pardon for Asia Bibi, a Christian woman convicted for blasphemy, and had criticized Pakistan's draconian blasphemy laws. His killer was hailed as a hero in much of Pakistan. Two months later, the highest-ranking Christian politician in the country, Shahbaz Bhatti, was shot dead as an infidel. Al Qaeda and the Pakistani Taliban claimed responsibility for the killing.[56]

Time and again, the Pakistani government makes it clear that blasphemous utterances are a form of terrorism, and that blasphemy should be punished as severely as terrorist acts. Resorting to acts of terrorism thus becomes the most logical and appropriate response to blasphemy and violation of religious sentiments. But that has not always been the case. What Pakistani novelist Kamila Shamsie calls "the violently offended Muslim"[57] is a recent development, as changing governments scramble to play the Islamic card in attempts to strengthen national identity across ethnic and tribal boundaries, to mobilize voters against archenemy India, and to boost the military against potential rival forces in society. A permanent alliance of military and mosque creates a platform for Islamists and supporters of jihad. The population, which suffers under the violence of the Islamists, is too frightened to challenge them and their ideology for fear of being branded apostates or heretics.

Islamification gained momentum in Pakistan after 1979—the year the Soviets invaded Afghanistan; Iran burst into revolution; and Islamic militants seized the Grand Mosque at Mecca, controlling Islam's holiest place for more than two weeks before being wiped out by security forces in a bloodbath whose toll reached hundreds, perhaps even thousands. But even before that year, Pakistani leader Zulfikar Ali Bhutto branded the minority Ahmadi Muslims as apostates and forbade them to call themselves Muslim. Later, General Zia-ul-Haq made Islamic law the basis of the country's system of justice and education. He widened the scope of blasphemy under the penal code; in 1990, the death penalty was made obligatory in cases of blasphemy.[58]

During British rule, not a single Muslim was convicted of blasphemy in what is today's Pakistan. And from the founding of the Pakistani state in 1947 until Zia-ul-Haq's introduction of new blasphemy codes, fewer than 10 cases were brought to court, and the majority of those ended in acquittal. Not a single case among them was filed by a Muslim against a non-Muslim. Since the mid-1980s, the number of blasphemy cases and extrajudicial killings of alleged blasphemers has exploded. The most conservative figure is around 500 cases, whereas other sources speak of 1,000 and even 5,000 blasphemy cases. Since 1990, 58 Pakistanis who had been charged with blasphemy were murdered by citizens taking the law into their own hands. Many of those charged were Ahmadi Muslims, Christians, Hindus, and Shia. Forced conversion became common. Before Zia-ul-Haq, Pakistan's blasphemy law protected any believer, whereas the new laws protect only Muslims.[59]

Blasphemy counts as one of the most heinous crimes possible in Pakistan, so when celebrated blasphemer Salman Rushdie was honored with a knighthood by Queen Elizabeth for his literary achievements in the summer of 2007, violent protests ensued. Pakistani Religious Affairs Minister Mohammad Ijaz-ul-Haq, son of former dictator Zia-ul-Haq, commented: "If someone blows himself up, he will consider himself justified. How can we fight terrorism when those who commit blasphemy are rewarded by the West?"[60]

It was remarkable insofar as that comment made it clear that in that political culture, blasphemy—a crime without a victim—is on a par with terrorism. That was again apparent when the Danish embassy in Islamabad was the subject of a terrorist attack in 2008, killing 6 and injuring 30 people. Al Qaeda declared that the attack was in retaliation for the Muhammad cartoons, warning that there would be more unless Denmark apologized. So much was predictable. But then Pakistan's ambassador to Denmark accepted the logic of al Qaeda when she blamed *Jyllands-Posten*. "It isn't just the people of Pakistan that feel they have been harassed by what your newspaper has begun. I'd like to know if your newspaper is satisfied with what it has done and what it has unleashed?" Fauzia Mufti Abbas asked a reporter from the paper following the attack.[61]

Those five examples show how many countries exploit the accusation of "defaming religion" in order to silence artists and critical voices. I am willing to concede that during the Cartoon Crisis, *Jyllands-Posten* and I may not have fully contemplated the consequences of our actions. But I do not grasp the difference between the Muhammad cartoons and the violations of which Kareem, Samodurov, Husain, Kambaksh, and Shaikh were accused. I am also dubious that the religious faithful—be they residents of Alexandria, Moscow, Mumbai, Mazar-i-Sharif, Islamabad, or Copenhagen—have a particular right not to be affronted. What would that imply for the rights of nonbelievers? In each of those cases, should we defend the right to offend or the right not to be offended?

Those questions are not intended to be rhetorical. The Muhammad cartoons reveal a number of dilemmas. Some Europeans appear to believe that we should use the distinction between majority and minority to distinguish between those who have the right to offend and those who do not. The Indian example, however, shows what that may precipitate—a majority insisting in the same way as a minority on the right not to be offended, doing so on the basis of the principle that all should be treated equally, and then exploiting that principle as a political weapon. And it raises the question of borders: If critics of the Muhammad cartoons had been consistent in their logic, they should have targeted *Jyllands-Posten* from the moment the cartoons were published in September 2005 until somewhere around the end of January 2006, when they were still mostly a domestic matter. From the moment the issue turned into a global crisis, however, the same critics should by their own logic have defended the new minority, that is, *Jyllands-Posten* and Denmark, against the offended Muslim masses around the world.

The problem with distinguishing between majority and minority is that societies all over the world have become so diverse that every minority will include individuals who in some way are in opposition to the group. If we think of the Muhammad issue as a conflict between a majority and a minority, we leave hanging those Muslims who insist on the right to practice their faith differently from the majority, just as we would continually be needing to second-guess who would be entitled to offend and who would not. Moreover, we would be sowing doubt about the necessity of wording principles concerning the rights of the individual across cultures, nations, religions, races, classes, majorities, and minorities. The idea of universal civil rights would be undermined.

As societies become increasingly multicultural, multiethnic, and multireligious, if we accept the idea that people have a right not to be offended, we will end up with a tyranny of silence, for almost any speech may be deemed offensive. The alternative is to define a minimal set of constraints on freedom of speech necessary for peaceful cohabitation. For me, the line should be drawn at inciting violence, the key issue being a clear and present danger that the speech will be followed by violence.

I believe Europe would be best equipped to cope with future challenges by using something like the First Amendment to the U.S. Constitution, which accords privileged status to freedom of speech. The more diverse a society, the greater the need for diversity of speech. We should amend articles of human rights conventions that seek to criminalize speech that incites hatred but that does not entail a clear and present danger of violence or discrimination. That kind of speech is seldom constructive, but the cost of forbidding it is high.

When I interviewed Salman Rushdie in the spring of 2009, he spoke of the existential and political significance of the right to tell one's own story. Rushdie's words gave me a sense of direction for this book. During the interview, I asked him to recommend three books to my readers; one of them was Kamila Shamsie's novel *Burnt Shadows*. I read it in 2009 while attending a seminar in Paris on immigration and integration. In the world she portrayed, loyalties were tested; betrayal was ambiguous; identities clashed on the battlefield and in residential suburbia. In a way, the novel and the seminar shared a theme: how to cope with diversity and difference. Life presents us with choices and dilemmas. Who are we, who are they, where do we all come from, and where—separately or together—are we going? Can people of different backgrounds, history, and religion live together in peace and harmony? Can we remain true to ourselves without pushing others away? In a world where we all encounter more strangers than ever before, those are the challenges we face.

I interviewed Kamila Shamsie in London in the autumn of 2009. We talked about her novel, and about Rushdie's view that we all have a fundamental, existential right to tell our own story. It was a perspective in which any breach of the right of free speech became not just a political crime, but a violation of human nature. I asked Shamsie if she agreed. She replied:

> One depressing thing about us humans is that we give up using our imagination. We can lose the ability both to create a narrative for our own lives and to understand others. It's strange because we start creating stories at a very early age. Telling stories establishes intimacy. What is my story, and how much do I want to share with you? Which of my stories do I need you to listen to in order for you to understand who I am? So yes, I do agree that it's very fundamental. It touches a profound need to create contact with our surroundings.

I asked if that meant for her that a link existed between the ability to empathize and telling stories.

"I believe there is," she said. "Some people are only interested in telling stories about themselves. But when we start talking about human beings as storytelling creatures, it's just as important to listen to the stories of others."[62]

Her words hit home. Storytelling was what the Cartoon Crisis had been all about: the freedom and the right to tell a story as one saw fit, and the right and ability of others to listen to it. Some had neither the right nor the opportunity to tell their stories because they were subjected to persecution and oppression. Some were frightened to tell their stories because they were fearful of the reactions. Still others told their stories but suffered threats, violence, or loss of liberty. Finally, there were those who had the right and the ability to tell their stories, but who experienced difficulty imagining worlds other than their own, or who just didn't want to listen to stories that made their perception of reality fall apart.

"Empathy" has become something of a buzzword at the beginning of the 21st century; people fling it around to show how good they are. Whenever the champions of goodness want to exclude anyone from the right company, they accuse them of lacking empathy. It's as though they have confused the meanings of "sympathy" and "empathy." To have sympathy for someone means having unconditional solidarity; if you disagree with a person for whom you have sympathy, you often choose to keep quiet about it. The imperative of sympathy follows the logic "either with me or against me." That is the perspective of the grievance fundamentalist. Empathy is different. You put yourself in the position of another and see them as they are, not as they prefer to be seen. It involves both proximity and distance. Being an object of empathy can mean being confronted with unpleasant truths about ourselves.[63]

It is symptomatic of the age in which we live that many people are unable to distinguish between sympathy and empathy. Grievance fundamentalism illustrates why: setting ourselves up as aggrieved victims means gaining an advantage. It's the same confusion regarding the distinction between tolerance and respect, which has been widespread ever since *The Satanic Verses* was published. Semantically, they have been turned on their heads and now serve the mindset of grievance fundamentalism instead of supporting and promoting individual liberty.

Empathy is founded on the notion of one common human nature, entailing rights for all humans, regardless of who and where we are. Among them are freedom of speech, freedom of religion, freedom of movement, the right not to be subjected to torture, and equality before the law. Only a small minority of countries actually uphold those fine principles. Denmark is one. So although many people during the Cartoon Crisis complained that Muslims were being discriminated against in Denmark, the truth is that Muslim citizens are more empowered there than in any Muslim country.

If we accept demands to safeguard particular cultures and religions against criticism, we come close to rejecting the idea of a universal human nature and universal civil rights. We tend toward the claim that humans are unable to understand one another across cultural divides: that belief is the basis of calls for special rights and differential rights, for example, for women or nonbelievers.

I was born and brought up in Denmark, a small liberal democracy that is one of the most stable and tolerant societies in the world, in which citizens enjoy greater freedoms and greater equality than almost anywhere else. That equality is widely apparent, not only in areas such as gender politics or access to education and medical aid but also with regard to freedom of religious exercise, the right to say no to religion, and the liberty to put whatever we think or feel into words, images, or sounds. Looking around the world, I can see that I belong to an extremely privileged group.

Nevertheless, it took people from other parts of the world, where liberty cannot be taken for granted, to teach me to appreciate freedom of speech.

The Soviet human rights movement taught me more about the foundations of freedom and its preconditions than my life and upbringing in one the freest countries in the world. It was a profound discovery that has marked my life. I am grateful to have experienced a totalitarian dictatorship: I was able to see how it intimidated its citizens and to observe individuals insisting on their right to live in freedom and dignity. They refused to submit to the tyranny of silence. And the story had a happy ending: the Soviet state disappeared.

Kamila Shamsie's words about exchanging narratives also affected me in a more personal way. She made me think about my own life and the importance of telling stories and listening to the stories of those closest to me.

The Cartoon Crisis gave me the chance to travel around the world to discuss why the individual's right to tell a story is so important, even if that story should offend and cause sorrow. It helped me reflect on how elements of my own life—people I had met, events I had experienced—shaped my viewpoints on freedom of speech and its perimeters. The process convinced me that no one should have the right to dictate to others what stories they should tell and in what way. That was Salman Rushdie's point. The moment we begin to restrict people's right to tell their story— the moment we begin to monitor and control speech, either to spare the reader discomfort or to safeguard the state—then freedom no longer prevails and from then on, the only question is how much unfreedom we will accept.

If we allow the distinction between words and action to crumble, and we forbid words, not because they incite crime but because they may cause affront, then we have limited our own right to tell a story by giving the listener a say in what stories we may tell and how they may be told. Danger lies that way. For when words run out, violence begins. If we forbid offensive speech, individuals will resort to direct action.

Afterword

We have avenged the Prophet!

Georges Wolinski's grave is blanketed with flowers. Some have begun to fade; others are fresh and fragrant. Many of the people who have come to pay their last respects to the legendary cartoonist have placed pens and pencils by his grave. Here and there, in the midst of the floral tributes, the eye is drawn to the slogan *Je suis Charlie*, white on black. The modest grave is tucked between an overbearing cross in granite and a couple of similarly grandiose statues reminiscent of another era. On a small marble stone, against a gilded background, there is an inscription: *Georges WOLINSKI, 1934–2015*.

The tragedy cannot be expressed more simply.

Wolinski's own humorous and anything-but-sentimental view on life had once prompted him to suggest quite a different fate for his mortal remains. Asked by Parisian daily *Le Monde* a few short years before his violent demise if he feared death, Wolinski dismissed the notion, adding, "I've told my wife to empty my ashes down the toilet so I can look at her ass every day."

Nevertheless, here he lies. Wolinski was buried in the middle of January 2015 in the Montparnasse cemetery on the south side of Paris. Elsewhere in the neat, 200-year-old cemetery lies Elsa Cayat, the psychoanalyst who every other week penned a column for *Charlie Hebdo* called *Le Divan* ("The Couch"). Cayat, too, was among the fatalities when the brothers Chérif and Saïd Kouachi forced their way into the offices of the satirical weekly magazine during an editorial meeting on January 7, 2015, murdering 11 staffers and subsequently gunning down and killing a policeman as they fled. A couple days later, one Jewish employee and three Jewish customers and a police officer were killed by Amedy Coulibaly during a siege at a kosher supermarket in the eastern part of Paris. Both Kouachi brothers and Coulibaly were shot and killed by security forces soon after the siege; all three terrorists claimed allegiance to ISIS or al-Qaeda in Yemen. The latter shortly afterward took responsibility for the attacks, stating that of the 11 names featured on the terrorist organization's "Most Wanted List" of individuals guilty of offending the Prophet Muhammad, only 10 now remained following the murder of *Charlie Hebdo*'s editor-in-chief. Among the names remaining are those of three Danes, including me.

The cemetery in Montparnasse is well known as the final resting place of a host of cultural luminaries, foreign as well as French. Here lie such poets and writers as Charles Baudelaire, Guy de Maupassant, Simone de Beauvoir, Jean-Paul Sartre, and Marguerite Duras, alongside the likes of Samuel Beckett, Susan Sontag, and the great figure of 20th-century Argentinian literature, Julio Cortázar. Now Wolinksi is among them.

A compatriot of Wolinski's from the western part of France has placed at the grave a drawing of a catlike figure flanked by two towers of pencils striving toward the sky. In tears, the figure says, "GEORGES, you inspired me for fifty years, in my drawings and in love. I have lost my elder brother."

I have come to Montparnasse to say goodbye to Georges Wolinski. We met on several occasions, and I appreciated his down-to-earth demeanor and his keen ability to spot hypocrisy in almost any guise. Yet for all his wisecracks, it wasn't hard for me to trace a tinge of melancholy that perhaps was attributable to Wolinski's losing his first wife at a young age. Wolinski and I first met in 2007. As *Jyllands-Posten*'s culture editor, I ran an excerpt of Wolinski's comic book *Merci, Hannukah Harry*, occasioning a joint visit to the annual comics festival at Angoulême in western

France. Wolinski had always said laughter was the shortest route between two people. Now he had been slain because of it.

The attack on *Charlie Hebdo* was a culmination of almost nine years of threats and intimidation by Islamists wishing to exact revenge for the magazine's ostensibly having offended Islam and the Muslim prophet Muhammad. In November 2011, the magazine's editorial offices were the target of an arson attack, when still-unidentified individuals petrol-bombed the premises during the night. That same night, the magazine's website was hit by hackers. These strikes came after *Charlie Hebdo* announced that the Prophet Muhammad would be featured as a "guest editor" of the magazine to mark the occasions of Libya having introduced a constitution based on Sharia law and of an Islamist party having won the first free elections in Tunisia. The front page of the issue, for which the magazine re-dubbed itself *Charia Hebdo*, was a caricature of Muhammad promising 100 lashes to anyone not prepared to die while laughing at the magazine's contents. *Charlie Hebdo* reacted to the petrol bombing with a front page showing a bearded man clad in traditional Muslim dress receiving a passionate kiss from a male cartoonist. The picture was accompanied by the words "Love is stronger than hate." Following the attack, the magazine moved to a new location on the Rue Nicolas-Appert in Paris's 11th arrondissement, where security was much improved, albeit still sorely inadequate in the end.

Ten months later, in September 2012, new caricatures of Muhammad appeared in *Charlie Hebdo* after the U.S. ambassador to Libya and three members of his staff were killed in a rocket attack in Benghazi, Libya, and further attacks had taken place on U.S. embassies in various locations throughout the Middle East and North Africa. Initially, these attacks seemed to have been sparked by a film called *Innocence of Muslims* that had appeared on YouTube and was criticized for blaspheming the Prophet Muhammad. Later, however, it became apparent that the Benghazi attack, which also involved storming and setting fire to the U.S. consulate building, had been anything but spontaneous. Subsequently, the French government endeavored in vain to persuade *Charlie Hebdo* from publishing any more cartoons depicting Muhammad.

At the time, the magazine's editor-in-chief, Stéphane Charbonnier, better known by the pen name of Charb, declared that *Charlie Hebdo* had no option but to continue "scorning, mocking, and ridiculing" Islam until doing so became as banal and uncontroversial as it was in the case of Catholicism. Behind those words lay the idea that one of the functions of religious satire is to keep religious doctrine and institutions in check, thereby ensuring that they not be made sacrosanct and inviolable or not be exploited to gain power or exert social control. Rather, religious satire demands that religious institutions instead be removed from their pedestal whenever they make claims that challenge the secular order or individual liberty. Despite the abolition of France's blasphemy laws in 1791 and the legal separation of church and state in 1905, this struggle between religious doctrine and secularism has carried over into the late 20th and early 21st centuries.

Charlie Hebdo's satire of Islam began in February 2006, during the global crisis ignited by the Muhammad cartoons published by *Jyllands-Posten*. A number of European newspapers had already republished the cartoons, which had quickly become famous, and at France's *Le Soir* the move had cost the managing editor his job.

"I believed we had to run *Jyllands-Posten*'s cartoons as documentation," explained Caroline Fourest when I spoke to her in February 2015 in Paris. "Everyone at [*Charlie Hebdo*] was shocked by the sacking of *Le Soir*'s editor for having republished your cartoons, and you were receiving threats. So, obviously we needed to run the drawings." Fourest was on the staff of *Charlie Hebdo* as a journalist and commentator from 2004 to 2010. Today, she spends most of her time making documentary films and writing books, and when we met she was finishing up an essay about the importance of defending the right to blasphemy.

But *Charlie Hebdo*, home to some of France's best and most popular cartoonists, didn't just rerun *Jyllands-Posten*'s cartoons in February 2006. *Charlie Hebdo* added its own cartoons, among them a front page depicting the Muslim prophet burying his face in his hands and grieving at the caption "It's hard being loved by jerks." The drawing came from the pen of Jean Cabut, who, like Wolinski, was a legend among French newspaper cartoonists and one of those killed in the January 2015 attack. An earlier draft of the front page had come from Wolinski, who imagined *Charlie Hebdo* interviewing Muhammad. Wolinski's take showed a grinning prophet, who exclaims, upon seeing *Jyllands-Posten*'s cartoons, "That's the first time the Danes ever made me laugh!"

According to Fourest, it was important to *Charlie Hebdo* to depict Muhammad as being on the side of secularity: "We talked a lot about that. 'Why do we always let the fanatics lay claim to him?' we argued. And the fact of the matter is that's the way Muhammad is always depicted in *Charlie Hebdo*. He's always been against the fundamentalists."

I first visited *Charlie Hebdo* in February 2007. The editor-in-chief at the time, Philippe Val, had asked me to be a witness in a court case that three Muslim organizations had brought against the magazine for inciting religious hatred. In the view of those organizations, such hatred was made evident by three cartoons: Cabut's front-page depiction of Muhammad bemoaning being loved by jerks, Kurt Westergaard's cartoon of Muhammad with a bomb in his turban, and Jens Julius Hansen's drawing in which Muhammad receives a group of suicide bombers in the afterlife with the words, "Stop, we've run out of virgins!" The second and third cartoons had both originally been run by *Jyllands-Posten*. Val explained to me afterward that he had invited me in order to demonstrate that I wasn't a racist in the employ of some extreme xenophobic pamphlet, as many of *Charlie Hebdo*'s critics claimed. To me, the alliance between *Charlie Hebdo* and *Jyllands-Posten* was illustrative of a core element in the debate about free speech in a multicultural democracy. Regardless of where we stood on the political spectrum—*Jyllands-Posten* is a libertarian-conservative newspaper whose political standpoint is right of center, whereas *Charlie Hebdo* is firmly left—we were standing together to defend the principles of secular democracy: freedom of speech, freedom of religion, and a society in which church and state are kept separate. In that way, we were demonstrating that defense of free speech transcended the political argument between right, left, and center in European politics.

Legal proceedings became the order of the day for *Charlie Hebdo* after Philippe Val and Jean Cabut relaunched the magazine in 1992. According to *Le Monde*, the magazine faced 48 court cases with 9 rulings against it, most of them for libel rather than religious insult. Fewer than one-third of the cases were for religious insult, and *Charlie Hebdo* was acquitted in all of them. Furthermore, *Le Monde*'s survey revealed that only 7 of *Charlie Hebdo*'s 523 front pages from 2005 to 2015 featured Islam. Three times that number satirized Christianity, and 10 lampooned several religions at once. By far the majority of the magazine's front-page cartoons poked fun at politicians, especially those of France's anti-immigration party Front National, and most others targeted economic and social issues and the worlds of sport and entertainment.

Taking the stand in court, I was asked by *Charlie Hebdo*'s counsel to explain the circumstances that had led *Jyllands-Posten* to publish the cartoons. I brought up the issue of self-censorship, as well as my friendships with Soviet dissidents, whose mocking of the communist ideology had led to their being incarcerated in prison camps and who latterly had become a point of reference for me in my understanding of what was at stake in the debate concerning the Muhammad cartoons. However, the object of my friends' criticism had been a political ideology; the object of

Charlie Hebdo's criticism was religious. Apart from that, I saw no difference between the two cases at all.

The counsel for the Muslim organizations attempted to sow doubt about our motive in running the cartoons and to uncover what he claimed to be hypocrisy and double standards, but it was clear that he had not done his homework. The opposing lawyer highlighted *Jyllands-Posten* editor-in-chief Carsten Juste's decision not to publish entries from an Iranian competition for cartoons satirizing the Holocaust and contrasted it with the paper's "racist" attacks on Muslims with its Muhammad cartoons. This strategy was doomed to fail. In the first place, on February 4, 2006, when the cartoon crisis was at its peak and Danish embassies in the Middle East were being set alight, *Jyllands-Posten* ran a page of cartoons from the Arab press, a number of which were clearly anti-Semitic in nature, including one claiming the Holocaust to be a figment of Jewish imagination. Second, some months later, *Jyllands-Posten* and a number of other Danish dailies of various political leanings had indeed published cartoons from the Iranian Holocaust cartoon competition. But this was not because we were anti-Semites: in the same way that our publication of the Muhammad cartoons was not an expression of any anti-Muslim sentiment, publication of the Iranian cartoons was a way to show our readers the kinds of things people were poking fun at in the Muslim world, where many had been incensed and offended by the Muhammad depictions. In that way, our readers could judge for themselves whether the violent reactions to the Muhammad cartoons throughout the Muslim world were reasonable.

In that particular instance, the court in Paris ruled in favor of *Charlie Hebdo*, but in January 2015, two dissatisfied Muslims exacted their horrific revenge for the magazine's insults to their faith. Eyewitnesses reported that the Kouachi brothers shouted, "We have avenged the Prophet!" upon fleeing *Charlie Hebdo*'s offices following the massacre. Fourest, who hurried to the scene immediately after the attack to offer support to her colleagues, learned that the two brothers had taken pains to make sure that Charb, the editor-in-chief who had publicly defended *Charlie Hebdo*'s religious satire since 2009, was among their victims. Apart from Wolinski, Charb was the *Charlie Hebdo* cartoonist I knew best. We had appeared together in Lyon in 2009 at a panel discussion on freedom of speech.

"Charb talked openly about the threats made to himself and to the magazine," Fourest told me. "He felt isolated and alone in his efforts to defend *Charlie Hebdo*, and he said it was getting increasingly difficult to stand up to the kind of intimidation they were receiving. He was deeply concerned." Fourest was scheduled to appear alongside Charb on a TV program on the evening of January 7. She received the news of his death while on the phone with the program's producer, discussing issues for the impending debate.

In the week that followed the *Charlie Hebdo* massacre, many French people were shocked when some Muslim students refused to take part in the remembrance ceremony for the victims and instead paid tribute to the perpetrators. According to *Le Figaro*, 54 people were arrested for publicly applauding the attack on *Charlie Hebdo*. At least 12 were convicted in court under the law against glorifying terrorism. At the same time, mosques and Islamic culture centers were vandalized throughout the country.

The attack on *Charlie Hebdo* marked, in one observer's words, the end of the idealism of May 1968 and its criticism of France's colonial past and institutional racism. Right from the start, *Charlie Hebdo* had seen itself as rebellious—a magazine that castigated power and stood up for vulnerable minorities like Muslims from the former French colonies. In 1996, Charb, along with *Charlie Hebdo*'s founder François Cavanna and then editor-in-chief Philippe Val, launched a petition containing some 174,000 signatures that called for a ban on Front National after several violent attacks on immigrants. In the petitioners' view, this party violated the principle embodied in the French declaration of human rights of equality before the law and incited discrimination against certain groups of people. Now the rebels of the Parisian barricades of the 1960s and 1970s had been murdered by the sons of those they had sought to defend.

Val, Charb's predecessor as editor-in-chief, was equally concerned when we met for lunch in February 2015 in the Latin Quarter, close to the cafés where French intellectuals hung out in the decades following World War II. We wanted to mull over the state of the world and to enjoy each other's company. Val was worried about his 10-month-old son's future in France and was indignant about what he sees as the cowardice of intellectuals in the struggle for secular values. France, he said, is under threat from a new totalitarian ideology whose aggressive anti-Semitism, insistence on supremacy, and willingness to use violence in many ways harks back to Nazism. Val was horrified by the complacency with which murders and attacks on Jews were met by many of his fellow citizens.

Val is a gaunt man; the clutching grief that I had seen in his face on television and in other images a month prior had given way to something less severe. I saw him weep on TV at the loss of his friends. That afternoon, though, his voice cracked only once, when speaking of Wolinski and Cabut, the two cartoonists to whom he felt most attached and with whom he had maintained long-lasting friendships. Apart from that, Val's grief had been superseded by anger and the urge to put into words what is happening in French society. A month previously, Val declared that, with the attacks on *Charlie Hebdo* and the Jewish supermarket, France was changed forever.

Val had famously once asked, "What kind of a civilization are we if we cannot ridicule those who fly planes into skyscrapers and blow up passenger trains?" I asked him how he viewed satire now. "Satire has two aims," he told me. "First, it wants to make us laugh when nothing is funny anymore. Satire adds to our existence an element of play when everything becomes too difficult. In that way, it helps us stay free. Second, satire also works as a kind of vengeance against those who have erred. It's extremely effective, and unlike other ways of exacting revenge, it leaves no dead."

Val was outraged by the many people who have suggested that *Charlie Hebdo*, by virtue of its merciless satire and lampooning of radical Islam, is itself at least partly to blame for the killing of its staff members:

> People say we shouldn't have poured petrol on the flames, that we should have been more careful about baiting our executioners. "Those who challenge evil do so at their own risk"—that's how the argument goes. But these critics don't seem to be able to see that this was the same logic that legitimized collusion with the Nazi occupiers during World War II. We won't put up with that anymore. We can't let those arguments pass.

On a February morning in 2015, I met with Gérard Biard, Charb's successor as *Charlie Hebdo*'s editor-in-chief. The sun was shining in Paris, but it was bitterly cold and the wind chopped up the waves on the Seine. Fifty-six-year-old Biard is half-Italian and grew up in a suburb of Paris politically dominated by communists. It was in Bible school as a child that he first began to question his faith. The priests there were of working-class backgrounds and instilled in Biard the idea that faith was a private issue between an individual and God, thereby paradoxically initiating a process that eventually led to Biard's declaring himself an atheist. As a young man he studied Italian and was later employed by an insurance company before realizing that he had taken a wrong turn. After that, Biard began working in theater, where he met Philippe Val and followed him to *Charlie Hebdo* when the magazine was relaunched in 1992. Politically, Biard stands left of center and describes himself as a social democrat.

I met Biard in the grand Place des Vosges, the French capital's oldest square. Two security guards accompanied him. We entered a maze-like building, proceeded down a narrow corridor, veered off, and continued down another corridor that was barely wide enough for two people to pass each other. At the end of yet another corridor, we entered an empty room, sunlight slanting down sporadically through grubby windows, and sat down to talk.

Biard was quiet and maintained a relaxed tone at all times. He is alive only by chance, having been on holiday in London on the day of the January 7 attack on *Charlie Hebdo*'s offices. Like Philippe Val, Biard is disturbed by the relativism that has since spread through certain circles of French society:

> A month after the attack some people are already falling back into the classic stance: "No, of course cartoonists should not be murdered, but. . . ." It's hypocritical and utterly irresponsible. It insists upon a moral connection between the perpetrators and their victims. First, they're saying there's a legitimate motive behind the atrocity, even though they condemn violence, and second, they're claiming the victims aren't entirely without blame. In that way, they put the terrorists and their victims on par. It concerns me that these critics don't understand what is at stake. What's under fire here is the democratic value of free speech, which includes the right to caricature and the right of blasphemy. If you equate those who insist on that right in a democratic society with those who call for its abolition and are willing to kill in order to achieve that, then you're undermining the very concept of free speech.

Reluctant to see the place where his friends and colleagues were murdered, Biard has not yet been back to the editorial offices after the massacre, and he is coming to terms with fear as a fact of life. The security agents who look after him are a constant reminder that his life is in danger, but his fear vanishes the moment he sits down behind the computer to write a piece for *Charlie Hebdo*.

In Biard's view, self-censorship remains widespread in French culture when it comes to Islam. He believes that this is an issue of fear on the one hand and discomfort with confronting a sensitive issue on the other. Biard believes that reducing their identity solely to religion undermines the citizenship of many Muslims, their citizenship being wholly independent of religious belief and affiliation. Religion is irrelevant, Biard says:

> In a way you're dissociating Muslims from their citizenship. That's what the Islamists and segments of the left wing want. When we attack Islamism, we are defending Muslims as equal citizens who are first and foremost French—citizens of a republic built on secular principles and the notion of equality before the law. Many people think that criticizing the religion is the same as criticizing those who believe in it, but that's not the case. Targeting Islamism is not the same as targeting Muslims. Islamism makes political demands, so it's more than a religion. Many people fail to understand that. But in countries where Islamism has come to the forefront, they understand only too well. Free thinkers in the Muslim world support us and say, no, you mustn't give up, you have to carry on.

For Biard, secularism is paramount: "It guarantees that no religion can make special political demands. It's no coincidence that the countries in which religious minorities are deprived of their rights and subjected to persecution are the same as those in which religion has been given political power." Biard takes issue with identity politics and the fact that some people are more concerned with what makes them different from their fellow citizens than with what they share. He defends the republican value of separation of church and state, as well as the secular order that safeguards the principle of equality before the law and that provides no special rights to any religion or ideology.

These are the same principles that some Muslims challenged after the publication of the Muhammad cartoons in *Jyllands-Posten* 10 years ago. Biard stresses the fundamental difference between targeting ideas and targeting individuals, which I agree is an important distinction. I made the same point myself during the Cartoon Crisis when critics compared cartoons of a religious figure like the Prophet Muhammad to anti-Semitic cartoons in the Nazi magazine *Der Stürmer*. Ideas, both religious and nonreligious, need to be challenged, and protecting them against ridicule and mockery goes against Enlightenment values. Ideas don't enjoy any rights, but human beings do.

All of the former and current members of *Charlie Hebdo*'s editorial team with whom I spoke supported France's legislation against hate speech, including the country's Gayssot Act of 1990, which prohibits Holocaust denial, and another law that makes it illegal to glorify terrorism.

For Philippe Val, the boundary of free speech must be drawn at inciting hatred, and he is a firm advocate of France's prohibition of Holocaust denial. Caroline Fourest finds there is a great deal of confusion as to where the line of free speech should be drawn. In her opinion, there should be no restrictions on criticizing or mocking ideas and symbols—that being intrinsic to France's historical development into a modern democracy—but inciting hatred against individuals is another matter. Both she and Gérard Biard are also in favor of laws outlawing Holocaust denial. And along with Val, Fourest and Biard support laws criminalizing the glorification of terrorism, which have been used against Muslims who applauded the killings of *Charlie Hebdo*'s staff members.

I concur with Val, Fourest, and Biard to the extent that racist opinion and anti-Semitism must be opposed. I also believe there is a difference between, on the one hand, scorning, mocking, and ridiculing a religious doctrine and religious symbols and figures (i.e., blasphemy) and, on the other, denigrating the memory of 6 million Jews exterminated during World War II by denying that the Holocaust took place. Unlike these three journalists, however, I believe this difference to be moral in nature and therefore not a legal issue. Rather, it is a culture war that rightly ought to be played out in classrooms and in public debate, not in the courts. I fail to see how Holocaust denial entails inciting violence against Jews, regardless of whether insistence on such a repugnant and reprehensible lie represents anti-Jewish sentiment. Nor do I believe that criminalizing Holocaust denial and incitement to hatred against Jews can prevent acts of violence against the Jewish community.

The former Yugoslavia criminalized incitement to ethnic hatred, and even telling ethnic jokes or waving a national flag at a soccer match carried a prison sentence. But the law could do nothing to prevent ethnic cleansing, wholesale murder, or war as the country disintegrated in the early 1990s. Similar legislation existed in the Soviet Union, where it did nothing to stop ethnically motivated violence and murder when armed conflicts broke out—also in the early 1990s—between Armenians and Azerbaijanis, Abkhazians and Georgians, Ossetians and Georgians, and Uzbeks and Kyrgyz.

I think the above-mentioned examples from Yugoslavia and the Soviet Union indicate that laws are ineffective tools to prevent ethnic or racial violence. Before violence erupted, hate-speech laws were used to silence critical voices. After ethnic wars broke out, the laws were used only against the enemy, not to maintain social cohesion. In fact, so-called hate-speech laws are very often used to oppress minorities rather than to protect them. This is the case in authoritarian regimes in particular, although not exclusively so. With reference to hate-speech legislation in the Netherlands, Dutch politician Geert Wilders has called for the Koran to be outlawed, while several European countries have banned Muslim women from covering their faces in public. Danish human rights activist Jacob Mchangama puts it this way:

> The freedoms that (sometimes) allow bigots to bait minorities are also the very freedoms that allow Muslims and Jews to practice their faiths freely. By further eroding these freedoms, no one is more than a political majority away from being the target rather than the beneficiary of laws against hatred and offense.[1]

If the motive for criminalizing certain speech is indeed to stop incitement to hatred, we would surely—as American professor of constitutional law Robert Post[2] has pointed out—need to ban a lot more than is the case at present, given the somewhat loosely worded nature of legislation in Europe. A large number of films, books, computer games, religions, and political ideologies would have to be consigned to that category if we were to be in any way consistent. Post thus maintains that all laws against hate speech are governed by social conventions and not by the wish to ban speech that objectively incites hatred, discrimination, violence, or any other harm. These laws end up enforcing a dominant group's conception of what is socially acceptable—that is, a culturally and historically determined notion of what it means to show respect. This becomes problematic in a multicultural democracy with varying opinions on right and wrong and what constitutes hate speech. As Post argues, one man's vulgarity is another's lyric. Or more appropriately with respect to faith, what is sacred to one faith community may be blasphemous to another.

Laws against hate speech in a multiethnic society also impose the norms of one group on all other groups. This is a democratic problem, and one of the reasons public debate in the United States does not exclude speech and opinions that may be deemed hateful or offensive: to do so would undermine the equality of citizens in public discussion and sow doubt as to the legitimacy of government. Here is where the link between tolerance, liberty, and equality in a multicultural society becomes clear. To ensure equality, public debate must allow all utterances of opinion, regardless of their nature; and in a society such as the United States, which was founded on immigration, the government must remain neutral when it comes to the nature of its citizens' speech. The culturally, ethnically, and religiously diverse democracy cannot allow the exclusion from the public domain of certain opinions, however reprehensible or unpleasant they may be. Conversely, opinions deemed by the majority to be morally correct and constructive cannot be favored. Government must not be more committed to one group's norms to the disadvantage of another group's. All speech must be protected in the same way, as long as it does not directly incite violence.

Unlike in Europe, the United States refrains from playing the arbiter of taste, although its citizens do the job admirably themselves: the United States is afflicted with identity politics and grievance fundamentalism to the point where one hardly knows whether to laugh or cry. So-called trigger warnings are now commonplace at American universities, wherein professors are obliged to warn their students if the curriculum will include material that may trigger trauma responses. This has led to calls for trigger warnings to be applied to Ovid's poetry, Virginia Woolf's *Mrs. Dalloway*, and F. Scott Fitzgerald's *The Great Gatsby*.

Many universities have established safe zones to which students may retreat if they encounter ideas that may disturb their mental balance, and anyone who says anything that might be construed as a threat to the psychological comfort of other students is likely to be accused of microaggression. The term "microaggression" originally described the unintentional and unconscious discrimination of blacks by whites. It has come to describe similar alleged attacks against women, homosexuals, the poor, the disabled, and anyone else who might claim status as a marginalized minority.

Notably, on the occasion of PEN American Center presenting its Freedom of Expression Courage Award to *Charlie Hebdo*, a number of prominent writers revealed themselves unable to distinguish between criticizing ideas and religious symbols on the one hand and attacking individuals on the other. Similarly, students at some universities have gotten into the habit of forcing cancellations of invited speakers whose opinions differ from their own.

All this suggests that, despite a considerably more robust protection of constitutional freedom of expression in the United States than in Europe, contemporary American society itself exhibits strong cultural tendencies that in practice place that very freedom under threat—either because of fear or because of the widespread misconception that any utterance that may be deemed insulting must necessarily be an expression of intolerance and ought therefore not be uttered at all.

But why is the state so differently empowered in Europe and the United States when it comes to stepping in to curb the speech of its citizens? According to Robert Post, this is due both to a deeply entrenched distrust of government among Americans and to strong forces that have always exerted pressure to limit the latitude and power of government. Moreover, the individual and individual rights constitute the fulcrum of all U.S. debate surrounding the balance between government and citizen. To ensure the democratic legitimacy of government, it is therefore necessary to provide widespread protection of the rights of citizens to express themselves freely and without hindrance, the fear being that otherwise government will exploit legislation in order to punish speech with which it does not agree.

In Europe, Post argues, the situation is different. Here, there is a long tradition of the individual submitting to the state and displaying exaggerated respect for whoever holds power, whether a dictator, a president, a duke, a monarch, or the head of a church. Moreover, in Europe, the common good is generally given far greater weight than in the United States. In Post's view, Americans have a much smaller need to confirm their identity as a society by protecting and maintaining the norms that in Europe motivate legislation against hate speech.

Post is of the opinion that, in a multicultural society, hate-speech laws and other violation codes may work contrary to their own intentions, breeding negative social consequences insofar as criminalizing certain opinions may prompt some groups to view the laws as selective, targeting them as an expression of the supremacy of others. This is exactly the case with many Muslims in France, which on the one side adheres to a very strong anti-clerical tradition legitimizing religious criticism such as that practiced by *Charlie Hebdo*, but on the other side exhibits some of Europe's toughest legislation against hate speech, the aim of which is mostly to protect Jews against anti-Semitism and Holocaust denial, which are widespread among Muslims. Legislation outlawing hate speech may thereby contribute to an erosion of democratic cohesion and social unity across societal groups.

Four days after saying goodbye to my friends and colleagues in Paris, the tragedy I had been fearing for years finally happened: my home city of Copenhagen was the scene of an attack whose motivation and execution echoed what had occurred in Paris. On Saturday, February 14, 2015, a 22-year-old Muslim gunman of Palestinian descent, born and raised in Denmark, struck first at a café debate on the subject of blasphemy and art, killing one attendee, a 55-year-old filmmaker who tried to stop him. Some hours later, the gunman shot and killed a Danish Jew, who was minding the door for a bat mitzvah at the city's main synagogue. With 80 guests inside the synagogue and an audience of 30 gathered for the café debate, had the killer been able to gain entry to the two events, what ensued would surely have been a bloodbath.

The Danish government should have insisted on the right to free speech, especially because the killings in Copenhagen were a clear attack on freedom of expression, religion, and assembly. Instead, it reacted to the attack with a proposal to retain the country's blasphemy law and increase surveillance activities. The perpetrator behind the deadly attacks in Copenhagen frequented a mosque run by Hizb-ut-Tahrir, and a number of politicians called for a ban on the organization, which wants to abolish democracy and establish a caliphate based on the Koran. Thus, the response to these attacks against the right of assembly and Denmark's Jewish community was to move toward restricting freedom of speech and religion.

This brings me back to two central points:

First, it is necessary in a liberal democracy to distinguish between words and actions, and to legislate only against speech that incites violence. We are all individually responsible for our own interpretations of what is said by others, and we alone translate our reactions into actions, as Kenan Malik has suggested.[3] Between talk and action stands a conscious individual with the ability to judge what is right and wrong. Words alone can never cause us to act, as though by the push of a button. Words have consequences only if we decide that they should. Humans are not robots or animals whose behavior is dictated by external stimuli alone. Humans are equipped with reason and the capability of rational thought and may thus consciously decide how to react to words, if at all.

Second, in the debate over how a liberal democracy ought to react to terrorism, it is important to bear in mind that outlawing speech is the closest a society can get to controlling people's thoughts. Utterances occupy a zone somewhere between thoughts (with which no authority can interfere, no matter how hard totalitarian dictatorships may try) and actions, which in some instances may and should be prohibited by law.

It is not prohibited to think that black people belong to an inferior race, that non-Muslims are less worthy than Muslims and therefore cannot claim the same rights, or that women are less intelligent than men and thus unsuitable for certain kinds of work. But if, on the basis of such opinions, you in practice discriminate against blacks, non-Muslims, or women by denying them equality and the rights enjoyed by others, all proponents of liberal democracy concur that you are thereby in breach of a fundamental democratic principle. If, however, you merely say that blacks, non-Muslims, and women do not deserve the same rights as do other citizens in your society, without discriminating against them in practice, a large measure of disagreement exists as to what to do.

The liberal answer—the one to which I subscribe—is that thoughts and utterances have more in common than do utterances and actions, and this is why we ought not outlaw racist speech, although we should still punish discriminatory actions. A less liberal answer would be that utterances beget actions, and that some utterances, even if they do not directly incite violence, should therefore also be criminalized. The nonliberal answer insists that words are actions, legitimizing the banning of utterances on a large scale.

Ten years after the publication of the Muhammad cartoons, the illiberal approach to free speech is on the rise across Europe and in the United States, although in America the threat to free speech doesn't primarily come from the lawmakers and courts but from cultural forces and social pressure. The influx of immigrants and asylum seekers from the Middle East, Central Asia, and Africa has caused new tensions in Europe. For years, if not decades, to come, the question at the top of Europe's political agenda will be how to manage the growing diversity of culture, religion, and ethnicity while at the same time protecting fundamental liberties like freedom of speech.

Unfortunately, it looks like freedom of speech will be sacrificed on the altar of cultural, religious, and ethnic diversity. European politicians and human rights groups are of the opinion that the growing diversity of culture needs less diversity of speech, while the logical answer to the new challenge would be to accept that more diversity of culture and religion would be followed by more diverse kinds of speech, including speech that may be perceived as blasphemous and offensive to some. That's important for equality and freedom. Recently, in accordance with a European Union (EU) framework decision from 2008, Věra Jourová, the EU commissioner for justice, consumers, and gender equality, called on all member states to pass laws criminalizing certain forms of hate speech and Holocaust denial. She said, "If freedom of expression is one of the building blocks of a democratic society, hate speech, on the other hand, is a blatant violation of that freedom. . . . It must be severely punished." She also insisted that "member states must firmly and immediately investigate and prosecute racist hatred. . . . I find it disgraceful that Holocaust denial is a criminal offense in only 13 member states."

It seems obvious that laws criminalizing Holocaust denial in an increasingly diverse Europe will be accompanied by demands from other groups—ethnic, cultural, and religious—to protect what's sacred to them against ridicule and mockery as well. There is also strong support for criminalizing hate speech in the European Parliament. A recent expert report recommended that the European Commission initiate infringement proceedings against member states that have failed to fully implement the framework decision and have even suggested blocking those websites that feature hate speech. It seems that the EU's slogan of "United in Diversity" does not extend to the full realm of opinions.

At the national level, all EU member states have in place laws against hatred and sometimes even offense, and such laws are frequently enforced. The European Court of Human Rights has long refused to protect hateful and sometimes even offensive expressions aimed at particular groups, although it has not bothered to define what "hate speech" really means. The Council of Europe's human rights commissioner has gone even further, proposing a Europe-wide ban on gender-based hate speech and Holocaust denial. The government of Germany has passed new regulations that make it possible to shut down websites that feature hate speech. Chancellor Angela Merkel has called on Facebook and other social media enterprises to regulate speech on their platforms.

Free speech is in bad standing. I published the cartoons of the Prophet Muhammad 10 years ago to focus on two issues: (a) Do people commit self-censorship when it comes to Islam, and (b) if yes, is the self-censorship based in reality, or is the fear driving it just a product of people's prejudices and imagination? Today, it's clear that the answer to both questions is yes. Self-censorship is widespread, and the fear driving it is real. People challenging religious taboos have been killed.

The Muslims of Europe have to confront Islam's concepts of blasphemy and apostasy. Muslims have every right to feel offended by cartoons of their prophet, but they don't have any right to react with intimidation, threats, and violence.

Translated by Martin Aitken

Notes

Chapter 1. From Where I Stand

[1]Habib Toumi, "Doha Media Freedom Center Head Quits," *Gulfnews* (Dubai), June 24, 2009.

[2]In the fall of 2011, I was granted a visa to Russia; since then, I have had no problems entering the country.

[3]John Hansen and Kim Hundevadt, *Provoen og profeten:Muhammedkrisen bag kulisserne* (Copenhagen: Jyllands-Postens Forlag, 2006); Jytte Klausen, *The Cartoons That Shook the World* (London: Yale University Press, 2009).

[4]Per Stig Møller, "Europas rolle i forhold til omverdenen," in *Europas værdier og rolle i verden*, Charlotte Antonsen and Ole Buchardt Olesen, eds. (Copenhagen: Peter la Cour, 2007), pp. 11–19; Peter Berger and Anton Zijderveld, *In Praise of Doubt: How to Have Convictions without Becoming a Fanatic* (New York: HarperCollins, 2009).

[5]Interview with Salman Rushdie, May 15, 2009, Copenhagen.

[6]On the question of culture and political order and change, see Lawrence Harrison, *The Central Liberal Truth: How Politics Can Change a Culture and Save It from Itself* (New York: Oxford University Press, 2006); Francis Fukuyama, *Trust: Human Nature and the Reconstitution of Social Order* (New York: Simon and Schuster, 1995); and Lawrence Harrison and Samuel Huntington, *Culture Matters: How Values Shape Human Progress* (New York: Basic Books, 2005).

[7]Richard Bernstein, "German Cartoon of Suicide Bombers Angers Iran," *New York Times*, February 17, 2006. The cartoon was published February 10, 2006.

Chapter 2. Mass Murder and Satire

[1]Maria Gomez is a pseudonym; she wishes to remain anonymous.

[2]Lawrence Wright, "The Terror Web," *New Yorker*, August 2, 2004. The account of how the terror strike unfolded is based on Wright's article.

[3]"Spain Remembers Victims of Madrid," *The Guardian* (London), March 11, 2005.

[4]Fernando Reinares, "Al-Qaeda Is Back," *National Interest*, August 1, 2010, http://nationalinterest.org/article/al-qaeda-is-back-3348; "The Madrid Bombings and Global Jihadism," *Survival* 52, no. 2 (April–May 2010); "Spain Remembers," *The Guardian* (London).

[5]Victoria Burnett, "7 Are Acquitted in Madrid Bombings," *New York Times*, November 1, 2007; Paul Hamilos and Mark Tran, "21 Guilty, 7 Cleared over Madrid Train Bombings," *Guardian*, October 31, 2007.

Chapter 3. From Moscow to Muhammad

[1]I spoke with Sergei Kovalev on a number of occasions when I was living in Moscow. The conversation cited took place in the autumn of 2002. The human

301

rights movement had a keen eye for the dangers presented by group rights at the cost of the individual and his or her rights. My friend Kronid Lyubarsky, about whom I write in detail in a later chapter, pointed out in a talk he gave in 1992 that, following the coup in 1917, the Bolsheviks introduced a legal novelty: "Rights were not guaranteed for the individual, but for a certain group, however big. The Declaration of Rights proclaimed after the October Revolution was entitled: 'Declaration of Rights of the Working and Exploited People.' . . . Anyone not belonging to the working class and the exploited people was automatically deprived of his or her rights." See Kronid Lyubarsky, "The Development of the Concept of Human Rights: History and Perspectives," in *Kronid—Izbrannye stati K. Lyubarsky* (Moscow: Rossiyskiy Gosudarstvenny Universitet, 2001), pp. 263–64.

[2]Amos Oz, *Hvordan man kurerer en fanatiker* (Copenhagen: Gyldendal, 2004), p. 19.

[3]Orla Borg, "Terrorens religiøse ammunition," *Jyllands-Posten* (Aarhus), September 11, 2005.

[4]Ayaan Hirsi Ali, "Kære Theo," *Jyllands-Posten* (Aarhus), November 2, 2005. The letter Bouyeri left at the scene of the crime can be read at http://www.militantislammonitor.org/article/id/312.

[5]Morten Skjoldager, *Truslen indefra: De danske terrorister* (Copenhagen: Lindhart og Ringhof, 2009), p. 32.

[6]Rasmus Blicher, "Klovens grænser," *Jyllands-Posten* (Aarhus), September 18, 2005.

[7]Troels Pedersen of the Danish news agency Ritzaus Bureau was the journalist who initially interviewed Kåre Bluitgen about his difficulties finding an illustrator. I am hugely indebted to Troels Pedersen for having allowed me access to his recording of that interview, from which parts of this chapter derive. I later interviewed Kåre Bluitgen myself, as well as Nanna Gyldenkærne, publishing editor of Copenhagen publishers Høst & Søn, on the circumstances surrounding the publication of Bluitgen's 2006 book *Koranen og profeten Muhammeds liv* (*The Koran and the Life of the Prophet Muhammad*).

[8]Oleg Grabar, "Seeing and Believing," *New Republic*, October 30, 2009; Catharina Raudevere, Gudebilleder, "Billedforbud i Islam," in: *Gudebilleder. Ytringsfrihed og religion i en globaliseret verden* (Copenhagen: Tiderne skifter, 2006), pp. 28–43; Klaus Rothstein and Mikael Rothstein, "Bomben i turbanen," Copenhagen, 2006.

[9]Claus Seidel, chairman of the Danish cartoonists' society, later confirmed that my proposal to the cartoonists was open. For a transcript of Claus Seidel's interview on his communication with me and understanding of the project on the radio program *Orientering*, broadcast by Danmarks Radio, see "Muhammed-tegner: Invitationen var åben," *Jyllands-Posten* (Aarhus), January 18, 2008.

[10]Flemming Rose, "Muhammeds ansigt," *Jyllands-Posten* (Aarhus), September 30, 2005; Ulla Dubgaard, "Er kunstneres selvcensur og frygt for fundamentalister reel?" *Information* (Copenhagen), September 9, 2005; Klaus Rothstein, "Profetens ansigt," *Weekendavisen* (Copenhagen), January 27, 2006.

[11]Klaus Rothstein, "Profetens ansigt."

[12]Flemming Rose, *Amerikanske Stemmer* (Viby: Indsigt, 2006), pp. 51–66.

[13]Søren Kassebeer, "Ali-oversættere vil være anonyme," *Berlingske Tidende* (Copenhagen), September 23, 2005; Helsingin Sanomat, "Publisher Says 'Technical Error' Led to Omission of Book Critical of Islam," *Helsingin Sanomat* (Helsinki), September 19, 2005.

[14]John Latham on the origins of *God Is Not Great*, http://www.tate.org.uk/britain/exhibitions/latham/transcript.

[15]David Smith, "Artist Hits at Tate 'Cowards' over Ban," *Observer* (London), September 25, 2005.

[16]Tate press statement about *John Latham in Focus*, http://www.tate.org.uk/about/press-office/press-releases/tate-press-statement-about-john-latham-focus.

[17]Louzla Darabi's comments on *Scène d'amour* can be found on the website of Galerie Peter Herrmann at http://galerie-herrmann.com/arts/darabi/Answers_Louzla_Darabi.htm. In the summer of 2010, Darabi penned another piece on the work in the Swedish tabloid *Expressen* in which, under the headline "The Terror of Censorship," she states: "When 'Scène d'Amour' was censored I received threats from fundamentalists and was hounded by the media. Being unused to such things at the time, I was an easy target for manipulation. I made the mistake of accepting that 'Scène d'Amour' be replaced by another painting. . . . The citizens of our societies have laid down their arms, the social contract entailing that the State is duty-bound to protect them. But what happens when the State shies away? In such instances, the State allows barbarism to prevail. This was what happened when 'Scène d'Amour' was subjected to censorship." *Expressen*, June 10, 2010. Jesper Stein Larsen and Tom Hermansen, "Den farlige selvcensur," *Jyllands-Posten* (Aarhus), October 1, 2005.

[18]Darabi, "The Terror of Censorship"; Larsen and Hermansen, "Den farlige selvcensur."

[19]The British government's bill against inciting religious hatred is dealt with in the anthology *Free Speech Is No Offense*, Lisa Appignanesi, ed. (London: Penguin, 2005), which contains the open letter to the home secretary signed by 400 writers, as well as Rushdie's and Atkinson's essays.

[20]Andrew Higgins, "Blame It on Voltaire: Muslims Ask French to Cancel 1741 Play," *Wall Street Journal*, March 6, 2006.

[21]"Marlowe Rewrite 'Draws Criticism,'" *BBC News*, November 24, 2005.

[22]For the court's decision, see http://hudoc.echr.coe.int/sites/eng/pages/search.aspx?i=001-70113# (enter itemid "001-70113").

[23]Jakob Nielsen, "Imamer Kræver medvind i medierne," *Politiken* (Copenhagen), September 21, 2005; Mikkel Thastum and Louise Scheibel, "Imamer kræver positive medier," *Jyllands-Posten* (Aarhus), September 21, 2005.

[24]Ben Lewis, *Hammer and Tickle: A History of Communism Told through Communist Jokes* (London: Weidenfeld & Nicolson, 2008); Milan Kundera, *En Spøg* (Copenhagen: Gyldendal, 1967); Dora Shturman and Sergei Tikhtin, *Sovetskii Soiuz v zerkale politicheskogo anekdota* (London: Overseas Publications Interchange, 1985).

[25]Jens-Martin Eriksen and Frederik Stjernfeldt, *Adskillelsens politik: Multikuluralisme—ide og virkelighed* (Copenhagen: Lindhardt og Ringhof, 2008), pp. 237–61; Anthony Julius, *Transgressions: The Offenses of Art* (Chicago: University of Chicago Press, 2003). Both deal with offensive images.

[26]Mikkel Bøgh, "Virkningshistorier: Billeder, tvivl og blasfemi," *Kritik* no. 185 (2007): 37–41.

[27]W. J. T. Mitchell, *What Do Pictures Want? The Lives and Love of Images* (Chicago: University of Chicago Press, 2005).

[28]Asbjørn Grønstad and Øyvind Vågnes, "An Interview with W. J. T. Mitchell," *Image and Narrative*, November 2006, http://www.imageandnarrative.be/inarchive/iconoclasm/gronstad_vagnes.htm.

[29]Mitchell, *What Do Pictures Want?* p. 131.

[30]Julius, *Transgressions*, pp. 57–60.

[31]Ibid., pp. 25–51.

[32]Robert Hughes, *Culture of Complaint: The Fraying of America* (New York: Oxford University Press, 1993), pp. 155–203; Jack Fritscher, "What Happened When: Censorship, Gay History and Mapplethorpe," in *Censorship: A World Encyclopedia*, Derek Jones, ed. (New York: Routledge, 2001), pp. 67–98.

[33]A transcript of the debate in Congress concerning Andres Serrano's *Piss Christ* can be read at http://www.csulb.edu/~jvancamp/361_r7.html.

[34]Mitchell, *What Do Pictures Want?* p. 130.

[35]On the controversy about Chris Ofili's *Madonna*, see Carol Vogel, "Holding Fast to His Inspiration: An Artist Tries to Keep His Cool in the Face of Angry Criticism," *New York Times*, September 28, 1999; David Barstow and David M. Herszenhorn, "Museum Chairman Broached Removal of Virgin Painting," *New York Times*, September 28, 1999; Gustav Niebuhr, "Anger over Work Evokes Anti-Catholic Shadow," and "Mary's Power as Icon," *New York Times*, October 3, 1999; and Michael Kimmelman, "A Madonna's Many Meanings in the Art World," *New York Times*, October 5, 1999.

[36]Mitchell, *What Do Pictures Want?* p. 130.

[37]Ibid., p. 142.

Chapter 4. The Infamous Ability of Humans to Adapt

[1]I have interviewed Kurt Westergaard several times; the last time was in the spring of 2010.

[2]On al Shabaab in Denmark, see Michael Taarnby and Lars Hallundbæk, *Al-Shabaab: The Internationalisation of Militant Islamism in Somalia and the Implications for Radicalization in Europe* (Copenhagen: Denmark Ministry of Justice, 2010).

[3]"Summit Considers Terrorism, Moderation in Muslim World," Associated Press, December 7, 2005.

[4]*Gulf Daily News* (Bahrain), December 8, 2005.

[5]Eva Bendix, *Man siger tak: En bog om en pige og hendes far* (Copenhagen: Gyldendal, 2003).

[6]Rasmus Kreth, *Pilestræde under pres: De Berlingske blade 1933–1945* (Copenhagen: Gyldendal, 1998), p. 131.

[7]Ibid., p. 78.

[8]Gregers Dirckinck-Holmfeld, *Tør: Hvor andre tier, en krønike om Ekstra Bladet*, vol. 1 (Copenhagen: Ekstra Bladet, 2003), p. 192.

[9]Poul Henningsen, *Kulturkritik*, vol. 3 (Copenhagen: Rhodos, 1973), pp. 44–48.

[10]Julius Streicher, "Nuremberg Trial Judgements," http://www.jewishvirtuallibrary.org/jsource/Holocaust/JudgeStreicher.html.

[11]In his book *Perestroika: New Thinking for Our Country and the World* (New York: HarperCollins, 1987), Mikhail Gorbachev, in accordance with Marxist-Leninist ideology, claimed that the nationality question was solved in the Soviet Union. A few months later, movements for national independence initiated a political process that led to the dissolution of the Soviet Union.

[12]Louis Greenspan and Cyril Levitt, eds., *Under the Shadow of Weimar: Democracy, Law, and Racial Incitement in Six Countries* (London: Praeger, 1993), pp. 15–37.

[13]Aryeh Neier, *Defending My Enemy: American Nazis, the Skokie Case, and the Risks of Freedom* (New York: Dutton, 1979), p. 3.

[14]Ibid., p. 167.

[15]Agnès Callamard, "Fighting Racism through Freedom of Expression" (keynote address, ECRI Expert Conference, Strasbourg, November 16–17, 2006).

[16]Aryeh Neier, "Free Speech for All," *Index on Censorship* 37, no. 3 (2008): 20–25.

[17]"Banned Books," *The Independent* (London), January 22, 2010. For information on the ban of Vladimir Nabokov, D. H. Lawrence, and William S. Burrough, see http://www.independent.co.uk/arts-entertainment/books/features/banned -books-you-could-have-been-jailed-for-reading-1876200.html; of John Steinbeck, see http://bannedbooks.world.edu/2012/08/12/banned-books-awareness-the-grapes -of-wrath; of James Joyce, see http://bannedbooks.world.edu/2012/02/20/banned -books-awareness-ulysses; of Henry Miller, see http://www.thefileroom.org /documents/dyn/DisplayCase.cfm/id/1275; of Allen Ginsberg, see James Campbell, "To Save America," *The Guardian* (London), February 6, 2007.

[18]Anders Heger, "Voltaire Light," *Morgenbladet* (Oslo), September 21, 2007.

[19]Ibid.

[20]Ibid.

[21]"Günter Grass Says Danish Cartoons Recall Nazi Era," *New York Times*, February 17, 2006.

[22]"Government Renames Islamic Terrorism as 'Anti-Islamic Activity' to Woo Muslims," *Daily Mail* (London), January 17, 2008.

[23]Muslim Council of Britain, http://www.mcb.org.uk/index.php?option=com _content&view=article&id=1531&Itemid=94.

[24]Riazat Butt, "Archbishop Backs Sharia Law for British Muslims, *The Guardian* (London), February 7, 2008.

[25]Martin Gilbert, *The Holocaust: The Jewish Tragedy* (London: HarperCollins, 1987).

[26]Victor Klemplerer, *Jeg vil aflægge vidnesbyrd til det sidste: Dagbøger 1933–1941* (Copenhagen: Gyldendal, 2000), p. 15.

[27]*Why Democracy? De forbandede tegninger*, directed by Karsten Kjær (2007).

Chapter 5. The Pathway to God

[1]Manifesto of the Council of Ex-Muslims of Britain, http://ex-muslim.org.uk /manifesto/.

[2]Morten Skjoldager, "Tunesere er anklaget for at true statens sikkerhed," *Politiken* (Copenhagen), July 2, 2008.

[3]Pernille Ammitzbøll and Kristoffer Pinholt, "Terrormistænkte levede dobbeltliv," *Jyllands-Posten* (Aarhus), February 15, 2008.

[4]Olivier Roy, *Globalized Islam: The Search for a New Ummah* (New York: Columbia University Press, 2004).

[5]Hans Magnus Enzensberger, "The Terrorist Mindset: The Radical Loser," *Der Spiegel* (Hamburg), December 20, 2006.

Chapter 6. Aftershock I

[1]*Jyllands-Posten* (Copenhagen), "Terror og frihed," October 28, 2009.

[2]For an account of the charges against Headley, see *United States of America v. David Coleman Headley*, http://www.justice.gov/usao/iln/pr/chicago/2009/pr1207 _01a.pdf. For a summary of the case against Headley, see http://www.justice .gov/usao/iln/pr/chicago/2009/pr107_01b.pdf. For his confession, see the plea

agreement, http://www.hindu.com/nic/headleyplea.pdf. For an account of the charges against Tahawwur Rana, see *United States of America v. Tahawwur Hussain Rana*, http://www.justice.gov/usao/iln/pr/chicago/2009/pr1027_01a.pdf.

[3]The profile of Headley is based on the following sources: Sebastian Rotella, "The Man Behind Mumbai," *ProPublica* (New York), November 13, 2010; Sebastian Rotella, "Mumbai: The Plot Unfolds, Lashkar Strikes and Investigators Scramble," *ProPublica* (New York), November 14, 2010; Jane Perlez, "American Terror Suspect Traveled Unimpeded," *New York Times*, March 25, 2010; Joseph Tanfani, "From Pakistan to Philadelphia: A Terror Suspect's Journey," *Philadelphia Inquirer*, November 19, 2009; Joseph Tanfani, John Shiffman, and Kathleen Brady Shea, "Terror Suspect Was Drug Dealer, Then Informant," *Philadelphia Inquirer*, December 13, 2009; Gerald Posner, "Making of a Terrorist," *Daily Beast*, December 8, 2009; Philip Shenon, "A Terrorist Immigration Service," *Daily Beast*, December 8, 2009; Bruce Riedel, "Al-Qaeda's American Mole," *Daily Beast*, December 15, 2009; and Ginger Thompson, "A Terror Suspect with Feet in East and West," *New York Times*, November 22, 2009.

[4]Stephen Tankel, "Lashkar e-Taiba: From 9/11 to Mumbai," International Centre for the Study of Radicalisation and Political Violence, April–May 2009, http://www.ps.au.dk/fileadmin/site_files/filer_statskundskab/subsites/cir/pdf-filer/Tankel_01.pdf; Jayshree Bajoria, "Profile of Lashkar e-Taiba," Council on Foreign Relations, January 14, 2010; Bruce Riedel, "What Pakistan's Terrorists Want," *Daily Beast*, May 4, 2010.

[5]Husain Haqqani, "The Ideologies of South Asian Jihadi Groups," Carnegie Endowment for International Peace, March 20, 2005.

[6]Puk Damsgaard Andersen, "Terroren rykkede helt tæt på," *Jyllands-Posten* (Copenhagen), June 3, 2008; Puk Damsgaard Andersen, "Far sover, så du skal ikke græde," *Jyllands-Posten* (Copenhagen), June 8, 2008.

[7]Ilyas Kashmiri was killed in 2011, presumably by a drone strike. See Ron Moreau, Sami Yousafzai, and Christopher Dickey, "Al Qaida Commander Ilyas Kashmiri Killed in U.S. Predator Strike," *Daily Beast*, June 4, 2011.

[8]Nicholas Kulish, "New Terrorism Case Confirms That Denmark Is a Target," *New York Times*, September 17, 2007.

[9]Kenan Malik, *From Fatwa to Jihad: The Rushdie Affair and Its Legacy* (London: Atlantic Books, 2009).

[10]Erik Jensen, "Det er jo pissenemt at opføre sig ordentligt," *Politiken* (Copenhagen), February 4, 2006.

[11]Jytte Klausen, *The Cartoons That Shook the World* (London: Yale University Press, 2009). p. 65.

[12]Ibid.

[13]Mohammad Hashim Kamali, *Freedom of Expression in Islam* (Cambridge: Islamic Texts Society, 1997).

[14]*Hardtalk*, BBC, February 3, 2006.

[15]The following is based on John Hansen and Kim Hundevadt, *Provoen og profeten: Muhammedkrisen bag kulisserne* (Aarhus: Jyllands-Postens Forlag, 2006).

[16]Klausen, *Cartoons That Shook the World*, pp. 175–80.

[17]Ibid., p. 81.

[18]Ibid., p. 168.

[19]Allan Sørensen, "Stormuftien i Jerusalem: Danmark er et let offer," *Kristeligt Dagblad* (Copenhagen), Feburary 7, 2006.

[20]Vebjørn Selbekk, "Tegningerne som ryster Danmark," *Magazinet* (Bergen), January 19, 2006.

[21]Klausen, *Cartoons That Shook the World*, p. 75.

[22]Associated Press, January 31, 2006.

[23]Hansen and Hundevadt, *Provoen og profeten*.

[24]Ritzaus Bureau, February 28, 2006.

[25]"OIC Calls for Emergency Meeting on Cartoon Issue OIC," *Arab News* (Jeddah), February 18, 2006.

[26]Hansen and Hundevadt, *Provoen og profeten*.

[27]Ibid.

[28]Gwladys Fouché, "Danish Paper Rejected Jesus Cartoons," *The Guardian* (London), February 6, 2006.

[29]For a transcript of the interview, see *American Morning*, CNN.com, February 8, 2006, http://edition.cnn.com/TRANSCRIPTS/0602/08/ltm.01.html.

[30]"Arabiske streger," *Jyllands-Posten* (Copenhagen), February 4, 2006.

Chapter 7. Aftershock II

[1]Obed Minchakpu, "Religious Riots in Nigeria Leave Hundreds Dead," *Christianity Today* (Carol Stream, IL), October 1, 2001; "Nigeria's Sharia Split," *BBC News*, October 15, 2001.

[2]Jefferson Morley, "Cartoons Not the Only Cause of Nigeria Violence, a Daily Survey of What the International Online Media Are Saying," *Washington Post*, February 22, 2006.

[3]John Hansen and Kim Hundevadt, *Provoen og profeten:Muhammedkrisen bag kulisserne* (Copenhagen: Jyllands-Postens Forlag, 2006).

[4]Ulla Dubgaard, "Er kunstneres selvcensur og frygt for fundamentalister reel?" *Information* (Copenhagen), September 9, 2005; Klaus Rothstein, "Profetens ansigt," *Weekendavisen* (Copenhagen), January 27, 2006.

[5]Patrick Jonsson, "Jihad Jane Alleged Target Lars Vilks: I Have an Axe Here," *CSM*, March 10, 2010.

[6]Jack Katzenell, "Israeli Woman Convicted of Distributing Mohammed as Pig Leaflets," Associated Press, December 20, 1997.

[7]Nick Gillespie, "Why We're Having an Everybody Draw Mohammed Contest on Thursday, May 20," *Reason.com*, May 18, 2010.

[8]Ben Hoyle, "Artists Too Frightened to Tackle Radical Islam," *The Times* (London), November 19, 2007.

[9]Vebjørn Selbekk, *Truet af Islamister* (Oslo: Genesis, 2006).

[10]Kristian Lindberg, "Hån, spot og rumrejser," *Berlingske Tidende* (Copenhagen), September 26, 2008.

[11]Michael Bo, "Den er sjov. Den kommunikerer. Og tog kort tid at lave," *Politiken* (Copenhagen), September 24, 2008.

[12]For those who find themselves unconvinced as to the extent of self-censorship, please consult the website Fri Debat, http://www.fridebat.nu. It includes a timeline tracking examples around the world.

[13]Per Stig Møller, "Værdiernes kollision," *Berlingske Tidende* (Copenhagen), July 27, 2009.

[14]On the background of the call to outlaw incitement to hatred and war propaganda as worded in the conventions on human rights, see Manfred Novak,

"UN Covenant on Civil and Political Rights," *CCPR Commentary*, 2nd rev. ed. (Kehl, Germany: Engel, 2005).

[15]Dieter Grimm, "Freedom of Speech in a Globalized World," in *Extreme Speech and Democracy*, Ivan Hare and James Weinstein, eds. (Oxford: Oxford University Press, 2009), p. 21.

[16]Ivan Hare, "Extreme Speech under International and Regional Human Rights Standards," in Hare and Weinstein, *Extreme Speech and Democracy*, pp. 62–80.

[17]United Nations Human Rights Commission, International Covenant on Civil and Political Rights, http://www.ohchr.org/en/professionalinterest/pages/ccpr.aspx.

[18]United Nations Human Rights Commission, International Covenant on the Elimination of All Forms of Racial Discrimination, http://www.ohchr.org/EN/ProfessionalInterest/Pages/CERD.aspx.

[19]According to the British government's Equality Bill of 2010, vegans and teetotalers should be accorded the same degree of protection against discrimination as religious groups. See Marie Woolf, "Don't Mock My Lentils: Vegans to Get Discrimination Rights," *Sunday Times* (London), March 7, 2010.

[20]Tim Black, "After the Convention, What Next for Liberty?" *Spiked* (London), March 2, 2009.

[21]Dominique Moïsi, *The Geopolitics of Emotion: How Cultures of Fear, Humiliation, and Hope Are Reshaping the World* (New York: Anchor, 2009).

[22]Jacob Mchangama, "Fri tale: Om venstrefløjens multikulturalistiske udvanding af ytringsfriheden," in *Friheden flyver: En debatbog om mangfoldighed*, Dennis Nørmark, ed. (Copenhagen: Cepos, 2010).

[23]Anne Weber, *Manual on Hate Speech* (Strasbourg: Council of Europe Publishing, 2009).

[24]Robert Post, "Hate Speech," in Hare and Weinstein, *Extreme Speech and Democracy*, pp. 123–38.

[25]Vagn Greve, *Bånd på hånd og mund: Straffforfølgelse eller ytringsfrihed* (Copenhagen: Djof, 2008).

[26]Ibid.

[27]Flemming Ytzen, "Radikal næstformand anmelder drabschef," *Politiken* (Copenhagen), March 6, 2010.

[28]Steven Lukes, *The Curious Enlightenment of Professor Caritat* (New York: Verso, 1996).

[29]Ronald Dworkin, "The Right to Ridicule," *New York Review of Books*, March 23, 2006.

[30]Flemming Rose, *Amerikanske Stemmer* (Viby: Indsigt, 2006), pp. 117–27.

[31]Anthony Lewis, *Freedom for the Thought That We Hate: A Biography of the First Amendment* (New York: Basic Books, 2007).

[32]Guy Carmi, "Dignity versus Liberty: The Two Western Cultures of Free Speech," *Boston University International Law Journal* 26, no. 2 (Fall 2008): 277–374; Guy Carmi, "Dignity—The Enemy from Within: A Theoretical and Comparative Analysis of Human Dignity as a Free Speech Justification," *University of Pennsylvania Journal of Constitutional Law* 9, no. 4 (2007): 958–1001; Adam Liptak, "U.S. Court Is Now Guiding Fewer Nations," *New York Times*, September 18, 2008.

[33]European Union law website, http://eur-lex.europa.eu/LexUriServ/LexUriServ.do?uri=CELEX:32008F0913:en:NOT.

[34]James Weinstein, "An Overview of American Free Speech Doctrine," in Hare and Weinstein, *Extreme Speech and Democracy*, pp. 81–91.

[35]Peter Walker, "Man Guilty of Inciting Murder at Cartoon Protest," *The Guardian* (London), July 5, 2007.

[36]Dirk Voorhoof, "European Court of Human Rights: Case of *Leroy v. France*," IRIS Legal Observations of the European Audiovisual Observatory, 2009.

[37]Weinstein, "An Overview," in Hare and Weinstein, *Extreme Speech and Democracy*, pp. 84–85.

[38]Ibid., pp. 81–91.

[39]C. Edwin Baker, "Autonomy and Hate Speech," in Hare and Weinstein, *Extreme Speech and Democracy*, pp. 139–57.

[40]Liptak, "U.S. Court Is Now Guiding Fewer Nations"; Carmi, "Dignity versus Liberty."

[41]Interview with author, Amsterdam, January 22, 2009. See also Paul Scheffer, *Immigrant Nations* (London: Polity, 2011).

[42]Lewis, *Freedom for the Thought That We Hate*, pp. 11–112.

[43]Michael Scammell, "Censorship and Its History: A Personal View," in *Information, Freedom and Censorship*, Kevin Boyle, ed. (London: Times Books, 1988), pp. 1–19.

[44]Carmi, "The Enemy from Within."

[45]John Stuart Mill, *On Liberty and Other Writings*, Stefan Collini, ed. (Cambridge: Cambridge University Press, 1989); Richard Reeves, *John Stuart Mill: Victorian Firebrand* (London: Atlantic Books, 2007).

[46]Uffe Ellemann-Jensen, *Vejen, jeg valgte* (Copenhagen: Gyldendal, 2007).

[47]Declaration of the Rights of Man and Citizen, http://www1.curriculum.edu.au/ddunits/downloads/pdf/dec_of_rights.pdf.

[48]Douglas Murray, "Fire in a Crowded Theatre," *Standpoint* (London), March 2009; Tim Black, "Britain Is Not a 'Crowded Theatre,'" *Spiked* (London), February 16, 2009.

[49]The context of Oliver Wendell Holmes's wording, "The most stringent protection of free speech would not protect a man falsely shouting fire in a theater and causing a panic," is illuminated by Anthony Lewis, *Freedom for the Thought That We Hate*.

[50]Alan Dershowitz, "Shouting 'Fire!'" *Atlantic Monthly*, January 1989, p. 72.

[51]Jeevan Vasagar, "Schools Drop Holocaust Lessons," *The Guardian* (London), April 2, 2007.

Chapter 8. From Russia with Love

[1]Kronid Lyubarsky, *Kronid: Izbrannye stati K. Lyubarskogo* (Moscow: Rossiiskii Gos. Gumanitarnyi Universitet, 2001), p. 60.

[2]Ibid., pp. 54–60.

[3]Interview with author, May 1993.

[4]The standard work on the history of Soviet dissent is Ludmila Alekseyeva's *Istoriya Inokomysliya v SSSR: Noveishiy period* (1984). English translation: *Soviet Dissent: Contemporary Movement for National, Religious, and Human Rights* (Middletown, CT: Wesleyan University Press, 1987). For an early history of the Moscow Helsinki Group, see Paul Goldberg, *The Final Act: The Dramatic, Revealing Story of the Moscow Helsinki Watch Group* (New York: Morrow, 1988). The history of the human rights movement is presented from more personal angles in the memoirs of those who took part: Andrei Amalrik, *Zapiski Dissident* (Moscow: Slovo, 1991); Yuri Orlov, *Opasnye mysli: Memuary iz russkoi zhizni* (Moscow:

Argumenty I Fakty, 1992); Anatoly Marchenko, *To Live Like Everyone* (New York: Holt, 1989) and *My Testimony* (New York: Penguin, 1971); Lyudmila Alexeyeva and Paul Goldberg, *The Thaw Generation: Coming of Age in the Post-Stalin Era* (Pittsburgh: Pittsburgh University Press, 1993); Andrei Sakharov, *Memoirs* (New York: Knopf, 1990); Boris Weil, *Osobo Opasny* (London: OPI, 1980); Natan Sharansky, *Fear No Evil* (New York: Random House, 1988); and Yelena Bonner, *Alone Together* (New York: Vintage, 1986).

[5]Andrei Sakharov, *Progress, Coexistence, and Intellectual Freedom* (New York: Norton, 1968). (The *New York Times* published the full text on July 22, 1968.)

[6]Goldberg, *The Final Act*; G. V. Kuzovkin, ed., *K istorii moskovskoi khelsinskoi gruppy* (Moscow: Zatsepa, 2001); Lyudmila Alexeyeva, *Dokumenty Moskovskoi Helsinskoi Gruppy* (Moscow: Zatsepa, 2001).

[7]Alexeyeva and Goldberg, *The Thaw Generation*, p. 292.

[8]Märta-Lisa Magnusson, ed., *The Louisiana Conference on Literature and Perestroika* (Esbjerg, Denmark: South Jutland University Press, 1989).

[9]Kronid Lyubarsky, "Islam i Musulman'e," in *Strana i Mir* (Almaty), 1990, no. 4.

[10]Nadezhda Mandelstam, *Hope against Hope* (New York: Scribner, 1970).

[11]Aleksandr Solzhenitsyn, *The Oak and the Calf: Sketches of Literary Life in the Soviet Union* (New York: Harper and Row, 1980).

[12]Aleksandr Solzhenitsyn, *Arkhipelag Gulag* (Paris: YMCA Press, 1973).

[13]Vadim Medvedev's statement was related to me in the beginning of 1989 by the writer Viktor Astafyev.

[14]Aleksandr Solzhenitsyn, "Live Not by Lies," *Washington Post*, February 18, 1974.

[15]Amalrik, *Zapiski Dissident*, p. 37.

[16]A. V. Korotkov, S. A. Melchin, and A. S. Stepanov, eds., *Kremlevskiy Samosud: Sekretnye Dokumenty Politbyuro o Pisatele A. Solzhenitsyne* (Moscow: Rodina, 1994).

[17]Ibid., pp. 319–26.

[18]Ibid., p. 361.

[19]Ibid., p. 353.

[20]Interview with author, September 2, 2007.

[21]Natan Sharansky, *The Case for Democracy: The Power of Freedom to Overcome Tyranny and Terror* (New York: Public Affairs, 2004), pp. 39–64.

[22]Ibid., p. 40.

[23]Jacob Mchangama, "Fri tale: Om venstrefløjens multikulturalistiske udvanding af ytringsfriheden," in *Friheden flyver: En debatbog om mangfoldighed*, ed. Dennis Nørmark (Copenhagen: Cepos, 2010), pp. 94–95.

[24]Flemming Rose, "Muhammeds ansigt," *Jyllands-Posten* (Copenhagen), September 30, 2005.

[25]Ibid.

Chapter 9. Questioning the Harassers

[1]*Jyllands-Posten* (Copenhagen), March 2, 2006. For the full text in English, see *BBC News*, March 1, 2006, http://news.bbc.co.uk/2/hi/europe/4764730.stm.

[2]Riazat Butt, "New Ex-Muslim Group Speaks Out," *The Guardian* (London), June 22, 2007. See also the websites of the Council of Ex-Muslims of Britain, http://ex-muslim.org.uk/; Zentralrat der Ex-Muslime, http://www.ex-muslime.de; and Centralrådet för ex-muslimer i Skandenavien, http://www.ex-muslim.net.

[3]Nina Shea and Paul Marshall, *Silenced: How Apostasy and Blasphemy Codes Are Choking Freedom Worldwide* (Oxford: Oxford University Press, 2011); Ibn Warraq, ed., *Leaving Islam: Apostates Speak Out* (Amherst, MA: Prometheus, 2003).

[4]*Submission: Part 1*, Theo van Gogh and Ayaan Hirsi Ali, 2004, http://www.youtube.com/watch?v=G6bFR4_Ppk8.

[5]Ayaan Hirsi Ali, *Ayaan: Opbrud og oprør* (Copenhagen: Jyllands-Postens Forlag, 2006), p. 335; Ayaan Hirsi Ali, *Infidel* (New York: Free Press, 2007).

[6]A wealth of material on Maryam Namazie's activities and her commitment can be found on her website: http://www.maryamnamazie.com.

[7]For a selection of Afshin Ellian's columns translated into English, see Social Affairs Unit, http://www.socialaffairsunit.org.uk/blog/archives/000644.php.

[8]Ludmila Alekseyeva, *Soviet Dissent: Contemporary Movement for National, Religious, and Human Rights* (Middletown, CT: Wesleyan University Press, 1987).

[9]All 65 issues of the *samizdat* periodical *Khronika tekuschikh sobytiy* (*Chronicle of Current Events*), which appeared from 1968 to 1982, are collected at http://www.memo.ru/history/DISS/chr/.

[10]Phillipe Demenet, "Adam Michnik: The Sisyphus of Democracy," *UNESCO Courier* (Paris), September 2001.

[11]Kathleen Parthé, "For Their Freedom and Ours: Alexander Herzen and the Liberation of Poland," Skalny Center newsletter, University of Rochester, 2012.

Chapter 10. A Victimless Crime

[1]The Story of Michael Servetus is based on Roland Bainton, *Hunted Heretic: The Life and Death of Michael Servetus* (Providence, RI: Blackstone Editions, 2005); Perez Zagorin, *How the Idea of Religious Toleration Came to the West* (Oxford: Princeton University Press, 2003); and Lawrence and Nancy Goldstone, *Out of the Flames* (New York: Broadway Books, 2003).

[2]Quoted in Zagorin, *Religious Toleration*, p. 77.

[3]This is a key point in Benjamin Kaplan's *Divided by Faith: Religious Conflict and the Practice of Toleration in Early Modern Europe* (London: Belknap Press, 2007).

[4]Zagorin, *Religious Toleration*, pp. 114–22. The following is based on Zagorin's account.

[5]Quoted in Stefan Zweig, chap. 7 in *The Right to Heresy, or How John Calvin Killed a Conscience: Castellio against Calvin* (New York: Viking Press, 1936), http://www.gospeltruth.net/heresy_toc.htm.

[6]Zagorin, *Religious Toleration*, p. 119.

[7]Michael Walzer, *On Toleration* (London: Yale University Press, 1997), pp. 14–36.

[8]I thank Magnus Ranstorp for the Swedish example concerning the Rosengården public housing complex in Malmö. Ranstorp is one of the authors of the cited report.

[9]See "Sharia Law in Britain: A Threat to One Law for All and Equal Rights," a report by One Law for All, June 2010, http://www.onelawforall.org.uk/wp-content/uploads/New-Report-Sharia-Law-in-Britain_fixed.pdf.

[10]Walzer, *On Toleration*, pp. 30–35.

[11]The Cairo Declaration on Human Rights in Islam, August 5, 1990, http://www1.umn.edu/humanrts/instree/cairodeclaration.html.

[12]The strong influence of the EU on the UN Human Rights agenda in the years after the end of the Cold War and its decline since 2000 are documented by Richard Gowan and Franziska Brantner, "The EU and Human Rights at the

UN: 2009 Review," European Council on Foreign Relations, http://ecfr.3cdn.net /c85a326a9956fc4ded_qhm6vaacc.pdf.

[13]See Koenraad Elst's postscript in Daniel Pipes, *The Rushdie Affair: The Novel, the Ayatollah and the West*, 2nd ed. (London: Transaction Publishers, 2003), pp. 257–89.

[14]Karin Deutsch Karlekar, "Press Freedom in 2009: Broad Setbacks to Global Media Freedom," overview essay for the report *Freedom of the Press 2010* (New York: Freedom House, 2010).

[15]On the decline of freedom of expression and freedom of the press in Western Europe, see statement by Article 19, "Western Europe: Freedom of Expression in Retreat in 2009," December 21, 2009, http://www.article19.org/pdfs/press /western-europe-freedom-of-expression-in-retreat-in-2009.pdf.

[16]Ann Elizabeth Mayer, "From Islamic Particularism to Pseudo-Universalism: The Organization of the Islamic Conference and Its Resolutions on Combating 'Defamation of Religions'" (unpublished paper, University of Pennsylvania, 2010).

[17]Morten Vestergaard, "Kritik af religion er velkommen," *Jyllands-Posten* (Copenhagen), October 28, 2008.

[18]United Nations Human Rights Commission, International Covenant on Civil and Political Rights, http://www.ohchr.org/en/professionalinterest/pages/ccpr .aspx.

[19]Anne Weber, *Manual on Hate Speech* (Strasbourg: Council of Europe Publishing, 2009).

[20]Ibid.

[21]Stephanie Farrior, *Molding the Matrix:* "The Historical and Theoretical Foundations of International Law Concerning Hate Speech," *Berkeley Journal of International Law* 14, no. 1 (1996): 3–98.

[22]Vestergaard, "Kritik af religion er velkommen."

[23]Kenan Malik, *From Fatwa to Jihad: The Rushdie Affair and Its Legacy* (London: Atlantic Books, 2009).

[24]See, for example, Matt Cherry, "Blasphemy 2010: An Old Whine in New Battles," International Humanist and Ethical Union, March 10, 2010, http://iheu .org/content/blasphemy-2010-old-whine-new-battles.

[25]Mayer, "From Islamic Particularism to Pseudo-Universalism."

[26]Ibid.

[27]See, for example, P. K. Abdul Ghafour, "OIC Chief: Global Action to Fight Islamophobia Is Needed," *Arab News* (Jeddah), May 2012.

[28]Nina Shea and Paul Marshall, *Silenced: How Apostasy and Blasphemy Codes Are Choking Freedom Worldwide* (Oxford: Oxford University Press, 2011).

[29]Abdul Kareem Nabeel Suleiman (Kareem Amer), "The Naked Truth of Islam as I Have Seen in Alexandria," Free Kareem Coalition, October 22, 2005. The story of Kareem Amer is based on information contained on the website, http://www .freekareem.org.

[30]Abdul Kareem Nabeel Suleiman (Kareem Amer), "The Events of Al-Azhar Inquisition," March 15, 2006; "The University of Terrorism," May 7, 2006; "Your Blessings, O Azhar," October 28, 2006. All articles are available on the Free Kareem Coalition website, http://www.freekareem.org. To access the articles, click on **About** at the top of the page; in the fourth paragraph, click on **what he said**.

[31]Magdy Samaan, "Prison Didn't Change Me: Kareem Amer," *Daily News Egypt* (Cairo) July 12, 2007.

[32]Konstantin Akinsha, "Orthodox Bulldozer," *Art News* (New York), May 1, 2003.

[33]Quoted from the guilty verdict, March 28, 2005, Tagansky Court, Moscow, http://old.sakharov-center.ru/museum/exhibitionhall/religion_notabene/hall _exhibitions_obvinenie.htm.

[34]Steven Lee Myers, "In Test of Free Speech, Russian Court Rules against Art Show," *New York Times*, March 28, 2005.

[35]Edward Kline, "Art on Trial: The Case of Samodurov, Vasilovskaya and Mikhalchuk" (briefing paper, Andrei Sakharov Foundation, March 11, 2005), http://asf.primetask.com/cgi/ASFdbs.pl?&pass=&action=Linkview&link_res _doc=kline-artOntrial-brief.1110648245.html.

[36]European Court of Human Rights, Partial Decision as to the Admissibility of Application no. 3007/06 by Yuriy Samodurov and Lyudmila Vasilovskaya against Russia, December 15, 2009, http://www.article19.org/data/files/pdfs/analysis /russia-first-decision-yuriy-samodurov.pdf.

[37]Ros Wynne-Jones, "Film Director Fights Blasphemy Ban," *The Independent* (London), March 28, 1996; "Artists Defend Banned Film on St. Theresa's Visions," *New York Times*, December 9, 1989; Patricia Wynn Davies, "Archaic Blasphemy Law Faces Last Judgment," *The Independent* (London), November 25, 1996.

[38]Quoted from the decision by the European Court of Human Rights in *Wingrove v. the United Kingdom*, http://original.religlaw.org/template.php?id=370.

[39]Quoted from the guilty verdict, http://old.sakharov-center.ru/museum /exhibitionhall/religion_notabene/hall_exhibitions_obvinenie.htm.

[40]Yuri Samodurov, March 10, 2003, http://old.sakharov-center.ru/museum /exhibitionhall/religion_notabene/.

[41]Frederik Stjernfelt, "Må vi se Jul I Valhal," *Weekendavisen* (Copenhagen), February 17, 2006.

[42]Sakharov Museum, "Public Debate on Taboos in Modern Russian Art," March 28, 2007, http://old.sakharov-center.ru/museum/exhibitionhall/forbidden -art/tabu-art/texts/.

[43]Yelena Bonner, letter to Sakharov Museum, March 16, 2007, http://old .sakharov-center.ru/museum/exhibitionhall/forbidden-art/discussion/.

[44]Sergei Kovalyov, "My Opinion on the Exhibition," http://old.sakharov-center .ru/museum/exhibitionhall/forbidden-art/discussion/sergey-kovalev/.

[45]Salil Tripathi, *Offense: The Hindu Case* (London: Seagull Books, 2009). Husain's story is based on Tripathi's book and Somini Sengupta, "A Muslim Artist and Hindu Images: It's a Volatile Mix," *New York Times*, June 16, 1998; and Somini Sengupta, "An Artist in Exile Tests India's Democratic Ideals," *New York Times*, September 9, 2008.

[46]Jerome Starkey, "He Just Shared an Article with Friends. What's the Problem?" *The Independent* (London), February 1, 2008.

[47]Jochen-Martin Gutsch, "Free Speech Case Tests Afghanistan," *Der Spiegel* (Hamburg), May 19, 2008.

[48]Ibid.

[49]Kim Sengupta, "Sayed Pervez Kambaksh: How He Was Sentenced to Die," *The Independent* (London), February 25, 2009.

[50]Austin Dacey and Colin Koproske, *Islam and Human Rights: Defending Universality at the United Nations* (New York: Center for Inquiry, 2008).

[51]Younus Shaikh, "Living among the Believers," International Humanist and Ethical Union, February 1, 2002, http://iheu.org/content/living-among-believers.

[52]Barry Bearak, "Death to Blasphemers: Islam's Grip on Pakistan," *New York Times*, May 12, 2001.

[53]Ibid.

[54]Ibid.

[55]"Dr. Younus Shaikh Free!" International Humanist and Ethical Union, January 23, 2004.

[56]Shea and Marshall, *Silenced*, pp. 99–100.

[57]Kamila Shamsie, *Offense: The Muslim Case* (London: Seagull Books, 2009).

[58]Shea and Marshall, *Silenced*, p. 86.

[59]Mohammad Nafees, "Blasphemy Laws in Pakistan: A Historical Overview," Center for Research and Security Studies, Islamabad, 2012.

[60]Tom Hundley, "Rushdie, Britain Stir Muslim World's Fury, *Chicago Tribune*, June 20, 2007.

[61]Kristoffer Pinholt, "Pakistan's Ambassadør Kritiserer JP," *Jyllands-Posten* (Copenhagen), June 4, 2008.

[62]Interview with author, November 27, 2009.

[63]"Klager, krav og krenkelser," *Dyade*, no. 4 (2008).

Afterword

[1]Jacob Mchangama, "European Leaders Have Long Compromised Free Speech," January 16, 2015, https://www.indexoncensorship.org/2015/01/jacob-mchangama-european-leaders-long-compromised-free-expression/.

[2]Robert Post, "Hate Speech," in *Extreme Speech and Democracy* (Oxford, U.K.: Oxford University Press, 2009), pp. 123–38.

[3]Kenan Malik, *From Fatwa to Jihad: The Rushdie Affair and Its Legacy* (London: Atlantic Books, 2009), p. 189–90.

Index

Aandehullet (journal), 77–78
Abbas, Fauzia Mufti, 271
ABC, 134
Abderrahmane, Slimane Hadj, 97
Abdullah (king of Saudi Arabia),
    77
Abu Laban, Ahmad, 36, 121–22
ACLU. *See* American Civil
    Liberties Union
actions
    distinction between speech and,
        80, 114, 148, 160–61, 254
    incited by speech, in Holocaust,
        81–82, 84, 145–46
adapt, infamous ability of humans
    to, 73, 77
Ad-Dustur (newspaper), 135
Afghanistan
    media coverage of, 32
    religious defamation in,
        responses to, 264–67
Afghan Journalists Association,
    266
Akkari, Ahmed, 123–24
Al-Azhar University, 250, 252
Alekseyeva, Lyudmila, 173–76
Al Jazeera (television station), 136
Alliance of Civilizations, 131
al Qaeda. *See* Qaeda, al

Amalrik, Andrei, 183
ambassadors, Muslim, in Cartoon
    Crisis, 3, 78, 121, 124
Amer, Abdul Kareem Nabeel
    Suleiman, 250–53
American Civil Liberties Union
    (ACLU), 83
American Morning (television
    program), 133–35
Amnesty International, 86, 189
Andersen, Kresten Vestbjerg,
    144
Andreasen, Victor, 117
Annan, Kofi, 131
anti-Islamic activity, use of term,
    90
anti-Semitism
    in caricatures, 57, 58, 89–90
    in cartoons, 135–36
    Muhammad cartoons compared
        to, 89–91
    in speech, 82–83, 146–47
Anzour, Najdat, 162–63
apartheid, South African, 74, 87,
    212–13, 214
apostasy
    death penalty and threats for,
        93, 198, 209
    right of, 93, 197–98, 209–10, 223–24

appeasement
  of Nazi Germany, 77, 80–81
  in response to Cartoon Crisis,
    78, 116
  of Soviet Union, 187
Appignanesi, Lisa, *Free Speech Is
  No Offense*, 303n19
Arab League, 123, 125
Arab News (newspaper), 135
Arbour, Louise, 121, 127
art
  censorship by museums, 48–51,
    61, 259
  differences in interpretation of
    offensiveness of, 59–63
  language used to represent, 63
  religious defamation in, 253–61
  right to offend with, 51, 60–63
  self-censorship by artists,
    141–43
  speech as, 87–88
  Westergaard cartoon of
    Muhammad as, 60
Article 19 (organization), 85, 242
assassination attempts, against
    Westergaard. *See also* death
    threats
  in 2007, 67, 70
  in 2008, 13, 93–94
  in 2010, 68–69, 78, 111
Ates, Seyran, 86
Atkinson, Rowan, 51
Austria, hate speech banned in,
    147
Aznar, José María, 20, 21

Bæklund, Rachel, 118
Balkh University, 264
Bangladesh, 267
Barbican Theatre (London), 52
Bashir, Omar al-, 210
BBC, 90, 122
Begin, Menachem, 143
Belov, Vasiliy, 255
Bendix, Hans, 73, 77–78
Berlingske Tidende (newspaper), 79,
    119, 144
Bharatiya Janata Party, 262
Bharat Mata (Husain), 262–63
Bhatti, Shahbaz, 269
Bhutto, Zulfikar Ali, 107, 270
Biard, Gérard. 288–91
Bibi, Asia, 269
Bill of Rights, U.S., 230
bin Laden, Osama, 34, 43
blasphemy
  calls for global ban on, 130, 131
  as form of terrorism, 269–71
  as punishable by death, 114, 116,
    121, 265–70
  terrorism as response to, 113–14
  updating of legislation on, 139,
    153
  violence as response to, 115–16
Blix, Ragnvald, 79
Bluitgen, Kåre
  biography of Muhammad by,
    39–40, 41, 45–46, 141, 302n7
  Muhammad cartoons targeting,
    55
BNP. *See* British National Party
Bøgh, Mikkel, 58

Bojesen, Bo, 73
bombs. *See also* Madrid train
    bombings
    in London underground
        bombings of 2005, 49
    in Westergaard cartoon of
        Muhammad, 2, 54, 57–58,
        75, 100
Bonner, Elena, 256, 259–60
Bouyeri, Mohammad, 36–37, 217
boycott, of Danish goods, 127, 128
Brezhnev, Leonid, 185
Britain. *See also* London
    censorship of film in, 256
    Equality Bill of 2010 in, 308n19
    libel cases in, 242
    proposed ban on speech
        criticizing religion, 51,
        303n19
    protests over Muhammad
        cartoons in, 156
    Sharia law in, 237
British Empire, 237
British National Party (BNP),
    157
Brooklyn Museum of Modern Art,
    61–62
Burroughs, William S., *Naked
    Lunch*, 87
Bush, George H. W., 240
Bush, George W., 43, 191

Cabut, Jean, 283–84
Callamard, Agnès, 85
Calvin, Jean, 225–26
Calvin, John, 230–32, 235

Defense of Orthodox Faith, 231
canonic alibi, 60
caricatures
    anti-Nazi, 78–81
    anti-Semitic, 57, 58, 89–90
    vs. illustrations, 41
Carlsen, Annette, 42
cartoon(s). *See also* Muhammad
    cartoon(s); *specific cartoonists*
    anti-Nazi, 78–81
    Christians and Jews in, 74,
        133–36
    about Holocaust, 134–36
    vs. illustrations, 41–43
Cartoon Crisis. *See* Muhammad
    Cartoon Crisis
Castellio, Sebastian, *Concerning
    Heretics*, 231–32
casualties
    of Cartoon Crisis, 3, 111, 130, 139
    of Madrid train bombings, 19–20
    of protests against Rushdie's *The
        Satanic Verses*, 114
Catholic Inquisition, 225–33
Caution, Religion! exhibition,
    253–58, 260
Cavanna, François, 286
Cavling, Ole, 80
Cayat, Elsa, *Le Divan* ("The Couch"),
    279
censorship. *See also* self-censorship
    as act of violence, 6
    of art, 48–49, 61, 257–58
    of film, 164, 165, 256, 262
    of literature, 52–53, 87–88, 182,
        240, 262

OIC's attempts to globalize, 242–45

of theater, 221–22

Central Council of Ex-Muslims in Germany, 208

Chafiq, Chahla, 195

Chakrabarti, Shami, 49

Charbonnier, Stéphane (Charb), 282, 286–88

Charlie Hebdo (magazine), 27, 196, 279–96

arson and cyber attack against, in 2011, 281

cartoons of Islam in, 281, 283

court cases against, 284–85

reprinting of *Jyllands–Posten* Muhammad cartoons, 282–83

terrorist attack against, in 2015, 279–80, 281, 283, 285–86, 289

Charta 77, 197

Chechen War, First, 30

China, "abuse" of freedom of speech in, 146

Christianity

art as offensive to, 61–63

in cartoons, 74, 134, 142–43

essential beliefs of, 231–32

power of images in, 59

Reformation in, 225–29

schisms in, 228

Christoffersen, Thorbjørn, 143–45

Chronicle of Current Events, 169, 176, 221

civilians, Islam on killing of, 36

Clausen, Erik, 257

closed societies. *See also specific countries*

free speech in, vs. open societies, 44, 81

human rights in, 188–89

potential for change in, 8

storytelling in, vs. open societies, 6

CNN, 133–34

Coetzee, J. M., 139

Cold War, democracy movements during, as threat to stability, 115

comedians. *See* humor

Committee for the Defense of the Honor of the Prophet, 125, 126

Committee for the Protection of Afghan Journalists, 266

Congress, U.S., censorship of art in, 61

Constitution, Afghan, 265–66

Constitution, U.S.

Bill of Rights in, 230

First Amendment of, 142, 156, 273. *See also* speech, freedom of

Corcoran Gallery of Art (Washington, D.C.), 61

Coulibaly, Amedy, 280

Council of Europe, 147

Council of Ex-Muslims, 196–97, 209

cultural diversity

and ethnic clashes in former Soviet states, 30, 292

and human rights, 8–9, 197

Czechoslovakia
  Prague Spring in, 221
  Warsaw Pact invasion of, 172,
    221, 224
Czech Republic, 87

Dacey, Austin, *Islam and Human
  Rights*, 266
Dagbladet (newspaper), 141
Daily Champion (newspaper), 140
Daily Independent (newspaper),
  140
Daniel, Yuli, 171, 220
Danish, Sarwar, 266
Danish Film School, 163
Danish Institute of Human Rights,
  85
Danish Islamic Society, 121
Danish People's Party, 54, 55
Danish Refugee Council, 119
Danish Security and Intelligence
  Services (PET)
  Rose under protection of, 121
  Sørensen (Karim) under, 94–95
  on terrorist attack planned
    against Denmark in 2009,
    103, 111, 112
  Westergaard under protection
    of, 67–71
Danish Union of Journalists, 86
Danmarks Radio, 113
Darabi, Louzla
  No Name Fever exhibition, 50
  Scène d'amour, 50, 303n17
death penalty
  for apostasy, 93, 209

for blasphemy, 114, 116, 121,
  265–70
for heresy, 225–32
deaths. *See* casualties
death threats. *See also*
    assassination attempts
  against Muslim dissidents, 209,
    214
  in response to Muhammad
    cartoons, 54–55, 86, 115
  against Rose, 103–4
  for speaking out against Islam, 198
Declaration of Rights of the
  Working and Exploited
  People (1918), 302n1(ch3)
Declaration of the Rights of Man
  (1789), 163, 230, 309n47
Declaration on Human Rights in
  Islam, 240–41, 249, 311n11
defamation cases, in Germany,
  rise of, 242. *See also* religious
    defamation
democracies. *See also specific
  countries*
  during Cold War, as threat to
    stability, 115
  individual vs. group rights in, 236
  in Middle East, opposition to, 128
  right to offend in, 11, 155
  storytelling in, 6
  unconditional free speech in,
    81, 155
Denmark
  embassies of, attacks and
    protests at, 3, 92, 111, 130,
    156, 255, 271

foreign office of, 78, 79

homogeneity of culture of, 119, 234

housing shortage in, 117

imams' criticism of media coverage in, 43, 53, 125

and Nazi Germany, 77–81

protests over Muhammad cartoons in, 124

terror attack planned for 2009 in, 103–13

depictions of Muhammad. *See* Muhammad, depictions of

Dershowitz, Alan, 165

Deuchar, Stephen, 48–49

Diéne, Doudou, 127

dignity, right of, 156

dissidents

in fear societies, role of, 190–92

as inspiration for Rose in Cartoon Crisis, 119, 192, 223

Muslim. *See* Muslim dissidents

religious, 229

search for utopia by, 222–23

Soviet. *See* Soviet dissidents

diverse societies

vs. homogeneous societies, free speech in, 12, 158, 160, 273

Muslim societies as, 249

tyranny of silence in, 12, 273

diversity, cultural

and ethnic clashes in former Soviet states, 30, 292

and human rights, 9, 197–98

Dolfuss, Engelbert, 79

double-thinkers, 190

doubt, role of, 5

dung, in art, 62–63

Dworkin, Ronald, "The Right to Ridicule," 154–55

Dylan, Bob, 93, 225

education, gender segregation in, 210, 252

Egypt

"abuse" of freedom of speech in, 146

in Cartoon Crisis, role of, 124–28

dissidents in, 191

elections of 2005 in, 95

religious defamation in, responses to, 250–53

Egyptian Spring, 127–28

Ekstra Bladet (newspaper), 79–80, 117–18

elections

Egyptian, of 2005, 127

Iranian, of 2009, 10

Spanish, impact of Madrid train bombings on, 19–21

Ellemann-Jensen, Uffe, 78, 163–64

Ellian, Afshin, 14, 213–20

death threats against, 214

on Muhammad cartoons, 219–20

Soviet dissidents compared to, 220

embassies, Danish, attacks and protests at, 3, 92, 111, 130, 156, 255, 271

empathy

link between storytelling and, 274–75

vs. sympathy, 275

empires, approaches to tolerance in, 237

England. *See* Britain

Enzensberger, Hans Magnus, 102

Equality Bill of 2010 (Britain), 308n19

Ergüven, Abdullah Riza, *Yasak Tümceler (The Forbidden Phrases)*, 52–53

Eriksen, Jens-Martin, *Adskillelsens politik*, 57

erotic literature, censorship of, 87–88

ETA (Euskadi Ta Askatasuna), and Madrid bombings, 20

ethnic clashes, in former Soviet states, 30, 292

EU. *See* European Union

Europe. *See also specific countries*
codification of human rights in, 147

hate speech legislation in, 85, 147–53

on misunderstandings as cause of conflict, 35

Muhammad cartoons reprinted in, 128–29

as part of Islamic world, 47

religious freedom in, origins of, 229–30

self-hatred in culture of, 217–18

tolerance in, conceptions of, 235–39

vs. United States, free speech in, 12, 155–60, 273

welfare states in, crisis of, 149

European Convention for the Protection of Human Rights, 147

European Council, 244

European Court of Human Rights, 52–53, 147, 156–57, 244, 256, 258

European Union (EU)
in Cartoon Crisis, 78, 124–25, 130–31

and democracy in Middle East, 127

hate speech legislation in, 156

Holocaust denial banned in, 166

as model for world, 30

execution. *See* death penalty

ex-Muslims. *See* apostasy; Muslim dissidents; *specific people*

Expressen (newspaper), 303n17

expression, freedom of. *See* speech, freedom of

fanaticism, 34–35

FBI. *See* Federal Bureau of Investigation

fear, freedom undermined by, 149

fear societies, 187–92

Federal Bureau of Investigation (FBI), 103, 105, 109–10, 113

Figaro, Le (newspaper), 286

film
censorship of, 164, 165, 256, 262

self-censorship in, 143–45

"fire," crying, in crowded theater, 164–65

Fitzgerald, F. Scott, *The Great Gatsby*, 294

Fitna (film), 164, 165

flag burning, 157

Fogh Rasmussen, Anders, 3, 43, 53, 121, 124, 129

Forbidden Art—2006 exhibition, 259–61

Forefathers' Eve (Mickiewicz), 221–22

Fourest, Caroline, 196, 282, 283, 285–86, 291

France, self-censorship of theater in, 52

freedom(s). *See also* religious freedom; speech, freedom of
misunderstandings of price of, 215–17
of press, recent decline in, 241–42
relation between tolerance and, 12

Freedom of Expression in Islam, 121

Freedom House, 189, 241

Friedman, Milton, 208

Fritsch, Theodor, 83

Front National, 284, 286

Fukuyama, Francis, 239

gays
vs. ex-Muslims, marginalization of, 209
rights movement for, 213

Gayssot Act, 1990, 291

Gaza, 129

Gazeta Wyborcza (newspaper), 222

gender segregation, in education, 210, 252

Germany
defamation cases in, 242
drawing of Iranian soccer players in, 10
free speech vs. right of dignity in, 156
hate speech banned in, 147
Nazi. *See* Nazi Germany
Weimar, 82, 83–85, 145–46

Gheit, Ahmed Aboul, 124

Gilani, Daood Sayed. *See* Headley, David

Ginsberg, Allen, *Howl*, 87

Ginzburg, Aleksandr, 175

Giuliani, Rudy, 62

glasnost, 178

Glazunov, Ilya, 255

Goebbels, Joseph, 79, 83

Gogh, Theo van, murder of
media coverage of, 35–36, 126
motivations for, 36–37, 126, 198
self-censorship after, 45
threats made referencing, 50–51, 123
as "victim of free speech," 86

Gomaa, Ali, 125

Gomez, Maria (pseudonym), 13, 17–27
on day of Madrid bombings, 17–19, 20
effects of Madrid bombings on, 21–22
at trial of perpetrators of Madrid bombings, 13, 21–24

good manners, vs. self-censorship, 140, 145, 203–4
Gorbachev, Mikhail, 82, 176, 178–79, 304n11
Göring, Hermann, 79
Gothenburg (Sweden), Museum of World Culture in, 50–51
Grabar, Oleg, 25
Graff, Finn, 142–43, 145
Grass, Günter, 89–90
grievance culture, 90, 149, 152–53, 257–58, 275
groups, vs. individuals
  in conceptions of human rights, 8–9, 197, 301–2n1(ch3)
  in conceptions of tolerance, 235–39
  minorities as, 237
Guardian (newspaper), 19, 133
Gurevich, Alina, 253
Gyldenkærne, Nanna, 302n7

Halabi, Abu Rached el-, 97
Haqqani, Husain, 108
Hardtalk (television program), 122
harm principle, 162–63
Harvey, Marcus, 61–62
Hashim, Abdur Rehman, 112–13
hate speech. *See also* anti-Semitism
  bans on, as threat to freedom of speech, 150–52
  as cause of Holocaust, 84
  definitions of, 150–51, 244
  and distinction between words and actions, 114, 148, 160–61, 297

European legislation banning, 85, 147–53
  freedom of speech as antidote to, 83–85
  international conventions on, 147–48, 149–51
  U.S. legislation on, lack of, 155–60
Havel, Václav, 87, 222–23
Hayek, Friedrich von, 208
Headley, David, 105–13
Headley, Serrill, 106–7
Heger, Anders, 88
Helsinki Accords of 1975, 173
Helsinki Groups, 174–76, 179, 188, 221
Helsinki Watch Committee, 174
Helveg-Petersen, Niels, 78
Henningsen, Poul, 72–73, 77–81, 86–87
heresy, death penalty for, 225–32
Herzen, Aleksandr, 224
Hezbollah, 210
Hindley, Myra, 61–62
Hinduism, 237, 261–64
Hirsi Ali, Ayaan, 14, 198–208
  De maagdenkooi, translations of, 47
  on depictions of Muhammad, need for more, 200–201
  as fundamentalist, 217
  Infidel, 199
  liberalism of, 208
  on Muhammad cartoons, 195, 199–208
  Nomad, 199
  references to, in Cartoon Crisis threats, 126

Soviet dissidents compared
to, 220
in *Submission*, 198
as "victim of free speech," 86
Hirst, Damien, *This Little Piggy
Went to Market*, 62
Historia Mortis Serveti
(anonymous), 230
Hitler, Adolf, 77–85, 145–46
Hizb-ut-Tahrir, 81
Hlayhel, Raed, 97–98, 123–24
Holmes, Oliver Wendell, Jr., 164–65
Holocaust
cartoons about, 134–36, 285
denial of, 12, 85, 166–67, 291–92,
299
speech in incitement of, 81–82,
84, 146
homogeneous societies
Denmark as, 119, 234
vs. diverse societies, free speech
in, 12, 158, 160
homosexuals
vs. ex-Muslims, marginalization
of, 209
rights movement for, 213
Høst & Søn, 46
human nature
adaptation in, 73, 77
storytelling in, 6, 274
human rights
codification in Europe, 147
cultural differences and, 8–9,
197–98
history of struggle for universal,
14

for individuals vs. groups, 8–9,
197–98, 301–2n1(ch3)
Islamic conception of, 240–47
national self-determination in
conflict with, 30
in Soviet Union. *See* Soviet
human rights movement
as Western invention, 198, 241
Human Rights Commission, UN,
121, 127, 188, 242–43
Human Rights Council, UN, 130,
242–43
Human Rights Watch, 174
humor. *See also* caricatures; cartoon(s)
about Islam, Ellian's call for, 214
loss of context for, 10
self-censorship in, 37–38, 43, 47
Soviet restrictions on, 54
Husain, Maqbool Fida, 261–64
Bharat Mata, 263
Hussein, Saddam, 240
Hvam, Frank, 37–38, 43, 47

Ibrahim, Saad Eddin, 146, 191
identity(ies)
multiple, 235
Muslim, 235
of Sørensen (Karim), 101
Ihsanoglu, Ekmeleddin, 76–77,
131, 243–44, 245
Ijaz-ul-Haq, Mohammad, 271
illustrations, vs. cartoons, 41–42
images. *See also specific types*
language used to represent, 63
power of, 59–63
immigrant society model, 239

immigration
    Muslim, 54, 158–59
    phases of, 159
Independent (newspaper), 266
Index on Censorship (journal), 85, 160
India
    in British Empire, 237
    censorship in, 262–63
    religious defamation in,
        responses to, 261–64, 272
    terrorist attack of 2008 in, 112
Indian Penal Code, 263
individuals, vs. groups
    in conceptions of human rights,
        8–9, 197–98, 301–2n1(ch3)
    in conceptions of tolerance,
        235–39
    minorities as, 237
infidels, Islam on killing of, 36
Information (newspaper), 45, 46
Inner Mission, 72
Innocence of Muslims (film), 281
Inquisition, 225–33
insensitivity training, 12
International Convention on the
    Elimination of All Forms of
    Racial Discrimination, 147–48,
    150–51, 189, 248
international conventions,
    constraints on freedom of
    speech in, 147–48, 150–51. *See
    also specific conventions*
International Covenant on Civil
    and Political Rights, UN,
    147–48, 243–45, 248

international forums, attempts to
    ban offensive speech in, 12
International Helsinki Federation
    for Human Rights, 174
International Human Rights Day,
    85
International Press Institute, 179
Inter-Services Intelligence
    (Pakistan), 108
Iran
    attack on Danish embassy in, 92
    depictions of Muhammad in, 25
    elections of 2009 in, 10
    on German drawing of Iranian
        soccer players, 10–11
    Holocaust cartoons
        commissioned in, 134–36
    Muslim dissidents from, 208,
        210, 213–17
    revolution of 1979 in, 210,
        213–15
Iraq
    Kuwait invaded by, 240
    Spanish troops withdrawn from,
        19
Ireland, religious defamation
    legislation in, 246
Islam. *See also* Muslim(s)
    cartoons about. *See* Muhammad
        Cartoon Crisis
    global ban on criticism of, calls
        for, 123–25, 126, 130–32,
        242–47
    human rights in, 240–47
    jokes about, call for, 214
    legislation protecting, 90

relations between West and, after 9/11, 33

terrorism perpetrated in name of, 75, 76

totalitarian movement based on, 195–97, 202–3, 207

violence in, 32–37

Islamic Faith Society, 123

Islamic law. *See also* Sharia law
in Afghanistan, 265
on blasphemy as punishable by death, 121
on depictions of Muhammad, 25, 46–47
in European justice systems, 90
in Pakistan, 270

Islamic terrorists, use of term, 90

Islamic world, Europe as part of, 47

Islamophobia
ambiguity of concept, 3, 196, 248
calls for crack down on, 130, 245–46, 248

Israel, human rights in, 188–89

Jackson, Michael, 2

Jami, Ehsan, 86

Japan, cartoon about royal family of, 11

Jehovah's Witnesses, 160

Jespersen, Otto, 11

Jesus, in Westergaard's cartoons, 74, 134

Jews. *See also* anti-Semitism; Holocaust
cartoons of, 74, 133–136, 143

European Muslims compared with, 89–91, 243

"Jihad Jane," 141

jokes. *See* humor

Jones, Sherry, 199

Jordan, Muhammad cartoons reprinted in, 9

Jourová, Věra, 299

Joyce, James, *Ulysses*, 87

Juste, Carsten, 43, 132, 135

Jyllands-Posten (newspaper). *See also* Muhammad cartoon(s)
accused of anti-Muslim agenda, 121, 134
on Bluitgen's biography of Muhammad, 39–40
Christians and Jews in cartoons of, 74, 134
as international newspaper, 33
Rose as culture editor at, 33–35, 280
Rose as Moscow correspondent to, 2, 5, 29, 32–33
terrorist attack planned for 2009 against, 103–14
on violence in Islam, 36–37
Westergaard as freelance cartoonist at, 69, 73

Kabakov, Ilya, 259

Kambaksh, Sayed Pervez, 264–67

Kashmir, 267

Kashmiri, Ilyas, 109, 113, 306n7 (ch6)

Kassem, Ahmed, 121

Kazantzaki, Nikos, *The Last Temptation of Christ*, 262

KGB (Komitet gosudarstvennoy bezopasnosti), 169, 173, 176, 182–83, 224
Khomeini, Ayatollah, 14, 216, 217, 240, 246
Khrushchev, Nikita, 181, 182
King, Martin Luther, Jr., 225
Kissinger, Henry, 187
Kjær, Karsten, 92
Kjærsgaard, Pia, 55, 151
Klausen, Jytte, *The Cartoons That Shook the World*, 199
Klemperer, Victor, 91
Koestler, Arthur, 139
Koproske, Colin, *Islam and Human Rights*, 266
Koran
  artistic depictions of, 48–49
  comedians on, 11, 38, 43
  on violence against civilians, 36
Kosolapov, Alexander, 253–54, 257, 259
Kouachi, Chérif and Saïd, 279–80, 285–86
Kovalev, Sergei, 30–31, 260, 301–2n1(ch3)
Kruuse, Jens, 88
Ku Klux Klan, 157
Kulturweekend (magazine), 35
Kuwait, Iraqi invasion of, 240

labor camps
  Chinese, 146
  Soviet, 54, 178, 181–82
Larson, Gary, 25

Lashkar-e-Taiba (LeT), 108–9, 112–13
Latham, John, *God Is Great*, 48–49
Lawrence, D. H., *Lady Chatterley's Lover*, 87
legislation
  on blasphemy, 139, 153
  on hate speech, 85, 114, 147–53, 155–60, 296
  on Islam and Muslims, 90
  on offensive images, 63
  on public decency, 87
  on religious defamation, 51, 81, 83, 246, 303n19
Lenin, Vladimir, 182, 184–85, 259
Leroy, Denis, 156–57
LeT. *See* Lashkar-e-Taiba
Lévy, Bernard-Henri, 195
Lewis, Bernard, 46–47
libel, 242
Libération (newspaper), 1
Libya, protests in, 140
Life of Brian, The (film), 200, 211
Ligachev, Yegor, 177
literature
  censorship of, 52–53, 87–88, 182, 240, 262
  power of, 181
  self-censorship of, 199
  by Soviet dissidents, 171–72, 180–85, 220–21
London
  Barbican Theatre in, 52
  Royal Academy in, 61
  Tate Britain in, 48–49

underground bombings of 2005 in, 49

Louisiana Museum of Modern Art, 177

Lukes, Steven, *The Curious Enlightenment of Professor Caritat*, 153–54

Luther, Martin, 227–28

Lutheranism, 228, 230

Lykketoft, Mogens, 78

Lyubarsky, Kronid, 169–71, 301–2n1(ch3)

at conference on literature and perestroika, 177–79

death of, 171, 175

emigration of, 170, 176

return to Russia, 179

trial of, 169–70

Madrid train bombings (2004), 17–27

attribution of, 20–21

casualties of, 19–20

memorial to victims of, 26

motivations for, 26–27

political impact of, 19–21

trial of perpetrators of, 13, 21–24, 27

Magaard, Tina, 36, 37

Magazinet (newspaper), 143

"Make Peace, Not Love," 34

Makiya, Kanan, 169

Malik, Kenan, 114, 246, 297

Manar (TV station), 126

Mandela, Nelson, 87

Mandelstam, Nadezhda, *Hope against Hope*, 180–81

Mandelstam, Osip, 29, 180–81

Manet, Édouard, 63

Le déjeuner sur l'herbe, 59–60

Olympia, 60

Manji, Irshad, 195

manners, good, vs. self-censorship, 140, 145, 203–4

Mansour, Said, 37

Mapplethorpe, Robert, 60–61, 63

Markaz-ad-Dawa-wal-Irshad, 108

Marlowe, Christopher, *Tamburlaine the Great*, 52

Marx, Karl, 57, 201

Marxism, 201, 206–7

Matthesen, Anders, 115–16, 257

Mayer, Ann Elizabeth, 243

Mchangama, Jacob, 150, 293

media coverage. *See also specific publications*

of Cartoon Crisis, 124–26, 159

Danish, imams' criticism of, 43, 53, 125

of Madrid train bombings, 19

Mill on responsibilities of press in, 161–62

recent decline in freedom of press and, 241–42

self-censorship in, 2

of Soviet human rights movement, 173–74

of van Gogh's murder, 35

meditation, 118–19

Medvedev, Roy, 54

Medvedev, Vadim, 182

Meheri, Athmane, 97
Melchior, Arne, 74–75
Merkel, Angela, 300
Michnik, Adam, 222–23
Mickiewicz, Adam, *Forefathers' Eve*, 221–22
Middle East. *See also specific countries*
   opponents of democracy in, 127–28
   protests over Muhammad cartoons in, 127–30, 139–40
Mikhalkov, Nikita, 255
Mikkelsen, Brian, 54
Mikkelsen, Jørn, 40, 41, 47, 104
Miliband, David, 164, 165
Mill, John Stuart, *On Liberty*, 161
Miller, Henry, 87
   Sexus, 88
minority(ies)
   as collectives vs. individuals, 237–38
   free speech as restricted to, 6
   problems with distinction between majority and, 272
   weak, Muhammad cartoons as attack on, 161, 205–7, 211–12, 219
Mitchell, W. J. T., *What Do Pictures Want?*, 58–59, 63
Mohammed's Believe It or Else? (comic strip), 25
Moïsi, Dominique, 150
Møller, Arvid. *See* Spott, Niels
Møller, Per Stig, 146
Momani, Jihad, 9

Monde, Le (newspaper), 279, 284
Moore, Michael, 165
Morozov, Pavlik, 137
Morozov, Trofim, 137
Moscow, Sakharov Museum in, 253–61
Moscow Helsinki Group, 173–75
Moussa, Amr, 125
Movement for the Finality of the Prophet, 268
Mozaffari, Mehdi, 195
Mubarak, Hosni, 127, 146, 191, 252
Muhammad, depictions of. *See also* Muhammad cartoon(s)
   in Bluitgen's biography of Muhammad, 39–40, 41, 45–46, 141
   differences in Muslim responses to, 25
   Hirsi Ali on need for, 200–201
   imams' reasons for opposing, 25, 123
   Islamic law on, 25, 46–47
   by Muslims, 25
   by non-Muslims, 25, 46, 141–44
Muhammad cartoon(s), 40–65. *See also* Westergaard cartoon
   anti-Semitism of Nazi Germany compared to, 89–91
   as attack on weak minority, 161, 205–7, 211–12, 219
   commissioning of, 40–42
   content of, 2, 41–42, 54–58
   crisis over. *See* Muhammad Cartoon Crisis
   global ban on, calls for, 123

Headley (David) on, 110

vs. illustrations of Muhammad, 41–43

as inclusive vs. exclusive of Muslims, 64

initial reactions to, 64, 120–23

interpretations of, 57–61

issues leading to commissioning of, 33–40

opponents' role in spread of, 59

reprinted in European countries, 128–29

reprinted in Islamic countries, 9

as response to self-censorship, 2, 11, 40, 42–54

Rose on regrets about, 113–15

Sørensen (Karim) on, 99–100

text accompanying, 43–44, 192–93

Muhammad Cartoon Crisis, 120–38

ambassadors of Muslim countries in, 3, 78, 121, 124

and anti-Nazi cartoon crises, parallels between, 78–80

anti-Semitism in Nazi Germany compared to, 89–91

attempts at appeasement in, 77–78

boycott of Danish goods in, 127, 128

calls for global ban on religious defamation and, 123–25, 126, 130–32

coordination of Muslim response in, 123–25, 129–30

Danish embassies targeted in, 3, 92, 111, 130, 156, 255

deaths attributed to, 3, 111, 130, 139

death threats in, 54–55, 86, 115

democracy in Middle East and, 127–28

dissidents as inspiration for Rose in, 119–20, 192, 223

Egypt's role in, 124–28

escalation of, in 2006, 127–37

false claims made in, 125–27, 162–63

harm principle and, 163

historical context for, 233

manifesto on, 195–96, 208

mistakes made by Rose in, 132–36

misunderstandings in, 35

Muslim dissidents on, 195, 199–213, 219–220

origins and development of, 120–25

protests in Europe in, 124, 156

protests in Middle East in, 127–30, 140

protests in Nigeria in, 139–40

responsibility for, theories about, 3

Rose and *Jyllands-Posten* blamed for violence in, 114–16, 257, 271

Rose in public debates over, 122, 125, 132–37

subjects of cartoons in, 2, 41, 54–58

and terrorist attack planned against Denmark in 2009, 103–13 time between publication and, 120–21

U.S. response to, 158–60

Mumbai, terrorist attack of 2008 in, 112

Munajid, Muhammad Al-, 26

Museum of World Culture (Gothenburg), 50–51

Muslim(s)

depictions of Muhammad by, 25

European, compared with Jews, 89–91, 243

former. *See* apostasy; Muslim dissidents

identity of, 235

immigration of, 54, 158–59

legislation protecting, 90

response to Muhammad cartoons. *See* Muhammad Cartoon Crisis

in Spain, history of, 22

stereotypes of, in Muhammad cartoons, 57–58

terrorism by, terms used for, 90

U.S., integration of, 158–59

as weak minority, 161, 205–7, 211–12, 219

women, subjugation of, 198, 210, 264

Muslim Brotherhood, 127, 128, 250

Muslim Council of Britain, 90

Muslim dissidents, 195–224

on Cartoon Crisis, 195, 199–213, 219–20

Ellian as, 213–20

Hirsi Ali as, 198–208

manifesto on Muhammad cartoons signed by, 195–96, 208

Namazie as, 208–13

Soviet dissidents compared to, 13–14, 171, 191, 195, 220–24

Muslim World Conference, 77

My Country and the World (journal), 177–78

Mykle, Agnar, 88

Nabokov, Vladimir, *Lolita*, 87

Namazie, Maryam, 14, 208–13

death threats against, 209

on Muhammad cartoons, 195, 208–13

socialism of, 208

Soviet dissidents compared to, 220

Nasreen, Taslima, 195

National Endowment for the Arts, 61

national self-determination, human rights in conflict with, 30

National Socialism. *See* Nazi Germany

Nazi Germany, 77–85. *See also* Holocaust

Danish critics of, 77–81

Jews in, European Muslims compared to, 89–91

Nuremberg trials after, 81

restrictions on freedom of speech in rise of, 82–85

Nazi sympathizers, in United States, 83, 157

Neier, Aryeh, 83–84

Defending My Enemy, 84
  in *Index on Censorship*, 85
Netherlands, blasphemy
  legislation in, 153
New Republic (magazine), 25
New York, Brooklyn Museum of
  Modern Art in, 61–62
New York Review of Books, 155
New York Times (newspaper), 62,
  114, 268
New York Times Magazine, 133
Nigeria
  protests in, 139–40
  Sharia law in, 140
9/11
  Afghanistan after, 32
  as bin Laden's declaration of
    love, 34
  democracy in Middle East after,
    127
  free speech regarding, limits on,
    157
  Hirsi Ali on, 198–99
  relations between Islam and
    West after, 33
No Name Fever exhibition (Darabi),
  50
Norris, Molly, 142
Norway
  blasphemy legislation in, 153
  Muhammad cartoons reprinted
    in, 128
Norwood, Mark, 157
Novoye Vremya (newspaper), 179
Novy Mir (journal), 181
Nuremberg Laws of 1935, 91
Nuremberg trials, 81

Observer (newspaper), 49
offend, right to
  with art, 51–52, 60–63. *See also*
    offensive images
  in democracy, 11, 155
  for majority vs. minority, 272
offensive images
  attempts to destroy, as counter-
    productive, 59
  differences in interpretation of,
    59–63
  language used to represent, 63
  legislation on, 63
  sources of power of, 59–63
offensive speech, laws banning,
  12
Ofili, Chris, *The Holy Virgin Mary*,
  62–63, 304n35
OIC. *See* Organization of the
  Islamic Conference
Olmert, Ehud, 143
Once I Was Blind, Now I See (play),
  250
open societies. *See also*
  democracies
  free speech in, vs. closed
    societies, 81
  storytelling in, vs. closed
    societies, 6
Organisation for Economic Co-
  operation and Development,
  125
Organization for Security and Co-
  operation in Europe, 125

Organization of the Islamic
Conference (OIC), 240–50
calls for global ban on religious
defamation from, 123, 126,
130–32, 242–47
in Cartoon Crisis, 3, 76, 77, 121,
122–31, 248
Declaration on Human Rights in
Islam by, 240–41, 249
Orlov, Yuri, 173–74, 175
Orwell, George, 80
1984, 82
Osman Sayed, Rabei, 21–24
Ottoman Empire, 237
Oxford Union, 1
Oz, Amos, *How to Cure a Fanatic*, 34

Pakistan
attacks on Danish embassy in,
111, 255, 271
blasphemy in, responses to,
267–271
coup of 1977 in, 107
Headley (David) in, 106–9
women's role in, 106
Pakistani Taliban, 269
parliamentary elections, Spanish,
impact of Madrid train
bombings on, 19–21
Pearl, Daniel, 160
Pedersen, Abdul Wahid, 46
Pedersen, Troels, 302n7
PEN, 86
People's Party (Spain), 20
perestroika, 178, 304n11
Perry, Grayson, 142, 145

PET. *See* Danish Security and
Intelligence Services
Philadelphia Inquirer (newspaper),
107, 109
Picasso, Pablo, *Guernica*, 26, 71
Poland
censorship of theater in, 221–22
political crisis of 1968 in, 222
transition to democracy in, 115
Politburo, 183–85
political parties, Islamic, attempts
to ban, 81. *See also specific
parties*
*Political Prisoners in the Soviet
Union*, 177
political violence, in Nazi
Germany, 84–85
Politiken (newspaper), 25, 35, 113,
116, 144
Politkovskaya, Anna, 146
pornography, censorship of, 87–88
Post, Robert, 293, 295–96
Prague Spring, 221
predestination, 230
press coverage. *See* media
coverage
press, freedom of, recent decline
in, 241–42
Protestant Reformation, 225–30
protests, in Cartoon Crisis
in Europe, 124, 156
in Middle East, 127–30, 140
in Nigeria, 139–40
protests, in Soviet human rights
movement, 172
public decency laws, 87

public funding, of art, 61
Pushkin, Aleksandr, 260

Qaddafi, Mummar el-, 140
Qaeda, al
  in killings for blasphemy, 269
  and Madrid bombings, 20–21
  in planned attack on Denmark,
    110, 113
  retaliation for Cartoon Crisis, 271
Qaradawi, Yusuf al-, 128–29
Qasmi, Abdul Wahid, 268
Qatar, 261

racial discrimination. See also
    hate speech
  expansion of definition of, 149–52
  international conventions on,
    147–48, 150–51, 248
  religious defamation as, 246
radicalization, of Sørensen
    (Karim), 97–102
Rana, Tahawwur, 106–7
Random House, 199
Ranstorp, Magnus, 311n8 (ch10)
Rasputin, Valentin, 255
Reagan, Ronald, 74
Redeker, Robert, 86
Refn, Lars, 44
Reformation, 225–30
Rehman, Shabana, 86
Reinares, Fernando, 20–21
Rejsen til Saturn (film), 143–45
religious defamation. See also
    blasphemy
  in Afghanistan, 264–67

calls for global ban on, 123–24,
    126, 130–32, 242–47
  in Egypt, 250–53
  expansion of definition of, 246
  in India, 261–64, 272
  legislation on, 51, 81, 83, 246,
    303n19
  in Pakistan, 267–71
  as racism, 245–46
  in Russia, 253–61
religious freedom
  harm principle and, 163
  origins of, 229–32
religious radicalization, of
    Sørensen (Karim), 97–102
religious tolerance, 226–40
  debate over, in 1500s, 14, 226–32
  European conceptions of,
    235–39
  U.S. model of, 239
respect, vs. tolerance, 275
Ritzaus Bureau, 39, 302n7
Robert Mapplethorpe: The Perfect
    Moment exhibition, 61
Roof of the World (television series),
    162
Roosevelt, Eleanor, 245
Rose, Flemming
  career of, 5, 31–33, 119. See also
    Jyllands-Posten
  education of, 118–19, 179–80
  family of, 117
  wife of, 2, 5, 105, 234
  youth of, 117–19
Roshal-Fedorov, Mikhail, 259
Royal Academy (London), 61

Rushdie, Salman
    calls for global ban on criticism
        of Islam after, 123
    on crimes without victims, 113
    fatwa against, 14, 45, 240, 246, 256
    manifesto on Muhammad
        cartoons signed by, 195
    Pakistani protests over, 271
    on proposed ban on speech
        critical of religion, 51–52
    The Satanic Verses, 60, 114, 178,
        240, 262
    on storytelling, 5–6, 7, 273, 277
    as "victim of free speech," 86
    on *Vision of Ecstasy*, 256
Russia. *See also* Soviet Union
    "abuse" of freedom of speech
        in, 146
    Declaration of Rights in,
        301–2n1(ch3)
    religious defamation in,
        accusations of, 253–61
    visas for entry into, 2,
        301n2(ch1)
Russian Orthodox Church, 254–58
Russian Penal Code, 260

Saint-Genis-Pouilly (France), 52
Sakharov, Andrei
    "Reflections on Progress, Peaceful
        Coexistence, and Intellectual
        Freedom," 172, 221
    in Soviet human rights
        movement, 30, 176, 186, 187,
        222–23
    widow of, 256, 259–60

Sakharov Museum (Moscow),
    253–61
Salnikov, Vasily Ivanovich, 234
Samodurov, Yuri, 253–61
Sandahl, Jette, 51
satire
    aims of, 287–88
    anti-Nazi, 78–81
    loss of context for, 10
    of others' religions, 206–7
    Westergaard's approach to, 74
Saudi Arabia, terrorist groups
    funded by, 108
Scammell, Michael, 160
Scavenius, Erik, 79–80
Scheffer, Paul, 159
Schenck, Charles, 164–65
Schindler's List (film), 143
Schlesinger, Arthur, Jr., 176
Security and Intelligence Services
    (PET). *See* Danish Security and
    Intelligence Services
Seidel, Claus, 40, 42, 302n9
self-censorship
    advocates of, 139, 140
    by artists, 141–43
    by art museums, 48–51, 61, 259
    by cartoonists, 40
    by comedians, 37–38, 43, 47
    examples of, 49–53, 141–45,
        307n12
    in film, 143–45
    after Muhammad cartoons,
        141–45
    Muhammad cartoons as
        response to, 2, 11, 40, 42–54

by publishers, 199

in Soviet Union, 183–93

in theater, 52

self-criticism, in Western society, 34

self-determination, national, human rights in conflict with, 30

self-hatred, in European culture, 217–18

self-immolation, 237

Sensation: Young British Artists from the Saatchi Collection exhibition, 61–62

sensitivity training, 12

Serrano, Andres, 60–61

  Piss Christ, 61, 63

Servetus, Michael

  The Restoration of Christianity, 227

  trial and execution of, 10, 225–35

sex

  and Hinduism, 261

  and Islam, 50, 52–53

Sfeir, Antoine, 195

Shaaban, Muhammad, 125

Shabaab, al, 68

Shahadah, 57

Shaikh, Younus, 267–70

Shamsie, Kamila, 269, 273–74, 276

  Burnt Shadows, 273

Sharansky, Natan, 175, 186–92

Sharia law

  in Britain, 237

  and human rights, 241

in Nigeria, 140

in Sudan, 210

Sharon, Ariel, 135

Shihan (weekly), 9

silence, right to, 203–5. *See also* tyranny of silence

Sinyavsky, Andrei, 171–72, 177, 220

Slumdog Millionaire (film), 263

socialism, of Namazie, 208

societies. *See also* closed societies; diverse societies; homogeneous societies; open societies

  conceptions of tolerance in, 235–39

  free vs. fear, 187–92

Soir, Le (newspaper), 282

Solana, Javier, 78, 125, 130–31

Solzhenitsyn, Aleksandr, 181–85

  fund for aid of political prisoners, 170

  The Gulag Archipelago, 181–84

  "Live Not by Lies," 183, 186

  The Oak and the Calf, 181

  One Day in the Life of Ivan Denisovich, 181

  return to Russia, 87

Somalia, al Shabaab in, 68

Sørensen, Erik Abild, 56

Sørensen, Karim, 13, 93–102, 117

  assassination attempt against Westergaard, 13, 93–94

  family of, 93, 95–96

  on Muhammad cartoons, 99–100

  religious radicalization of, 97–102

Sots Art, 254

South Africa, apartheid in, 74, 87, 212–13, 214

South Park (television program), 141–42, 158

Soviet dissidents, 169–93
  Gorbachev influenced by, 176, 178–79
  as inspiration for Rose in Cartoon Crisis, 119–20, 192, 223
  Kovalev as, 30–31
  literature by, 171, 180–84, 220–21
  Lyubarsky as, 169–71
  Muslim dissidents compared to, 13–14, 170–71, 191–92, 195, 220–24
  self-censorship by, lack of, 182–93
  trials of, 169–70
  underground press of, 169
  unity among, difficulty of creating, 174–75

Soviet human rights movement. *See also* Soviet dissidents
  conference on literature and perestroika in, 177–79
  dispersal and resurgence of, 176–77
  foreign media coverage of, 173–74
  individual vs. group rights in, 9, 301–2n1(ch3)
  influence on Rose, 276
  insult codes used to silence, 170
  intellectual basis for, 172
  Kovalev in, 30–31

origins of, 172–73, 220–21
significant events in, 171–73, 221

Soviet Penal Code, 170

Soviet Union, 169–93. *See also* Russia
  ethnic clashes after collapse of, 30, 292
  freedom missing in, 5
  jokes in, restrictions on, 54
  labor camps of, 54, 178, 181–82
  nationality question solved by, 304n11
  prioritizing state over family in, 137
  Rose as foreign correspondent in, 2, 5, 29, 32–33
  self-censorship in, 182–93
  Solzhenitsyn in, 87
  tyranny of silence in, 5, 82, 119, 169
  Western views of cultural differences in, 8–9
  Western views on possibility of collapse of, 9, 176

Spain. *See also* Madrid train bombings
  on global ban on religious defamation, 131–32
  history of Muslims in, 22

Spanish Socialist Workers' Party, 20, 21

speech
  and actions, distinction between, 80, 114, 148, 160–61, 254
  as art, 87–88
  criticizing religion, legislation on, 51, 81, 83, 303n19

in incitement of Holocaust,
81–82, 84, 145–46
speaker vs. recipient of,
tolerance of, 244–45
violence and terrorism as
response to, 114, 145–46,
254–55
violence as antithesis of, 85
speech, freedom of
"abuse" of, 146–47
available responses to threats
against, 11–12
debate over boundaries of, 80–88
in diverse vs. homogeneous
societies, 12, 158, 160, 273
in Europe vs. United States, 12,
155–60, 273
vs. freedom to offend, 153
as hate speech antidote, 83–85
hate speech bans as threat to,
150–52
international conventions
constraining, 147–48, 149–51
in international forums, 12
relation between tolerance and, 13
religious pressure on, recent
examples of, 250–72
and storytelling, 6, 274–77
suppression of, as act of
violence, 6. *See also*
censorship; self-censorship
unconditional, in democracies,
81, 155
"victims" of, 86
in Weimar Germany, 82, 83–85,
145–46

Spiegel, Der (newspaper), 266
Spielberg, Steven, 143
Spott, Niels (pseudonym), 79–80
Springsteen, Bruce, 17
Stalin, Joseph, 54, 136–37, 182
Stauning, Thorvald, 79
Steinbeck, John, *The Grapes of
Wrath*, 87
stereotypes, Muslim, in
Muhammad cartoons, 57–58
Stjernfeldt, Frederik, 258
Adskillelsens politik, 57
storytelling
freedom of speech and, 5–7,
273–77
Rushdie on, 5–6, 7, 273, 277
Westergaard on, 71–72, 73
Streicher, Julius, 82, 83, 84, 89
Stürmer, Der (tabloid), 82, 89–90,
291
Submission (film), 126, 198
Sudan, Sharia law in, 210
Supreme Court, Indian, 261, 262
Supreme Court, Pakistani, 268
Supreme Court, U.S., 155–56, 160,
164–65
Sweden
censorship of art in, 50–51
constraints on freedoms of
Muslims in, 237
sympathy, vs. empathy, 275
Sysoev, Vyacheslav, 259

Tagesspiegel, Der (newspaper), 10
Taliban, 32, 269
Tantawi, Mohammad Sayed, 125

Taseer, Salman, 269
Tate Britain (London), 48–49
teetotalers, 308n19
Teresa of Avila, Saint, 256
terrorist attacks
  blasphemy as form of, 269–71
  in Denmark, planned for 2009,
    103–13
  funding for, 108
  in India, 112
  in London, 49
  in Madrid. *See* Madrid train
    bombings
  by Muslims, terms used for, 90
  perpetrated in name of Islam,
    75, 76
  as response to blasphemy, 114
  in United States. *See* 9/11
theater
  censorship of, 221–22
  self-censorship in, 52
Thestrup, Knud, 87
This Day (newspaper), 140
thoughts, and speech vs. actions,
  161
"Together Facing the New
  Totalitarianism" (manifesto),
  195–96, 208
tolerance. *See also* religious
  tolerance
  in *The Curious Enlightenment of
    Professor Caritat* (Lukes),
    153–54
  European conceptions of, 235–39
  of individuals vs. groups,
    235–39

relation between freedom and,
  13
vs. respect, 275
and right to offend, 152–53
of speaker vs. recipient of
  speech, 244–45
U.S. model of, 239
totalitarianism. *See also* closed
  societies; *specific countries*
  based on Islam, 195–96, 202–3,
    207
transgressive art, 60
Tretyakov Gallery, 258, 260
Tripathi, Salil, 261, 263
Trouw (newspaper), 200
T-shirt, Westergaard's cartoon of
  Muhammad on, 13, 21–24, 27,
  140
Turkey
  censorship of literature in,
    52–53
  on global ban on religious
    defamation, 131–32
tyranny of silence
  in diverse societies, 12, 273
  in Nazi Germany, 82
  in Soviet Union, 5, 82, 119, 169

UN. *See* United Nations
UNESCO, 1, 167
UNESCO Courier (magazine), 222
Ungermann, Arne, 73
United Nations (UN)
  calls for global ban on religious
    defamation in, 123, 126–27,
    130–32, 241–47

complaints about Muhammad cartoons to, 120–21

Human Rights Commission, 121, 127, 188, 242–43

Human Rights Council, 130, 243

International Covenant on Civil and Political Rights, 147–48, 243–45, 248

Namazie's work with, 210

Universal Declaration of Human Rights, 31, 119, 241, 245

United States

censorship of literature in, 87

vs. Europe, free speech in, 12, 155–60, 273

hate speech legislation in, lack of, 155–60

religious freedom in, origins of, 230

response to Cartoon Crisis in, 158–60

tolerance in, model of, 239

Universal Declaration of Human Rights, 31, 119, 241, 245

utopia, dissidents' search for, 222–23

Val, Philippe, 27, 196, 283, 284, 286–88, 291

van Gogh, Theo. *See* Gogh, Theo van

Vanguard (newspaper), 140

Vasilevskaya, Lyudmila, 256

vegans, 308n19

vegetarians, 151

Vichar Mimansa (magazine), 262

Vilks, Lars, 86, 141

Villumsen, Jørn, 42

violation codes, 13

violence

as antithesis of speech, 85

in Islam, 36–37

political, in Nazi Germany, 84–85

as response to blasphemy, 115–16

as response to speech, 114, 145–46, 254

suppression of freedom of speech as act of, 6

U.S. approach to speech inciting, 156

Visao (magazine), 89

Vision of Ecstasy (film), 256

Völkischer Beobachter, Der (newspaper), 78

Volkskrant, de (newspaper), 214

Voltaire, 88

Fanaticism, or Mahomet the Prophet, 52

Voronyanskaya, Elizaveta, 183

Wahhabism, 108

Walesa, Lech, 115

Wall Street Journal (newspaper), 160

Walzer, Michael, *On Toleration*, 236, 239

Warraq, Ibn, 195

Why I Am Not a Muslim, 34, 198

Warsaw Pact, Czechoslovakia invaded by, 172, 221, 224

Washington, D.C., Corcoran
Gallery of Art in, 61
Washington Post (newspaper), 140
Watan, Al- (newspaper), 135
weak minority, Muhammad
cartoons as attack on, 161,
205–7, 211–12, 229
Weekendavisen (newspaper), 45,
258
Weil, Boris, 177
Weimar Republic, free speech in,
82, 83–85, 145–46
Weldon, Fay, 256
Welt, Die (newspaper), 113
West
human rights as invention of,
198, 241
relations between Islam and,
after 9/11, 33
self-criticism in, 34
Westergaard, Gitte, 67–71
Westergaard, Kurt, 13, 67–76
assassination attempt against, in
2007, 67, 70
assassination attempt against, in
2008, 13, 93–94
assassination attempt against, in
2010, 68–69, 78, 111
atheism of, 71
career of, 69, 73–75
cartoons of Christians and Jews
by, 74, 133–34
education of, 72–73
on misunderstandings of
cultural codes, 75–76
under protection of PET, 67–71

reader reactions to cartoons of,
74–75
as target of planned 2009
terrorist attack, 103, 110–11
as "victim of free speech," 86
youth of, 71–73, 77, 116
Westergaard cartoon depicting
Muhammad
conception and drawing of, 75,
116
content of, 2, 54, 57–58
decision not to republish, 111
as hate speech, 244
interpretations of, 57–60
Sørensen (Karim) on, 99–100
at trial of perpetrators of Madrid
bombings, 13, 21–24, 27
on T-shirts, 13, 21–24, 27, 140
Westergaard's lack of regrets
about, 75, 76
Wikipedia, 163
Wilders, Geert, 164, 165, 219, 292
Wingrove, Nigel, 256
Wolinski,Georges, 279, 280–81, 283
Merci, Hannukah Harry, 280–81
women
in Muhammad cartoons, 56
Muslim, subjugation of, 198,
210, 264
in Pakistani society, 106
Woolf,Virginia, *Mrs. Dalloway*, 294
words. *See* speech
Worker–Communist Party of Iran,
208
World Association of
Newspapers, 2

World Cup, 10
World War II, Nuremberg trials
    after, 81. *See also* Holocaust;
    Nazi Germany

Yale University Press, 199
*Yasak Tümceler (The Forbidden
    Phrases)* (Ergüven), 52
Yerofeyev, Andrei, 258, 260

Zapatero, José, 20
Zia-ul-Haq, Muhammad, 107, 270,
    271

About the Author

FLEMMING ROSE is a Danish journalist and author, and served as foreign affairs editor and culture editor at the Danish newspaper *Jyllands-Posten*. During his tenure as culture editor, Rose was principally responsible for the September 2005 publication of the cartoons that initiated the Muhammad cartoons controversy in early 2006. Since then, he has been an international advocate for freedom of speech and regularly travels around the world to speak on the subject. In 2015 Rose was awarded the prestigious Publicist Prize from Denmark's national press club and received the Honor Award for defending free speech from the Norwegian Fritt Ord Foundation.

Cato Institute

Founded in 1977, the Cato Institute is a public policy research foundation dedicated to broadening the parameters of policy debate to allow consideration of more options that are consistent with the principles of limited government, individual liberty, and peace. To that end, the Institute strives to achieve greater involvement of the intelligent, concerned lay public in questions of policy and the proper role of government.

The Institute is named for Cato's Letters, libertarian pamphlets that were widely read in the American Colonies in the early 18th century and played a major role in laying the philosophical foundation for the American Revolution.

Despite the achievement of the nation's Founders, today virtually no aspect of life is free from government encroachment. A pervasive intolerance for individual rights is shown by government's arbitrary intrusions into private economic transactions and its disregard for civil liberties. And while freedom around the globe has notably increased in the past several decades, many countries have moved in the opposite direction, and most governments still do not respect or safeguard the wide range of civil and economic liberties.

To address those issues, the Cato Institute undertakes an extensive publications program on the complete spectrum of policy issues. Books, monographs, and shorter studies are commissioned to examine the federal budget, Social Security, regulation, military spending, international trade, and myriad other issues. Major policy conferences are held throughout the year, from which papers are published thrice yearly in the *Cato Journal*. The Institute also publishes the quarterly magazine *Regulation*.

In order to maintain its independence, the Cato Institute accepts no government funding. Contributions are received from foundations, corporations, and individuals, and other revenue is generated from the sale of publications. The Institute is a nonprofit, tax-exempt, educational foundation under Section 501(c)3 of the Internal Revenue Code.

CATO INSTITUTE
1000 Massachusetts Ave., N.W.
Washington, D.C. 20001
www.cato.org